The Inaugural Addresses of

President Thomas Jefferson,

1801 and 1805

Published with the generous assistance of

The Thomas Jefferson Foundation, Inc.

Charlottesville, Virginia

TH: JEFFERSON

St Memin del. & sc.

The Inaugural Addresses of President Thomas Jefferson, 1801 and 1805

Noble E. Cunningham, Jr.

UNIVERSITY OF MISSOURI PRESS, COLUMBIA AND LONDON

Publication of this book has been assisted by a generous gift from the
Martin S. and Luella Davis Publications Endowment.

Library of Congress Cataloging-in-Publication Data

Jefferson, Thomas, 1743–1826.
    The inaugural addresses of President Thomas Jefferson, 1801 and 1805 / Noble E.
Cunningham, Jr.
            p. cm.
    Includes bibliographical references and index.
    ISBN 0-8262-1323-5 (alk. paper)
    1. United States—Politics and government—1801–1809. 2. Presidents—United
States—Inaugural addresses. I. Cunningham, Noble E., 1926– II. Title.

J82.A3 2001
352.23'86'097309034—dc21
                                                                              00-049836

♾™ This paper meets the requirements of the
American National Standard for Permanence of Paper
for Printed Library Materials, Z39.48, 1984.

Designer: Stephanie Foley
Produced by: Regent Publishing Services
Typefaces: Palatino and Snell Roundhand

Frontispiece: mezzotint of Thomas Jefferson by Charles-Balthazar-Julien
Fevret de Saint-Mémin, 1805, from original drawing by Saint-Mémin, 1804.
Rare Book Room, Princeton University Library.

To Dana

Contents

Preface

Thomas Jefferson is widely recognized today as the principal author of the American Declaration of Independence. Less well known, but highly worthy of attention, are the addresses that Jefferson delivered at his two inaugurations as president of the United States, on March 4, 1801, and March 4, 1805. Jefferson's first inaugural address contained a succinct statement of his basic political principles and goals. Four years later, he reported on the implementation of those principles and his stewardship as president. Both addresses had far wider implications and applications.

Jefferson personally drafted each address, and he even made copies for the editor of the Washington, D.C., *National Intelligencer* to publish. From the first printings, the texts of both addresses were widely reprinted throughout the United States. They were also published in Canada and in Europe. Historians have previously recognized the importance of Jefferson's inaugural speeches, but little notice has been taken of their widespread circulation. Because the translations and publications of these addresses in Europe have gone largely unnoticed, readers may be surprised at the extent of the attention given abroad to both of the addresses.

Modern photographic and printing techniques provide ever closer glimpses of the past. Jefferson's inaugural addresses of two hundred years ago can now be widely read from texts in his own handwriting and from broadsides, leaflets, and newspapers of his own time. Today, readers may gain not only a sense of closeness to the past of Jefferson's day but also a clearer understanding of Jefferson's world of two centuries ago.

The two-hundredth anniversary of Jefferson's inauguration as president of the United States on March 4, 1801, provides an appropriate occasion to give wide recognition to Jefferson's memorable addresses.

The Inaugural Addresses of

President Thomas Jefferson,

1801 and 1805

Fig. 1-1. The Senate Wing of the unfinished United States Capitol, Washington, D.C. Watercolor by William R. Birch, 1800. Library of Congress.

Chapter I

Jefferson's Inaugural Address of March 4, 1801

Thomas Jefferson was the first president of the United States to be inaugurated in the new capital city of Washington, D.C., to which the offices of government moved from Philadelphia in the summer of 1800. The Capitol remained under construction with only the Senate chamber having been completed (fig. 1-1). Work also continued on the president's house, although the finished portions were in use. Public and private accommodations of the city were lacking in numbers and in conveniences, but after a close presidential election, excitement was high. At noon on March 4, 1801, in the oval-shaped Senate chamber, before a packed and enthusiastic audience, the principal author of the American Declaration of Independence took the oath of office as the third president of the United States.

The contrast between Jefferson's inauguration and that of his two predecessors was striking. Much ceremony and public display accompanied George Washington's inauguration in New York in 1789 and also characterized John Adams's inaugural in Philadelphia in 1797. Both Washington and Adams rode to their inaugurations in fancy carriages and wore swords when they took the oath of office. In contrast, Jefferson wore no sword and walked to his inauguration from Conrad and McMunn's boardinghouse on

New Jersey Avenue near the Capitol, escorted by Alexandria militia officers, marshals of the District of Columbia, and a delegation of members of Congress. "His dress was, as usual, that of a plain citizen, without any distinctive badge of office," one observer reported.[1] Samuel Harrison Smith, the editor of the Washington *National Intelligencer,* who was the first to publish the text of Jefferson's inaugural address, noted, "The manner in which it was delivered was plain, dignified, and unostentatious; the style is chaste, appropriate, and eloquent; the principles are pure, explicit, and comprehensive." The editor's wife, who was also among those crowded into the Senate chamber, penned a letter at the end of the day saying that she had "witnessed one of the most interesting scenes a free people can ever witness." She described Jefferson's address as "containing principles the most correct, sentiments the most liberal, and wishes the most benevolent, conveyed in the most appropriate and elegant language and in a manner mild as it was firm. If doubts of the integrity and talents of Mr. Jefferson ever existed in the minds

---

1. *National Intelligencer* (Washington), March 6, 1801; *Times* (Alexandria), March 6, 1801; *Examiner* (Richmond), March 13, 1801; Noble E. Cunningham, Jr., *In Pursuit of Reason: The Life of Thomas Jefferson,* 238–39.

of any one, methinks this address must forever eradicate them."[2]

In a letter to his South Carolina constituents, Representative Robert Goodloe Harper, a Federalist who had opposed Jefferson's election, wrote of the inauguration:

> The whole ceremony was conducted with the utmost propriety. As on the part of those who had supported the new President in the election, there was no unbecoming exultation; so his opposers manifested by their behaviour, a chearful acquiescence in the decision of the majority. They attended the ceremony; and after it concluded they paid a visit to the President, to express their respect to him as the Chief Magistrate of the nation, and their readiness to support him in the proper exercise of his authority. The speech which he delivered previous to taking the oath, was well calculated to inspire these sentiments, and to afford the hope of such an administration as may conduce to his own glory and the public good. Before the evening all was quiet, as if no change had taken place.[3]

More concisely, the new vice president, Aaron Burr, recorded: "The Day was serene and temperate—The Concourse of people immense—all passed off handsomely—great joy but no riot—no accident—The Papers contain Jefferson's Speech."[4]

If Jefferson directed little attention to his dress or to ceremony, he had given considerable care to what he would say. His speech on March 4, 1801, would be the first inaugural address to take its place among the great such addresses in American history. After two hundred years it still remains high among them.

President Washington, in deciding what remarks to make at his inauguration in New York in 1789, had rejected a lengthy address drafted by his secretary, David Humphreys, and turned to James Madison for help in preparing his speech. Still, the result lacked style and content. Although published in the newspapers and in at least one broadside, the address never attracted wide attention.[5] At the 1793 presidential inauguration in Philadelphia, when Washington took the oath of office for the second time, he offered a brief acknowledgment of only four sentences.[6] Three years later, in 1796, declining to be a candidate for reelection, Washington issued a farewell address that would provide the text by which his presidency would best be remembered.

President John Adams's inauguration, on March 4, 1797, was widely reported in the press, and the text of his inaugural address was published in the newspapers. While generating some praise from the Republican opposition, the speech also provoked criticism from Federalist extremists as being too "temporizing."[7] Adams's inaugural address never gained the attention that his successor's address would attract.

As the first president to be inaugurated following an election that transferred power in both the executive and the legislative branches from

2. *National Intelligencer,* March 6, 1801. Margaret Bayard Smith to Susan B. Smith, March 4, 1801, in Gaillard Hunt, ed., *The First Forty Years of Washington Society in the Family Letters of Margaret Bayard Smith,* 25–26. On celebrations of Jefferson's inaugurations, see Simon P. Newman, *Parades and the Politics of the Street: Festive Culture in the Early American Republic* (Philadelphia: University of Pennsylvania Press, 1997).

3. Harper to his constituents, March 5, 1801, in Noble E. Cunningham, Jr., ed., *Circular Letters of Congressmen to Their Constituents, 1789–1829,* 1:248.

4. Burr to Caesar A. Rodney, March 4, 1801, in Mary-Jo Kline and Joanne Wood Ryan, eds., *Political Correspondence and Public Papers of Aaron Burr,* 1:518.

5. W. W. Abbot, Dorothy Twohig, et al., eds. *The Papers of George Washington,* Presidential Series 2:152–57, 173–77; *Speech of His Excellency the President of the United States, to both Houses of Congress,* New York, April 30, 1789, printed by C. R. & G. Webster.

6. *General Advertiser* (Philadelphia), March 7, 1793.

7. *Aurora* (Philadelphia), March 6, 1797; *Argus* (New York), reprinted in the *Aurora,* March 10, 11, 1797; Page Smith, *John Adams,* 2:919–20.

one political party to another, Jefferson faced an unusual challenge in preparing his inaugural address. In drafting that speech, he would emphasize the same fundamental principles of public policy he had affirmed as a candidate during the presidential election of 1800. During that contest, Jefferson had given no speeches, for presidential candidates did not openly campaign for office. But he had written numerous letters to friends and political activists, and his views had become widely known.

Early in 1799, in a letter to Elbridge Gerry of Massachusetts, Jefferson penned one of the best and most succinct statements of his basic political views. With competition increasing for the approaching presidential election, the letter served as Jefferson's platform. He wrote:

I do then, with sincere zeal, wish an inviolable preservation of our present federal constitution, according to the true sense in which it was adopted by the States, that in which it was advocated by it's friends, and not that which it's enemies apprehended. . . . I am for preserving to the States the powers not yielded by them to the Union, and to the legislature of the Union it's constitutional share in the division of powers; and I am not for transferring all the powers of the States to the general government, and all those of that government to the Executive branch. I am for a government rigorously frugal and simple, applying all the possible savings of the public revenue to the discharge of the national debt; and not for a multiplication of officers and salaries merely to make partisans, and for increasing, by every device, the public debt, on the principle of it's being a public blessing. I am for relying, for internal defence, on our militia solely, till actual invasion, and for such a naval force only as may protect our coasts and harbors from such depredations as we have experienced; and not for a standing army in time of peace, which may overawe the public sentiment; nor for a navy, which by it's own expenses and the eternal wars in which it will

implicate us, grind us with public burthens, and sink us under them. I am for free commerce with all nations; political connection with none; and little or no diplomatic establishment. And I am not for linking ourselves by new treaties with the quarrels of Europe; entering that field of slaughter to preserve their balance, or joining in the confederacy of kings to war against the principles of liberty. I am for freedom of religion, and against all maneuvres to bring about a legal ascendancy of one sect over another; for freedom of the press, and against all violations of the constitution to silence by force and not by reason the complaints or criticism, just or unjust, of our citizens against the conduct of their agents. And I am for encouraging the progress of science in all it's branches; and not for raising a hue and cry against the sacred name of philosophy. . . . To these I will add, that I am a sincere well-wisher to the success of the French revolution, and still wish it may end in the establishment of a free and well-ordered republic; but I have not been insensible under the atrocious depredations they have committed on our commerce. The first object of my heart is my own country. In that is embarked my family, my fortune, and my own existence. . . .

These, my friend, are my principles; they are unquestionably the principles of the great body of our fellow citizens.[8]

In his inaugural address Jefferson reiterated some of these same statements of principles, offering a broad and comprehensive vision and appealing to his fellow citizens to unite behind him to realize it.

Although Jefferson had been planning what to say in his inaugural address for some time, it was not until February 17, 1801, that he finally knew that he would be inaugurated on March 4. The electoral-vote tie between Jefferson and the vice presidential nominee, Aaron Burr—caused by

8. Jefferson to Gerry, January 26, 1799, in Paul L. Ford, ed., *The Works of Thomas Jefferson*, 9:17–19.

the requirement that electors cast two votes without distinguishing between president and vice president—was not decided until February 17. Jefferson thus had only two weeks to put his inaugural address into final form.

When satisfied with the text of his address, Jefferson made a copy from which to read at the inauguration ceremony. That manuscript contained numerous abbreviations, enabling him to fit the text on two sheets of paper, written on both sides (fig. 1-2). Early in the morning on inauguration day, the president-elect gave a fully transcribed text of his speech (fig. 1-3) to newspaper editor Samuel Harrison Smith for publication in the Washington *National Intelligencer.* The following text, which may be considered Jefferson's final version, has been transcribed from the manuscript used by Smith in making the first printing of the address. Jefferson's own reading copy contained a few slight variations, but it was Smith's printing of the address that was copied and reprinted in other newspapers, broadsides, and pamphlets both in America and in Europe.

The Text of Jefferson's Address of March 4, 1801

Friends and fellow citizens

Called upon to undertake the duties of the first Executive office of our country, I avail myself of the presence of that portion of my fellow citizens which is here assembled to express my grateful thanks for the favor with which they have been pleased to look towards me, to declare a sincere consciousness that the task is above my talents, and that I approach it with those anxious and awful presentiments which the greatness of the charge, and the weakness of my powers so justly inspire. A rising nation, spread over a wide and fruitful land, traversing all the seas with the rich productions of their industry, engaged in commerce with nations who feel power and for-

get right, advancing rapidly to destinies beyond the reach of mortal eye, when I contemplate these transcendent objects, and see the honour, the happiness, and the hopes of this beloved country committed to the issue and the auspices of this day, I shrink from the contemplation, and humble myself before the magnitude of the undertaking. Utterly indeed should I despair, did not the presence of many, whom I here see, remind me, that, in the other high authorities provided by our constitution, I shall find resources of wisdom, of virtue, and of zeal, on which to rely under all difficulties. To you, then, gentlemen, who are charged with the sovereign functions of legislation, and to those associated with you, I look with encouragement for that guidance and support which may enable us to steer with safety the vessel in which we are all embarked, amidst the conflicting elements of a troubled world.

During the contest of opinion through which we have past, the animation of discussions and of exertions has sometimes worn an aspect which might impose on strangers unused to think freely, and to speak and to write what they think. But this being now decided by the voice of the nation, enounced according to the rules of the constitution, all will of course arrange themselves under the will of the law, and unite in common efforts for the common good. All too will bear in mind this sacred principle that though the will of the majority is in all cases to prevail, that will, to be rightful, must be reasonable; that the minority possess their equal rights, which equal laws must protect and to violate would be oppression. Let us then fellow citizens unite with one heart and one mind, let us restore to social intercourse that harmony and affection without which liberty, and even life itself, are but dreary things. And let us reflect that having banished from our land that religious intolerance under which mankind so long bled and suffered, we have yet gained little if we countenance a political intolerance, as despotic, as wicked, and capable of as bitter and bloody persecutions. During the throes and convulsions of the ancient world, during the agonizing spasms of infuriated man, seeking through blood and slaughter his long-lost liberty, it was not wonderful that the agitation of the billows should reach even this distant and peaceful shore; that this should be more felt and feared by some and less by others; and should divide opinions as to measures of safety. But every difference of opinion is not a difference of principle. We have called by different names brethren of the same principle. We are all republicans: we are all federalists. If there be any among us who would wish to dissolve this Union or to change it's republican form, let them stand undisturbed as monuments of the safety with which error of opinion may be tolerated, where reason is left free to combat it. I know indeed that some honest men fear that a republican government cannot be strong, that this government is not strong enough. But would the honest patriot in the full tide of successful experiment abandon a government which has so far kept us free and firm, on the theoretic and visionary fear, that this government, the world's best hope, may, by possibility, want energy to preserve itself? I trust not, I believe this, on the contrary, the strongest government on earth. I believe it the only one, where every man, at the call of the law, would fly to the standard of the law, and would meet invasions of the public order as his own personal concern. Sometimes it is said that man cannot be trusted with the government of himself. Can he then be trusted with the government of others? Or have we found angels, in the form of kings, to govern him? Let history answer this question.

Let us then, with courage and confidence, pursue our own federal and republican principles; our attachments to union and representative government. Kindly separated by nature and a wide ocean from the exterminating havoc of one quarter of the globe; too high-minded to endure the degradations of the others, possessing a chosen country, with room enough for our descendants to the thousandth and thousandth generation, entertaining a due sense of our equal right to use of our own faculties, to the acquisitions of our own industry, to honour and confidence from our fellow citizens, resulting not from birth, but from our actions and their sense of them, enlightened by a benign religion, professed indeed and practised in various forms, yet all of them inculcating Honesty, truth, temperance, gratitude and the love of man, ackneleging and adoring an overruling providence, which by it's dispensations proves that it delights in the happiness of man here, and his greater happiness hereafter; with all these blessings, what more is necessary to make us a happy and prosperous people? Still one thing more fellow citizens, a wise and frugal government which shall restrain men from injuring one another, shall leave them otherwise free to regulate their own pursuits of industry and improvement, and shall not take from the mouth of labor the bread it has earned. This is the sum of good government; and this is necessary to close the circle of our felicities.

About to enter, fellow citizens, on the exercise of duties which comprehend every thing dear and valuable to you, it is proper you should understand what I deem the essential principles of our government and consequently those which ought to shape it's administration. I will compress them within the narrowest compass they will bear, stating the general principle, but not all it's limitations.—Equal and exact justice to all men, of whatever state or persuasion, religious or political:—Peace, commerce and honest friendship with all nations, entangling alliances with none:—the support of the state governments in all their rights as the most competent administrations for our domestic concerns, and the surest bulwarks against anti-republican tendencies:—the preservation of the General government in it's whole constitutional vigour as the sheet anchor of our peace at home, and safety abroad:—a jealous care of the right of election by the people, a mild and safe corrective of abuses which are lopped by the sword or revolution where peaceable remedies are unprovided:—absolute acquiescence in the decisions of the majority, the vital principle of republics, from which is no appeal but to force, the vital principle and immediate parent of despotism:—a well disciplined militia, our best reliance in peace, and for the first moments of war, till regulars may relieve them:—the supremacy of the civil over the military authority;—economy in the Public expence, that labor may be lightly burthened:—the honest payment of our debts and sacred preservation of the public faith:—encouragement of agriculture, and of commerce as it's handmaid:—the diffusion of information, and the arraignment of all abuses at the bar of the public reason:—freedom of religion; freedom of the press; and freedom of person, under the protection of Habeas corpus:—and trial by juries, impartially selected. These principles form the bright constellation, which has gone before us and guided our steps through an age of revolution and reformation. The wisdom of our sages and blood of our heroes have been devoted to their attainment: they should be the creed of our political faith, the text of civic instruction, the touchstone by which to try the services of those we trust. And should we wander from them in moments of error or of alarm, let us hasten to retrace our steps, and to regain the road which alone leads to Peace, liberty and safety.

I repair then, fellow citizens, to the post you have assigned me. With experience enough in subordinate offices to have seen the difficulties of this the greatest of all, I have learnt to expect that it will rarely fall to the lot of imperfect man to retire from this station with the reputation, and the favor, which bring him into it. Without pretensions to that high confidence you reposed in our first and greatest revolutionary character, whose preeminent services had entitled him to the first place in his country's love—and destined for him the fairest page in the volume of faithful history, I ask so much confidence only as may give firmness and effect to the legal administration of your affairs. I shall often go wrong through defect of judgment. When right, I shall often be thought wrong by those whose positions will not command a view of the whole ground. I ask your indulgence for my own errors, which will never be intentional; and your support against the errors of others, who may condemn what they would not, if seen in all it's parts. The approbation implied by your suffrage is a great consolation to me for the past; and my future solicitude will be to retain the good opinion of those who have bestowed it in advance, to conciliate that of others by doing them all the good in my power, and to be instrumental to the happiness and freedom of all.

Relying then on the patronage of your good will, I advance with obedience to the work, ready to retire from it whenever you become sensible how much better choices it is in your power to make. And may that infinite power which rules the destinies of the universe lead our councils to what is best, and give them a favourable issue for your peace and prosperity.[9]

Samuel Harrison Smith published the above complete text in the *National Intelligencer* on the morning of March 4, 1801 (fig. 1-4). He had copies of his newspaper ready for distribution to members of Congress and visitors as they left the Senate chamber following the inauguration ceremonies and President Jefferson's delivery of his inaugural address.

---

9. Jefferson, inaugural address, March 4, 1801, manuscript (fig. 1-3) sent to Samuel Harrison Smith for publication in the *National Intelligencer,* Thomas Jefferson Papers, Library of Congress.

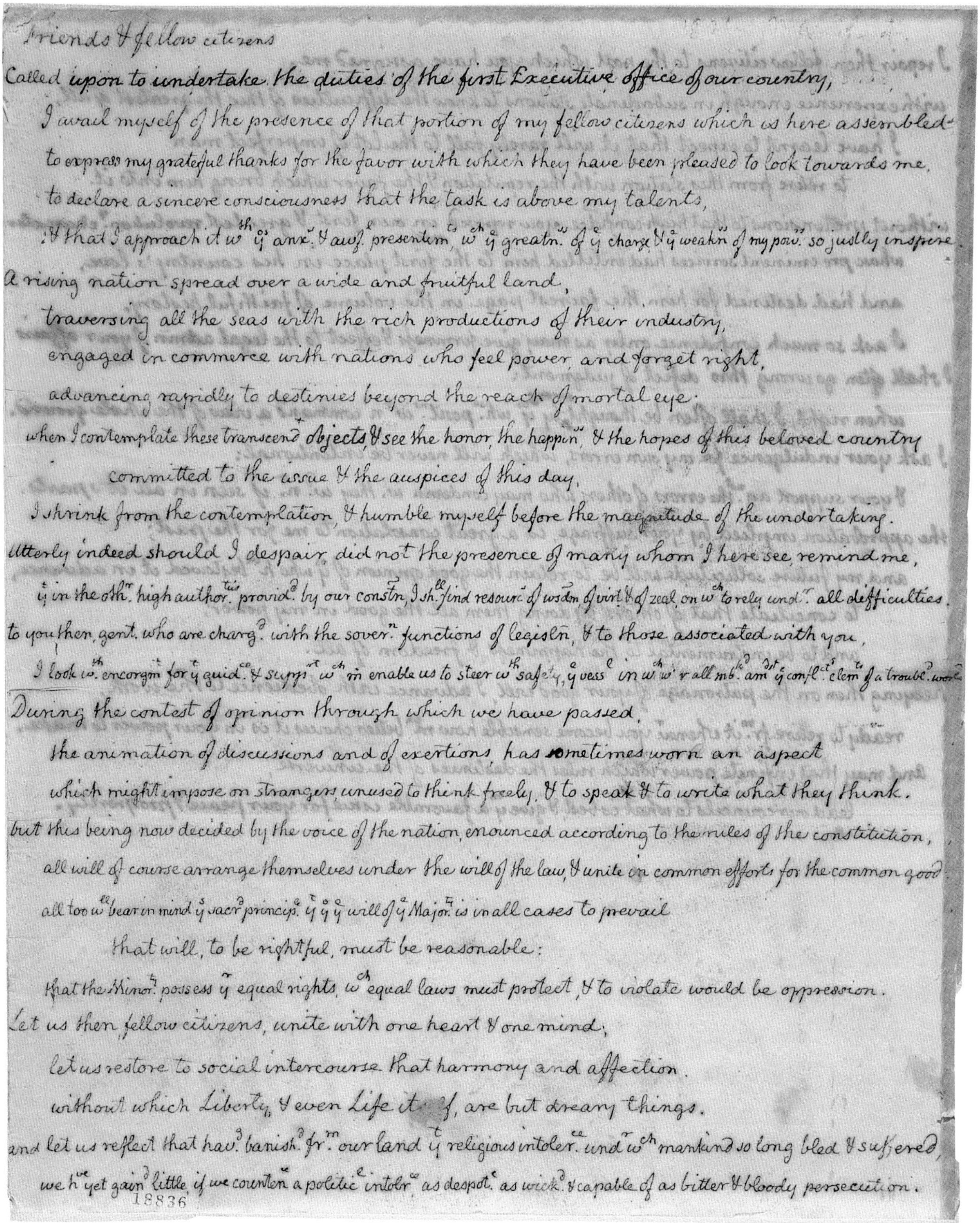

Friends & fellow citizens

Called upon to undertake the duties of the first Executive office of our country,

I avail myself of the presence of that portion of my fellow citizens which is here assembled,

to express my grateful thanks for the favor with which they have been pleased to look towards me,

to declare a sincere consciousness that the task is above my talents,

& that I approach it with those anxious & awful presentiments which the greatness of the charge & the weakness of my powers so justly inspire.

A rising nation spread over a wide and fruitful land,

traversing all the seas with the rich productions of their industry,

engaged in commerce with nations who feel power, and forget right,

advancing rapidly to destinies beyond the reach of mortal eye.

when I contemplate these transcendent objects, & see the honor, the happiness, & the hopes of this beloved country

committed to the issue & the auspices of this day,

I shrink from the contemplation, & humble myself before the magnitude of the undertaking.

Utterly indeed should I despair, did not the presence of many whom I here see, remind me,

that in the other high authorities provided by our constitution, I shall find resources of wisdom, of virtue & of zeal on which to rely under all difficulties.

to you then, gentlemen, who are charged with the sovereign functions of legislation, & to those associated with you,

I look with encouragement for that guidance & support which may enable us to steer with safety the vessel in which we are all embarked amidst the conflicting elements of a troubled world.

During the contest of opinion through which we have passed,

the animation of discussions and of exertions, has sometimes worn an aspect

which might impose on strangers unused to think freely, & to speak & to write what they think.

but this being now decided by the voice of the nation, enounced according to the rules of the constitution,

all will of course arrange themselves under the will of the law, & unite in common efforts for the common good.

all too will bear in mind this sacred principle, that tho' the will of the Majority is in all cases to prevail

that will, to be rightful, must be reasonable:

that the Minority possess their equal rights, which equal laws must protect, & to violate would be oppression.

Let us then, fellow citizens, unite with one heart & one mind;

let us restore to social intercourse that harmony and affection.

without which Liberty, & even Life itself, are but dreary things.

and let us reflect that having banished from our land that religious intolerance under which mankind so long bled & suffered,

we have yet gained little if we countenance a political intolerance as despotic, as wicked, & capable of as bitter & bloody persecution.

18836

Fig. 1-2. Thomas Jefferson's reading copy of his inaugural address delivered in the Senate Chamber, March 4, 1801. Library of Congress.

during the throes and convulsions of the antient world,

 dur.ᵍ the agonies ᵍ spasms of infuriat.ᵈ man, seeking through blood & slaughter his long lost liberty

it was not wonderful that the agitation of the billows should reach even this distant & peaceful shore:

that ij sh.ᵈ be more felt & fear.ᵈ by some, & less by others, & sh.ᵈ divide opinions as to measures of safety.

but every difference of opinion, is not a difference of principle.

we have called, by different names, brethren of the same principle.

we are all republicans: we are all federalists.

if there be any among us who wish to dissolve this union, or to change it's republican form,

 let them stand undisturbed, as monuments of the safety, wᵗʰ wᵗʰ error of opin. in b'tolerat.ᵈ whᵉ reas.ⁿ is left free to combat it.

I know ind.ᵈ ij some honest men hᵛᵉ fear.ᵈ ij a republicn govⁿᵐᵗ cann.ᵗ be strong; ij this goⁱ̃̃ⁿᵗ. is not strong enough.

 but wᵈ the honest patriot, in the full tide of succesf. experim. abandon a goⁱ̃ᵐᵗ wᶜʰ. so far kept us free & firm

  on ij theoretic & visionary fear ij ij govⁱ̃ᵐᵗ, the world's best hope, in, by possibilⁱᵗᵉ, want energy to preserve itself?

I trust not. I believe this, on the contrary, the strongest government on earth.

I believe it the only one where every man at the call of the law, would fly to the standard of the law:

 would meet invasions of public order, as his own personal concern.

Sometimes it is said ij Man cann.ᵗ be trust.ᵈ wᵗʰ ij govⁱ̃ᵐᵗ of himself. — Can he ij be trust.ᵈ wᵗʰ ij govⁱ̃ᵐᵗ of others?

 Or have we found angels in ij form of kings to govern him? — Let History answ.ʳ this question.

Let us ij plursͦᵉ wᵗʰ courᵃᵍᵉ & confidᵉ. our own feder. & republ.ⁿ princ. our attamᵗ to Union, & Representative govⁱ̃ᵐᵗ.

kindly separatᵈ by nature, & a wide ocean, from the exterminating havoc of one quarter of the globe,

 too high-minded to endure the degradations of the others;

possessⁱ̃ⁿʳ a chosen country, with room enough for our descend.ᵗ to the 1000.ᵗʰ & 1000.ᵗʰ generation;

entertain.ᵈ a due sense of our equal right, to ij use of our own faculties, to ij acquisitⁱᵒⁿˢ of our own industry,

 to honⁿ. & confidᶜᵉ frᵐ. our fel. cit. resultᵈ.ⁿ from birth, but frᵐ. our actions, & their sense of them,

enlightenᵈ. by a benign religion, professᵈ indeed & practsᵈ. in various forms,

 yet all of ij inculcatᵈ. Honesty, truth, temperⁿᶜᵉ gratitude, & the love of man,

acknoleᵍ.ᵈ & adoring an overruling providence, which by all it's dispensations proves

that it delights in the happiness of man here, & his greater happiness hereafter:

with all these blessings, what more is necessary to make us a happy and a prosperous people?

 still one thing more, fel. cit. a wise & frug.ᵈ govⁱ̃ᵐᵗ, wᶜʰ shall restrain men from injuring one another,

  shall leave them otherwise free to regulate their own pursuits of industry & improvement,

  18837 and shall not take, from the mouth of labor, the bread it has earned.

this is the sum of good govⁱ̃ᵐᵗ, & this is necessary to close the circle of our felicities.

about to enter fel. cit. on the exercise of duties, which comprehend every thing dear & valuable to you.

it is proper you should understand what I deem the essential principles of this governmt.

and consequently those which ought to shape it's administration.

I will compress them in ÿ narrowst compass ÿ wll bear, statg the genl principle, but not all it's limitations.

Equal & exact justice to all men, of whatever state or persuasion, religious or political:

Peace, commerce, & honest friendships with all nations, entangling alliances with none:

the support of the State-govmts in all their rights, as ÿ most competent admns for our domestic concer

and the surest bulwarks against anti-republican tendencies:

the preservn of the Genl govmt. in it's whole constinal vigor, as ÿ sheet anchor of our peace at home, & safety abro

a jealous care of the right of election by the people. a mild & safe corrective of abuses, wch r lopp'd by ÿ sword of revoln where peac remedies are unprov

absolute acquiescence in ÿ decisns of ÿ Majorty ÿ vitl princip. of republics, frm wch is no appeal but to force ÿ vit princip. & immedte par. of desp

a well discipld militia, our best reliance in peace & for ÿ first moments of war, till regulars may relieve the

the Supremacy of the Civil over the Military authority:

Economy in public expence, that labor may be lightly burthened:

the honest paiment of our debts, and sacred preservation of the public faith:

encouragement of Agriculture, & of Commerce as it's handmaid:

the diffusion of information, & arraignmt of all abuses at the bar of the public reason:

freedom of Religion, freedom of the press, & freedom of Person. under the protection of the Hab. corpus:

and trial by Juries, impartially selected.

these Principles form ÿ bright constelln wch hs gone before us & guid our steps, thro' an age of Revoln and Reformn.

the wisdom of our Sages, & blood of our Heroes, have been devoted to their attainment:

they should be the Creed of our political faith, the Text of civic instruction,

the Touchstone by which to try the services of those we trust;

and should we wander from them, in moments of error or alarm,

let us hasten to retrace our steps

and to regain the road which alone leads to Peace, Liberty & Safety.

I repair then, fellow citizens, to the post which you have assigned me.

with experience enough in subordinate stations to know the difficulties of this the greatest of all

I have learnt to expect that it will rarely fall to the lot of imperfect man

to retire from this station with the reputation & the favor which bring him into it.

without pretensions to that high confidce you reposed in our first & greatest revolutiony char

whose pre-eminent services had entitled him to the first place in his country's love,

and had destined for him the fairest page in the volume of faithful history,

I ask so much confidence only as may give firmness & effect to the legal admin of your af

I shall often go wrong thro' defect of judgment:

when right, I shall often be thought wrong by ys whse positns wch nt command a view of the whole gro

I ask your indulgence for my own errors, which will never be intentional:

& your support agnst the errors of others, who may condemn wt they wd nt, if seen in all it's pa

the approbation implied by your suffrage, is a great consolation to me for the past;

and my future sollicitude will be, to retain the good opinion of ys who hve bestowed it in adva

to conciliate that of others, by doing them all the good in my power;

and to be instrumental to the happiness & freedom of all.

Relying then on the patronage of your good will, I advance with obedience to the work,

ready to retire frm it whenevr you become sensible how mch better choices it is in your power to ma

and may that infinite power which rules the destinies of the universe,

lead our councils to what is best, & give ym a favorable issue for your peace & prosperity.

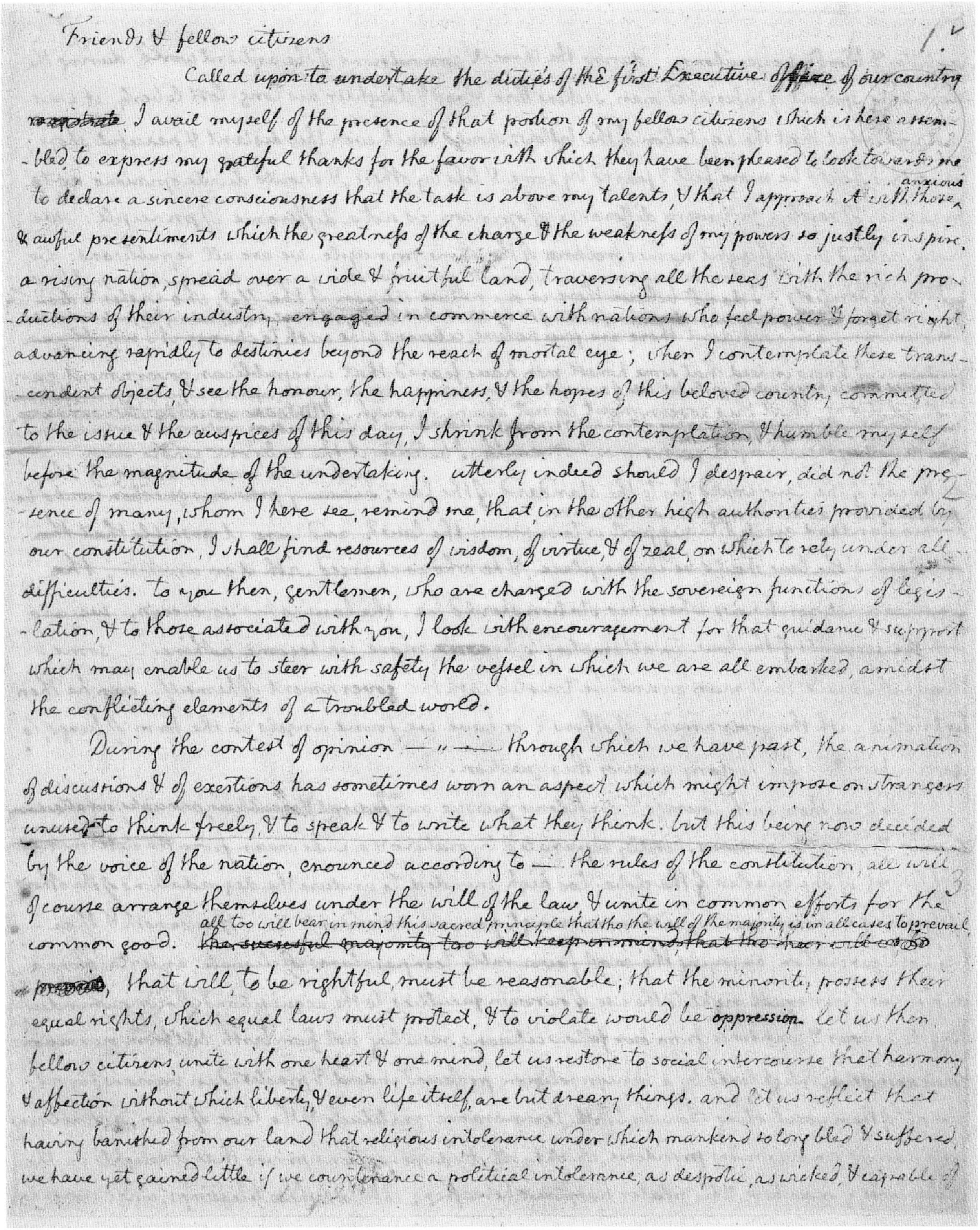
Friends & fellow citizens 1.
Called upon to undertake the duties of the first Executive office of our country ~~magistrate~~ I avail myself of the presence of that portion of my fellow citizens which is here assembled to express my grateful thanks for the favor with which they have been pleased to look towards me, to declare a sincere consciousness that the task is above my talents, & that I approach it with those anxious & awful presentiments which the greatness of the charge & the weakness of my powers so justly inspire. a rising nation, spread over a wide & fruitful land, traversing all the seas with the rich productions of their industry, engaged in commerce with nations who feel power & forget right, advancing rapidly to destinies beyond the reach of mortal eye; when I contemplate these transcendent objects, & see the honour, the happiness, & the hopes of this beloved country committed to the issue & the auspices of this day, I shrink from the contemplation, & humble myself before the magnitude of the undertaking. utterly indeed should I despair, did not the presence of many, whom I here see, remind me, that, in the other high authorities provided by our constitution, I shall find resources of wisdom, of virtue, & of zeal, on which to rely under all difficulties. to you then, gentlemen, who are charged with the sovereign functions of legislation, & to those associated with you, I look with encouragement for that guidance & support which may enable us to steer with safety the vessel in which we are all embarked, amidst the conflicting elements of a troubled world.
During the contest of opinion through which we have past, the animation of discussions & of exertions has sometimes worn an aspect which might impose on strangers unused to think freely, & to speak & to write what they think. but this being now decided by the voice of the nation, enounced according to the rules of the constitution, all will of course arrange themselves under the will of the law & unite in common efforts for the common good. ~~the successful majority too will keep in mind, that tho' their will is to prevail~~ all too will bear in mind this sacred principle that tho' the will of the majority is in all cases to prevail, that will, to be rightful, must be reasonable; that the minority possess their equal rights, which equal laws must protect, & to violate would be oppression. let us then, fellow citizens, unite with one heart & one mind, let us restore to social intercourse that harmony & affection without which liberty, & even life itself, are but dreary things. and let us reflect that having banished from our land that religious intolerance under which mankind so long bled & suffered, we have yet gained little if we countenance a political intolerance, as despotic, as wicked, & capable of

Fig. 1-3. Text, in Thomas Jefferson's handwriting, of his inaugural address of March 4, 1801, sent to Samuel Harrison Smith for publication in the Washington *National Intelligencer.* Library of Congress.

as bitter & bloody persecutions.   during the throes & convulsions of the antient world, during the agonising spasms of infuriated man, seeking thro' blood & slaughter his long-lost liberty, it was not wonderful that the agitation of the billows should reach even this distant & peaceful shore; that this should be more felt & feared by some & less by others; & should divide opinions as to measures of safety. but every difference of opinion, is not a difference of principle. we have called by different names brethren of the same principle. we are all republicans: we are all federalists. if there be any among us who would wish to dissolve this Union, or to change it's republican form, let them stand undisturbed as monuments of the safety with which error of opinion may be tolerated, where reason is left free to combat it.   I know indeed that some honest men fear that a republican government cannot be strong; that this government is not strong enough. but would the honest patriot, in the full tide of successful experiment, abandon a government which has so far kept us free and firm, on the theoretic & visionary fear, that this government, the world's best hope, may, by possibility, want energy to preserve itself? I trust not. I believe this, on the contrary the strongest government on earth. I believe it the only one, where every man, at the call of the law, would fly to the standard of the law, and would meet invasions of the public order as his own personal concern. sometimes it is said that man cannot be trusted with the government of himself. can he then be trusted with the government of others? or have we found angels, in the form of kings, to govern him? Let history answer this question.

Let us then, with courage & confidence, pursue our own federal & republican principles; our attachment to union & representative government. kindly separated by nature & a wide ocean from the exterminating havoc of one quarter of the globe; too high-minded to endure the degradations of the others, possessing a chosen country, with room enough for our descendants to the thousandth & thousandth generation, enjoying the most favourable temperatures of climate, entertaining a due sense of our equal right to the use of our own faculties, to the acquisitions of our own industry, to honour & confidence from our fellow citizens, resulting not from birth. but from our actions & their sense of them, enlightened by a benign religion, professed indeed & practised in various forms, yet all of them inculcating Honesty, truth, temperance, gratitude & the love of man, acknoleging and adoring an overruling providence, which by all it's dispensations proves that it delights in the happiness of man here. & his greater happiness hereafter; with all these blessings, what more is necessary to make us a happy & a prosperous people? still one thing more, fellow citizens. a wise & frugal government, which shall restrain men from injuring one another, shall leave them otherwise free to regulate their own pursuits of industry & improvement, & shall not take from the mouth of labor the bread it has earned. this is the sum of good government; & this is necessary to close the circle of our felicities.

About to enter, fellow citizens, on the exercise of duties which comprehend every thing dear & valuable to you, it is proper you should understand what I deem the essential principles of our government, & consequently those which ought to shape it's administration. I will compress them within the narrowest compass they will bear, stating the general principle, but not all it's limitations. — Equal & exact justice to all men, of whatever state or persuasion, religious or political: — Peace, commerce & honest friendships with all nations, entangling alliances with none: — the support of the state governments in all their rights, as the most competent administrations for our domestic concerns, & the surest bulwarks against anti-republican tendencies: — the preservation of the General government in it's whole constitutional vigour as the sheet anchor of our peace at home, & safety abroad: — free & frequent elections by the people in person, & the more frequent within the limits of their convenience, & the more a jealous care of the right of election by the people, a mild and safe corrective of abuses which are extensive the right of suffrage, the more perfectly within the definition of a genuine republic: lopped by the sword of revolution where peaceable remedies are unprovided: — — absolute acquiescence in the decisions of the majority, the vital principle of republics, from which is no appeal but to force, the vital principle & immediate parent of despotism: — a well disciplined militia, our best reliance in peace, & for the first moments of war, till regulars may relieve them: — the supremacy of the civil over the military authority: — economy in the public expence that labor may be lightly burthened: — the honest paiment of our debts & sacred preservation of the public faith: — encouragement of agriculture; and of Commerce as it's handmaid: the diffusion of information, & arraignment of all abuses at the bar of the public reason: freedom of religion; freedom of the press; & freedom of person, under the never ceasing protection of the Habeas corpus: — and trial by juries, impartially selected. these principles form the bright constellation, which has gone before us, & guided our steps through an age of revolution & reformation. the wisdom of our sages, & blood of our heroes have been devoted to their attainment: they should be the creed of our political faith; the text of civic instruction, the touchstone by which to try the services of those we trust; and should we wander from them in moments of error or of alarm, let us hasten to retrace our steps, & to regain the road which alone leads to Peace, liberty & safety.

I repair then, fellow citizens, to the post you have assigned me. with experience enough in subordinate offices to have seen the difficulties of this the greatest of all, I have learnt to expect that it will rarely fall to the lot of imperfect man to retire from this station with the reputation, & the favor which bring him into it. without pretensions to that high confidence you reposed in our first, and greatest revolutionary character ~~who was presented me~~, whose preeminent services had entitled him to the first place in his country's love ——, and destined for him the fairest page in the volume of faithful history, I ask so much confidence only as may give firmness & effect to the legal administration of your affairs. I shall often go wrong through defect of judgment. when right, I shall often be thought wrong by those whose positions will not command a view of the whole ground. I ask your indulgence for my own errors, which will never be intentional; and your support against the errors of others, who may condemn what they would not, if seen in all it's parts. the approbation implied by your suffrage, is a great consolation to me for the past; and my future solicitude will be, to retain the good opinion of those who have bestowed it in advance, to conciliate that of others by doing them all the good in my power, and to be instrumental to the happiness & freedom of all.

Relying then on the patronage of your good will, I advance with obedience to the work, ready to retire from it whenever you become sensible how much better choices it is in your power to make. and may that infinite power which rules the destinies of the universe, lead our councils to what is best, & give them a favorable issue for your peace and prosperity.

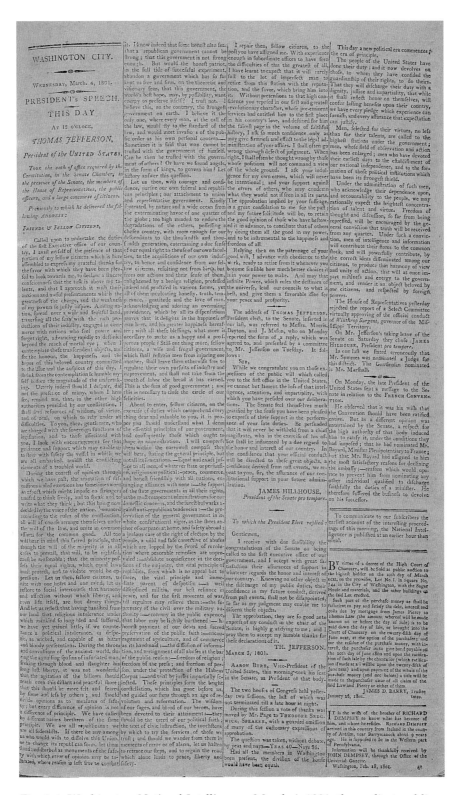

Fig. 1-4. Washington *National Intelligencer,* March 4, 1801, the earliest publication of Thomas Jefferson's first inaugural address. Library of Congress.

Fig. 2-1. Oil portrait of Thomas Jefferson, taken from life by Rembrandt Peale, 1800. The White House.

Chapter II

Words Widely Circulated

It was fortunate that Thomas Jefferson provided an advance copy of his inaugural address for publication, because the new president failed to make his weak voice heard in many parts of the chamber.[1] Moreover, interest in Jefferson's address reached far beyond those privileged to be in the Senate audience. "So great was the demand for this address," publisher Samuel Harrison Smith reported, "and so considerable the number of citizens surrounding the office in expectation of its appearing that the Press could scarcely keep pace with it." Smith also printed the speech in the *Universal Gazette,* the weekly edition of *National Intelligencer.*[2]

Once published in the *National Intelligencer* of March 4, 1801 (fig. 1-4), Jefferson's inaugural speech was widely reprinted. Both the Georgetown *Washington Federalist* (fig. 2-2) and the Alexandria *Times* printed the text the next day. Copies of the *National Intelligencer* and the *Washington Federalist* circulated through the country with remarkable speed. The Baltimore

American published the full text "by express from Washington," on March 5, the editor explaining: "At one o'clock this morning, a citizen whom the *American* feels proud in acknowledging as one of its best friends, handed the Editor the *National Intelligencer,* published at three o'clock yesterday afternoon."[3] The leading story under the *American* masthead reported the Baltimore celebration and the inauguration:

> Yesterday was a day of jubilee—it was devoted by the republicans of this city to the celebration of the first principle of a free government, the elective franchise. The morning was saluted by a discharge of cannon at Federal Hill, and sunrise was announced by the artillery of the Whig-Wham society, at the head of the Bason. The Observatory was elegantly decorated with colours, and the different shipping in the harbor displayed their flags.
>
> At 12 o'clock (supposed to be the moment of the President's taking the oath of office,) a grand salute was fired from both the places above mentioned. The citizens were generally divided into select parties and spent the afternoon with the utmost hilarity and good fellowship.

1. *National Intelligencer* (Washington, D.C.), March 4, 1801; Margaret Bayard Smith to Susan B. Smith, March 4, 1801, in Hunt, ed., *First Forty Years of Washington Society,* 25–26; Noble E. Cunningham, Jr., *The Process of Government under Jefferson,* 8–9.

2. *Universal Gazette* (Washington, D.C.), March 12, 1801.

3. The speech was also printed in the *Maryland Gazette* (Annapolis) on March 12.

Fig. 2-2. *Washington Federalist,* Georgetown, March 5, 1801. State Historical Society of Wisconsin.

Jefferson's address was printed in Philadelphia on March 7, 1801, in both the Republican *Aurora* and the Federalist *Gazette of the United States*. It appeared in New York in a broadside *From the Office of the Mercantile Advertiser,* "Monday, March 9, 1801, 10 o'clock, A.M." (fig. 2-3). The New York *American Citizen* published the text on March 10, and it appeared in the Newark *Centinel of Freedom* on the same day. The editor of the *Centinel* noted that the printing of Jefferson's address had excluded other important matter intended for that day's paper, but he added: "As nothing more gratifying to the public could employ our columns, we rely with confidence on the indulgence of our correspondents for the omission." *Kline's Carlisle Weekly Gazette,* published in Carlisle, Pennsylvania, included a supplement to the issue of March 11, printing the text in two broad columns, filling nearly a page (fig. 2-4).

To the south of Washington, the *Norfolk Herald* published Jefferson's speech in an Extra on March 9, and the Richmond *Virginia Argus* printed it on March 10. Copies of the inaugural speech reached Charleston, South Carolina, in time to be published in the *Times* on March 17 and in the *City Gazette* on March 18.

On Thursday afternoon, March 12, the sloop *Rising Sun,* from Alexander, Virginia, with Captain John Rhodes in command, arrived in Providence, Rhode Island, bringing a copy of Jefferson's inaugural speech. On Saturday, March 14, the *Providence Gazette,* published by John Carter, printed the complete text of the address.

Meanwhile, mail arriving in Boston on Friday night, March 13, brought copies of the text of Jefferson's speech to that city, and it was published in the *Columbian Centinel,* a Federalist paper, the following day. Appearing on Wednesdays and Saturdays, the *Columbian Centinel* thus scooped its rival, the Republican *Independent Chronicle,* which, publishing on

Mondays and Thursdays, would not print the text until Monday, March 16. Demand for copies of the address remained high, and the *Centinel* published the text again on March 18, after the previous printing had "fallen short of a supply for our Patrons." The following day, the editor of the *Independent Chronicle* prominently placed the following notice in his paper:

> This day will be published, at this office, on the finest imperial woven paper and a beautiful type,
> THE INAUGURAL SPEECH OF
> *THOMAS JEFFERSON,*
> PRESIDENT OF THE UNITED STATES,
> Delivered on the 4th of March 1801.
> The work will be executed with neatness, and in a form calculated to adorn the Parlours of all the *Federal Republicans.* A few copies will be struck on white satin--at different prices.

Printed in two columns, with a variety of fonts used to compose the heading and introductory commentary, the handsome print was designed to invite framing. Inconspicuously placed in the center of the decorative line separating the two wide columns can be seen in very small caps: "FROM THE CHRONICLE PRESS, BY ADAMS & RHOADES, COURT-STREET." (fig. 2-5). Abijah Adams and Ebenezer Rhoades were the editors of the Boston *Independent Chronicle.*

The *Massachusetts Spy, Or Worcester Gazette* published the text of Jefferson's inaugural address on March 18 under a heading "PERTINENT, JUDICIOUS, and CONCILIATORY ADDRESS." His address appeared on the front page of the Hartford, Connecticut, *American Mercury* (fig. 2-6), a Republican newspaper, on March 19, but it had already been printed in the Federalist *Connecticut Courant* on March 16. In Rhode Island, John Carter included the address in the Federalist *Providence Journal* on March 18.

In Boston, the *Mercury and New-England Palladium,* a semiweekly Federalist paper published by Alexander Young and Thomas Minns, offered an editorial on March 20 declaring:

> Since the election of Mr. Jefferson, the public mind has been falling from a point, where it lately trembled with anxiety and alarm. His Speech has removed the apprehensions of some, and disappointed the hopes of others. . . . His professions are fair and candid, as such we take them, and sincerely hope that all his general declarations will have a particular and exact fulfillment. And if, at any time, we remark upon errors in theory or practice, we shall do it from a solemn sense of duty, and in honorable manner. We have hitherto opposed Mr. Jefferson from principle. It will give us pleasure, in like manner, to support him.

Throughout the nation, in towns large and small, Jefferson's inaugural address was widely reprinted in both Federalist and Republican newspapers. In Harrisburg, Pennsylvania, the *Härrisburger Morgenröthe* published the full text in German on March 23. The *Farmers' Museum, or Literary Gazette* in Walpole, New Hampshire, printed the address on March 24. In Chillicothe, the seat of government of the Northwestern Territory, Nathaniel Willis, printer to the territorial legislature and publisher of the *Scioto Gazette,* printed the address in his paper on March 26. On the same date it appeared in the Peacham, Vermont, *Green Mountain Patriot.* In Lexington, Kentucky, James H. Stewart—who complained about the slowness of the mails—included Jefferson's speech in his *Kentucky Herald* on March 30.

From the early printings in newspapers, Jefferson's inaugural address would be reprinted not only throughout the United States but also in Europe. In addition to being republished in newspapers, the speech appeared in broadsides, pamphlets, and magazines. The *Connecticut Magazine* for March 1801, published in Bridgeport, printed the full text of the address of "Thomas Jefferson, Esq., who has long been at the head of what has been called the opposition party."[4] The *Baltimore*

Weekly Magazine published the speech, "by the particular request of a number of our readers," in its issue of May 13 (fig. 2-7).

Separate prints of the text of Jefferson's inaugural address of 1801 were widely available, most commonly printed on paper but also reproduced on satin, suitable for framing. A week after the inauguration, Mathew Carey had broadsides of Jefferson's inaugural speech ready for sale. In notices in both the Philadelphia *Aurora* and the *Gazette of the United States,* Carey described them as "elegantly printed (by [Hugh] Maxwell, in his best manner) on superfine wove paper, with a miniature likeness at the top" (fig. 2-8).[5] Carey also offered prints on satin. The paper prints, priced at one quarter of a dollar, sold rapidly. A few days before publication, Philadelphia printer John Means charged Carey three dollars for "printing 300 portraits of Jefferson at the Head of his Speech." Before the month was over, Carey was advertising the third edition of the broadside, and Means had printed another 279 Jefferson portraits on paper broadsides of the inaugural address and another 74 satin prints.[6]

At prices of $1.25 to $1.75, depending on the quality of the satin, Jefferson's admirers could purchase an elegant print. Carey's records show that at least 89 such satin prints were made. After Carey sent Jefferson one of the paper broadsides, Jefferson requested a satin print, which Carey promptly supplied.[7]

4. *Connecticut Magazine, and Gentleman's and Lady's Monthly Museum* 1 (March 1801): 186–89.

5. *Gazette of the United States* (Philadelphia), March 12, 1801; *Aurora* (Philadelphia), March 14, 1801.

6. Account books, Mathew Carey Papers, New-York Historical Society; *Aurora* (Philadelphia), March 27, 1801; Noble E. Cunningham, Jr., *The Image of Thomas Jefferson in the Public Eye: Portraits for the People,* 33–35.

7. *Aurora* (Philadelphia), March 9, 14, 1801; Account Books, Carey Papers; Carey to Jefferson, March 17, 31, 1801, Jefferson Papers, Coolidge Collection, Massachusetts Historical Society, microfilm edition, reel 5.

From the Office of the

Mercantile Advertiſer.

Monday, March 9, 1801, 10 *o'clock, A. M.*

WASHINGTON, March 2.

The Speaker laid before the houſe a letter from the Preſident of the United States elect, which was read as follows:

Waſhington, March 2, 1801.

"SIR,

"I beg leave through you, to inform the honorable houſe of repreſentatives of the United States, that I ſhall take the oath which the conſtitution preſcribes to the Preſident of the United States before he enters on the execution of his office, on Wedneſday the 4th inſt. at 12 o'Clock in the Senate chamber. I have the honor to be, with great reſpect, Sir, your moſt obedient, and moſt humble ſervant.

"THOMAS JEFFERSON."

The hon. Theodore Sedgwick, ſpeaker of the houſe of repreſentatives.

—

Waſhington, March 4, 1801.

"Encloſed is the Speech of the Preſident of the United States, delivered this day in the Senate Chamber of the Capitol, at 12 o'Clock. Mr. Burr had been ſworn into office at 11 o'clock.

"The aſſemblage of people was immenſe, and immediately upon the inauguration ſeveral diſcharges of artillery took place—there were about 1000 perſons in the Senate chamber, beſides the members of the Legiſlature, and not leſs than 150 Ladies.

"Mr. Adams left town at 4 o'clock this morning."

—

Friends and Fellow citizens,

Called upon to undertake the duties of the firſt Executive office of our country, I avail myſelf of the preſence of that portion of my fellow-citizens which is here aſſembled to expreſs my grateful thanks for the favor with which they have been pleaſed to look towards me, to declare a ſincere conſciouſneſs that the taſk is above my talents, and that I approach it with thoſe anxious and awful preſentiments which the greatneſs of that charge, and the weakneſs of my powers ſo juſtly inſpire. A riſing nation, ſpread over a wide and fruitful land, traverſing all the ſeas with the rich productions of their induſtry, engaged in commerce with nations who feel power and forget right; advancing rapidly to deſtinies beyond the reach of mortal eye; when I contemplate theſe tranſcendant objects, and ſee the honor, the happineſs, and the hope of this beloved country committed to the iſſue and the auſpices of this day, I ſhrink from the contemplation and humble myſelf before the magnitude of the undertaking. Utterly indeed ſhould I deſpair, did not the preſence of many, whom I here ſee, remind me, that, in the other high authorities provided by our conſtitution, I ſhall find reſources of wiſdom, of virtue, and of zeal, on which to rely under all difficulties. To you, then, gentlemen, who are charged with the ſovereign function of legiſlation, and to thoſe aſſociated with you, I look with encouragement for that guidance and ſupport which may enable us to ſteer with ſafety the veſſel in which we are all embarked, amidſt the conflicting elements of a troubled world.

During the conteſt of opinion through which we have paſt, the animation of diſcuſſions and of exertions has ſometimes worn an aſpect which might impoſe on ſtrangers unuſed to think freely and to ſpeak and to write what they think; but this being now decidedly the voice of the nation, announced according to the rules of the conſtitution, all will of courſe arrange themſelves under the will of the law, and unite in common efforts for the common good. All too will bear in mind this ſacred principle, that though the will of the majority is in all caſes to prevail, that will, to be rightful, muſt be reaſonable; that the minority poſſeſs their equal rights, which equal laws muſt protect, and to violate would be oppreſſion. Let us then, fellow citizens, unite with one heart and one mind, let us reſtore to ſocial intercourſe that harmony and affection without which liberty, and even life itſelf, are but dreary things. And let us reflect, that having baniſhed from our land that religious intolerance under which mankind ſo long bled and ſuffered, we have yet gained little, if we countenance a political intolerance, as deſpotic, as wicked, and capable of as wicked and bloody perſecutions. During the throes and convulſions of the ancient world, during the agonizing ſpaſms of infuriated man, ſeeking through blood and ſlaughter his long loſt liberty, it was not wonderful that the agitation of the billows ſhould reach even this diſtant and peaceful ſhore; that this ſhould be more felt and feared by ſome, and leſs by others; and ſhould divide opinions as to meaſures of ſafety; but every difference of opinion is not a difference of principle. We have called by different names brethren of the ſame principle. We are all republicans; we are all federaliſts. If there be any among us who would wiſh to diſſolve this union, or to change its republican form, let them ſtand undiſturbed as monuments of the ſafety with which error of opinion may be tolerated, where reaſon is left free to combat it. I know indeed that ſome honeſt men fear that a republican government cannot be ſtrong; that this government is not ſtrong enough. But would the honeſt patriot, in the full tide of ſucceſsful experiment abandon a government which has ſo far kept us free and firm, on the theoretic and viſionary fear, that this government, the world's beſt hope, may, by poſſibility, want energy to preſerve itſelf? I truſt not. I believe this, on the contrary, the ſtrongeſt government on earth. I believe it the only one, where every man, at the call of the law, would fly to the ſtandard of the law, and would meet invaſions of the public order as his own perſonal concern. Sometimes it is ſaid that man cannot be truſted with the government of himſelf. Can he then be truſted with the government of others? Or have we found angels in the form of kings, to govern him? Let hiſtory anſwer this queſtion.

Let us, then, with courage and confidence purſue our own federal and republican principles; our attachment to union and repreſentative government. Kindly ſeparated by nature and a wide ocean from the exterminating havoc of one quarter of the globe; too high-minded to endure the degradations of the others, poſſeſſing a choſen country, with room enough for our deſcendants to the thouſandth and thouſandth generation, entertaining a due ſenſe of our equal right to the uſe of our own faculties, to the acquiſitions of our own induſtry, to honour and confidence from our fellow citizens, reſulting not from birth, but from our actions and their ſenſe of them, enlightened by a benign religion, profeſſed indeed and practiſed in various forms, yet all of them inculcating honeſty, truth, temperance, gratitude and the love of man, acknowledging and adoring an over-ruling providence, which by all its diſpenſations proves that it delights in the happineſs of man here, and his greater happineſs hereafter; with all theſe bleſſings, what more is neceſſary to make us a happy and a proſperous people? Still one thing more, fellow-citizens, a wiſe and frugal government, which ſhall reſtrain men from injuring one another, ſhall leave them otherwiſe free to regulate their own purſuits of induſtry and improvement, and ſhall not take from the mouth of labour the bread it has earned. This is the ſum of good government; and this is neceſſary to cloſe the circle of our felicities.

About to enter, fellow citizens, on the exerciſe of duties which comprehend every thing dear and valuable to you, it is proper you ſhould underſtand what I deem the eſſential principles of our government, and conſequently thoſe which ought to ſhape its adminiſtration. I will compreſs them within the narroweſt compaſs they will bear, ſtating the general principle, but not all its limitations. Equal and exact juſtice to all men, of whatever ſtate or perſuaſion, religious or political—peace, commerce, and honeſt friendſhip with all nations, entangling alliances with none—the ſupport of the ſtate governments in all their rights as the moſt competent adminiſtrations for our domeſtic concerns, and the ſureſt bulwarks againſt anti-republican tendencies—the preſervation of the general government in its whole conſtitutional vigor, as the ſheet anchor of our peace at home, and ſafety abroad—a jealous care of the right of election by the people, a mild and ſafe corrective of abuſes which are lopped by the ſword of revolution where peaceable remedies are unprovided—abſolute acquieſcence in the deciſions of the majority, the vital principle of republics, from which is no appeal but to force, the vital principle and immediate parent of deſpotiſm—a well diſciplined militia, our beſt reliance in peace, and for the firſt moments of war, till regulars may relieve them—the ſupremacy of the civil over the military authority—economy in the public expence, that labor may be lightly burthened—the honeſt payment of our debts and ſacred preſervation of the public faith—encouragement of agriculture, and of commerce as its handmaid—the diffuſion of information, and arraignment of all abuſes at the bar of the public reaſon—freedom of religion—freedom of the preſs—and freedom of perſon, under the protection of the Habeas Corpus—and trial by juries impartially ſelected. Theſe principles form the bright conſtellation, which has gone before us, and guided our ſteps through an age of revolution and reformation. The wiſdom of our ſages, and blood of our heroes, have been devoted to their attainment—they ſhould be the creed of our political faith—the text of civic inſtruction, the touchſtone by which to try the ſervices of thoſe we truſt—and ſhould we wander from them in moments of error or alarm, let us haſten to retrace our ſteps, and to regain the road which alone leads to peace, liberty and ſafety.

I repair then, fellow-citizens, to the poſt you have aſſigned me. With experience enough in ſubordinate offices to have ſeen the difficulties of this greateſt of all, I have learnt to expect that it will rarely fall to the lot of imperfect man to retire from this ſtation with the reputation, and the favor, which bring him into it.——Without pretenſions to that high confidence you repoſed in our firſt and greateſt revolutionary character, whoſe pre-eminent ſervices had entitled him to the firſt place of his country's love, and deſtined for him the faireſt page in the volume of faithful hiſtory, I aſk ſo much confidence only as may give firmneſs and effect to the legal adminiſtration of your affairs. I ſhall often go wrong through defect of judgment. When right, I ſhall often be thought wrong by thoſe whoſe poſitions will not command a view of the whole ground. I aſk your indulgence for my own errors, which will never be intentional; and your ſupport againſt the errors of others, who may condemn what they would not if ſeen in all its parts. The approbation implied by your ſuffrage, is a great conſolation to me for the paſt; and my future ſolicitude will be, to retain the good opinion of thoſe who have beſtowed it in advance, to conciliate that of others by doing them all the good in my power, and to be inſtrumental to the happineſs and freedom of all.

Relying then on the patronage of your good will, I will advance with obedience to the work, ready to retire from it whenever you become ſenſible how much better choices it is in your Power to make.—And may that infinite power, which rules the deſtinies of the Univerſe, lead our councils to what is beſt, and give them a favourable iſſue for your peace and proſperity. THOMAS JEFFERSON.

United States, March 4, 1801.

—

On Monday, the late Preſident of the United States ſent a meſſage to the Senate in relation to the French Convention.

He obſerved that it was his wiſh that the Convention ſhould have been ratified entire. But as a different opinion was entertained by the Senate, a reſpect for the high authority of that body induced him to ratify it under the condition they had impoſed; that he had nominated Mr. Bayard, Miniſter Plenipotentiary to France; but that Mr. Bayard had aſſigned to him the moſt ſatisfactory reaſons for declining the embaſſy—reaſons which would operate to prevent him from nominating any other individual qualified to diſcharge faithfully the duties of a miniſter. He therefore ſuffered the buſineſs to devolve on his ſucceſſor.

Fig. 2-3. *From the Office of the Mercantile Advertiser,* "Monday, March 9, 1801, 10 o'clock, A.M.," Thomas Jefferson's inaugural address of March 4, 1801. New-York Historical Society.

SUPPLEMENT TO THE CARLISLE GAZETTE.

Wednefday, March 11, 1801.

Prefident's Speech.

THIS DAY, AT 12 O'CLOCK, *4th March*,

THOMAS JEFFERSON,

PRESIDENT OF THE UNITED STATES,

Took the oath of office required by the Constitution, in the Senate Chamber, in the presence of the Senate, the members of the House of Representatives, the public officers, and a large concourse of citizens.

Previously to which he delivered the following ADDRESS:

FRIENDS & FELLOW CITIZENS,

Called upon to undertake the duties of the firft Executive office of our country, I avail myfelf of the prefence of that portion of my fellow-citizens which is here affembled to exprefs my grateful thanks for the favour with which they have been pleafed to look towards me, to declare a fincere confcioufnefs that the tafk is above my talents, and that I approach it with thofe anxious and awful prefentiments which the greatnefs of the charge, and the weaknefs of my powers fo juftly infpire. A rifing nation, fpread over a wide and fruitful land, traverfing all the feas with the rich productions of their induftry, engaged in commerce with nations who feel power and forget right, advancing rapidly to deftinies beyond the reach of mortal eye; when I contemplate thefe tranfcendent objects, and fee the honour, the happinefs, and the hopes of this beloved country committed to the iffue and the aufpices of this day, I fhrink from the contemplation and humble myfelf before the magnitude of the undertaking. Utterly indeed fhould I defpair, did not the prefence of many, whom I here fee, remind me, that, in the other high authorities provided by our conftitution, I fhall find refources of wifdom, of virtue, and of zeal, on which to rely under all difficulties. To you, then, gentlemen, who are charged with the fovereign functions of legiflation, and to thofe affociated with you, I look with encouragement for that guidance and fupport which may enable us to fteer with fafety the veffel in which we are all embarked, amidft the conflicting elements of a troubled world. During the conteft of opinion through which we have paft, the animation of difcuffions and of exertions has fometimes worn an afpect which might impofe on ftrangers unufed to think freely, and to fpeak and to write what they think; but this being now decided by the voice of the nation, announced according to the rules of the conftitution, all will of courfe arrange themfelves under the will of the law, and unite in common efforts for the common good. All too will bear in mind this facred principle, that though the will of the majority is in all cafes to prevail, that will, to be rightful, muft be reafonable; that the minority poffefs their equal rights, which equal laws muft protect, and to violate would be oppreffion. Let us then, fellow-citizens, unite with one heart and one mind, let us reftore to focial intercourfe that harmony and affection without which liberty, and even life itfelf are but dreary things. And let us reflect that having banifhed from our land that religious intolerance under which mankind fo long bled and fuffered, we have yet gained little, if we countenance a political intolerance, as defpotic, as wicked, and capable of as bitter and bloody perfecutions. During the throes and convulfions of the ancient world, during the agonifing fpafms of infuriated man, feeking through blood and flaughter his long loft liberty, it was not wonderful that the agitation of the billows fhould reach even this diftant and peaceful fhore; that this fhould be more felt and feared by fome and lefs by others; and fhould divide opinions as to meafures of fafety; but every difference of opinion is not a difference of principle. We are all republicans: we are all federalifts. If there be any among us who would wifh to diffolve this Union, or to change its republican form, let them ftand undifturbed as monuments of the fafety with which error of opinion may be tolerated, where reafon is left free to combat it. I know indeed that fome honeft men fear that a republican government cannot be ftrong; that this government is not ftrong enough. But would the honeft patriot, in the full tide of fuccefsful experiment, abandon a government which has fo far kept us free and firm, on the theoretic and vifionary fear, that this government, the world's beft hope, may, by poffibility, want energy to preferve itfelf? I truft not. I believe this, on the contrary, the ftrongeft government on earth. I believe it the only one, where every man, at the call of the law, would fly to the ftandard of the law, and would meet invafions of the public order as his own perfonal concern.—Sometimes it is faid that man cannot be trufted with the government of himfelf. Can he then be trufted with the government of others? Or have we found angels in the form of kings, to govern him? Let hiftory anfwer this queftion.

Let us then, with courage and confidence, purfue our own federal and republican principles; our attachment to union and reprefentative government. Kindly feparated by nature and a wide ocean from the exterminating havoc of one quarter of the globe; too high minded to endure the degradations of the others, poffeffing a chofen country, with room enough for our defcendants to the thoufandth and thoufandth gene-

ration, entertaining a due fenfe of our equal right to the ufe of our own faculties, to the acquifitions of our own induftry, to honor and confidence from our fellow-citizens, refulting not from birth, but from our actions and their fenfe of them, enlightened by a benign religion, profeffed indeed and practifed in various forms, yet all of them inculcating honefty, truth, temperance, gratitude and the love of man acknowledging and adoring an overruling providence, which by all its difpenfations proves that it delights in the happinefs of man here, and his greater happinefs hereafter; with all thefe bleffings, what more is neceffary to make us a happy and a profperous people? Still one thing more, fellow-citizens, a wife and frugal government, which fhall reftrain men from injuring one another, fhall leave them otherwife free to regulate their own purfuits of induftry and improvement, and fhall not take from the mouth of labour the bread it has earned. This is the fum of good government; and this is neceffary to clofe the circle of our felicities.

About to enter, fellow citizens, on the exercife of duties which comprehend every thing dear and valuable to you, it is proper you fhould underftand what I deem the effential principles of our government, and confequently thofe which ought to fhape its adminiftration. I will comprefs them within the narroweft compafs they will bear, ftating the general principle, but not all its limitations.—Equal and exact juftice to all men, of whatever ftate or perfuafion, religious or political:—peace, commerce, and honeft friendfhip with all nations, entangling alliances with none:—the fupport of the ftate governments in all their rights, as the moft competent adminiftrations for our domeftic concerns, and the fureft bulwarks againft anti-republican tendencies:—the prefervation of the general government in its whole conftitutional vigor, as the fheet anchor of our peace at home, and fafety abroad:—a jealous care of the right of election by the people, a mild and fafe corrective of abufes which are lopped by the fword of revolution where peaceable remedies are unprovided:—abfolute acquiefcence in the decifions of the majority, the vital principle of republics, from which is no appeal but to force, the vital principle and immediate parent of defpotifm:—a well difciplined militia, our beft reliance in peace, and for the firft moments of war, till regulars may relieve them:—the fupremacy of the civil over the military authority:—economy in the public expence,' that labour may be lightly burthened:—the honeft payment of our debts and facred prefervation of the public faith:—encouragement of agriculture and of commerce as its handmaid:—the diffufion of information, and arraignment of all abufes at the bar of the public reafon:—freedom of religion; freedom of the prefs; and freedom of perfon, under the protection of the Habeas Corpus:—and trial by juries impartially felected. Thefe principles form the bright conftellation, which has gone before us, and guided our fteps through an age of revolution and reformation. The wifdom of our fages and blood of our heroes, have been devoted to their attainment:—they fhould be the creed of our political faith; the text of civic inftruction, the touchftone by which to try the fervices of thofe we truft; and fhould we wander from them in moments of error or of alarm, let us haften to retrace our fteps, and to regain the road which alone leads to peace, liberty and fafety.

I repair then, fellow citizens, to the poft you have affigned me. With experience enough in fubordinate offices to have feen the difficulties of this the greateft of all, I have learnt to expect that it will rarely fall to the lot of imperfect man to retire from this ftation with the reputation, and the favor, which bring him into it. Without pretenfions to that high confidence you repofed in our firft and greateft revolutionary character, whofe pre-eminent fervices had entitled him to the firft place in his country's love, and deftined for him the faireft page in the volume of faithful hiftory, I afk fo much confidence only as may give firmnefs and effect to the legal adminiftration of your affairs. I fhall often go wrong through defect of judgment. When right, I fhall often be thought wrong by thofe whofe pofitions will not command a view of the whole ground. I afk your indulgence for my own errors, which will never be intentional; and your fupport againft the errors of others, who may condemn what they would not if feen in all its parts. The approbation implied by your fuffrage, is a great confolation to me for the paft; and my future folicitude will be, to retain the good opinion of thofe who have beftowed it in advance, to conciliate that of others by doing them all the good in my power, and to be inftrumental to the happinefs and freedom of all.

Relying then on the patronage of your good will, I advance with obedience to the work, ready to retire from it whenever you become fenfible how much better choice it is in your power to make. And may that infinite power, which rules the deftinies of the univerfe, lead our councils to what is beft, and give them a favorable iffue for your peace and profperity.

On Saturday laft, THOMAS JEFFERSON, *then Vice-Prefident of the United States, and Prefident of the Senate, took leave of that body; on which occafion he delivered the following* ADDRESS:

Gentlemen of the Senate,

To give the ufual opportunity of appointing a Prefident pro tempore, I now propofe to retire from the chair of the Senate: and as the time is near at hand, when the relations will ceafe, which have for fome time fubfifted between this honourable houfe and myfelf, I beg leave before I withdraw to return them my grateful thanks for all the inftances of atten-

Fig. 2-4. *Supplement to the Carlisle Gazette,* Carlisle, Pennsylvania, March 11, 1801, publishing Thomas Jefferson's inaugural address of March 4. American Antiquarian Society.

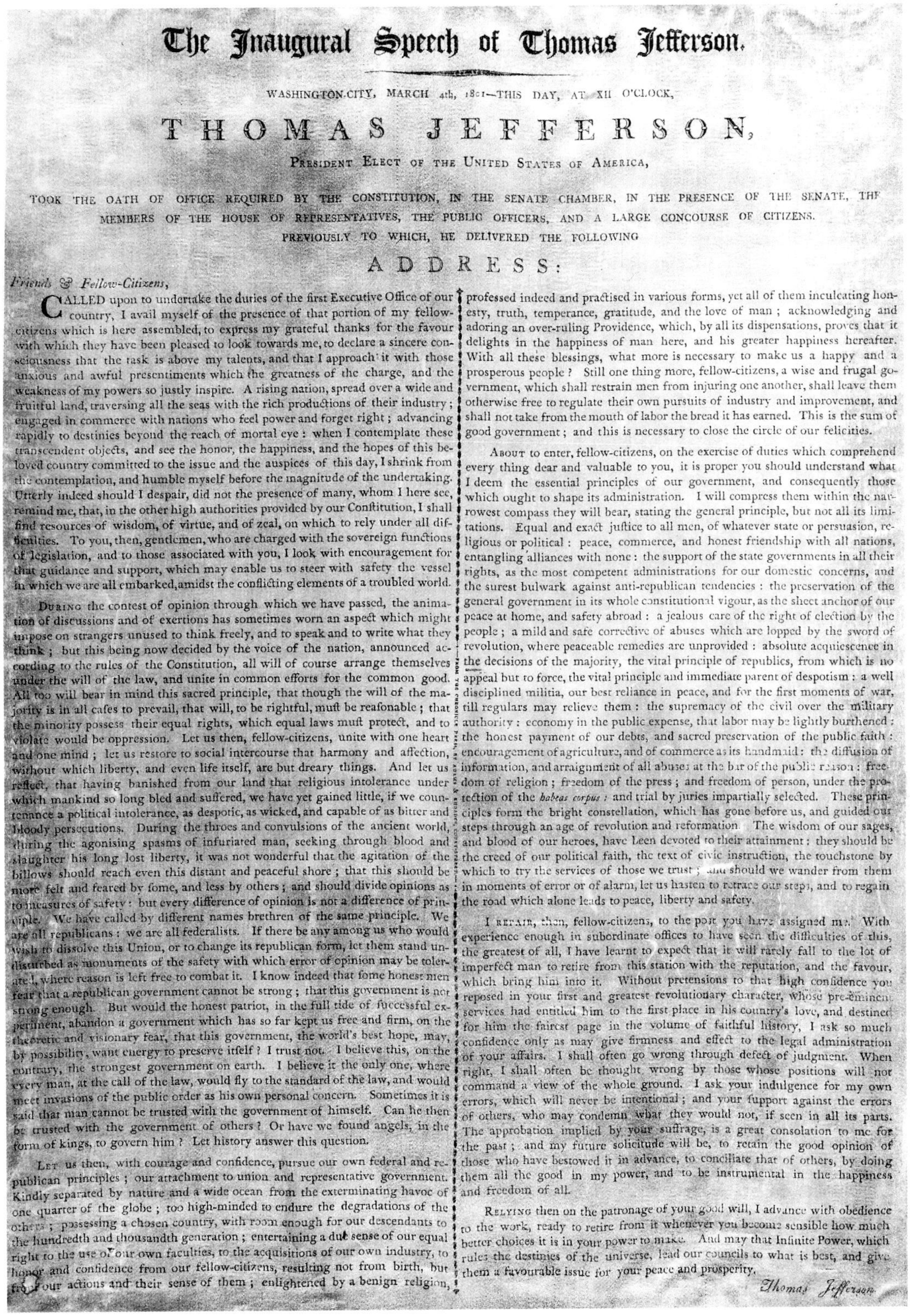

Fig. 2-5. *The Inaugural Speech of Thomas Jefferson. Washington City, March 4th, 1801.* Broadside, from the Chronicle Press, published by Adams and Rhoades, Court Street, [Boston, Mass., 1801]. American Antiquarian Society.

American Mercury.

PUBLISHED BY ELISHA BABCOCK—HARTFORD.

[—VOL. XVII.—]   THURSDAY, MARCH 19, 1801.   [—No. 872.—]

Fig. 2-6. *American Mercury,* Hartford, Connecticut, March 19, 1801. Beinecke Library, Yale University.

The Baltimore Weekly Magazine.

For ev'ry palate is our Banquet fit ;
Replete with Morals, Hist'ry, News & Wit.

WEDNESDAY, May 13, 1801.

By the particular request of a number of our readers, we insert the following

Speech

OF

Thomas Jefferson,

President of the United States —Delivered at his inauguration, March 4, 1801.

Friends & Fellow-Citizens,

CALLED upon to undertake the duties of the first executive office of our country, I avail myself of the presence of that portion of my fellow-citizens which is here assembled, to express my grateful thanks for the favour with which they have been pleased to look towards me, to declare a sincere consciousness that the task is above my talents, and that I approach it with those anxious and awful presentiments, which the greatness of the charge, and the weakness of my powers so justly inspire. A rising nation, spread over a wide and fruitful land, traversing all the seas with the rich productions of their industry, engaged in commerce with nations who feel power and forget right; advancing rapidly to destinies beyond the reach of mortal eye ; when I contemplate these transcendant objects, and see the honor, the happiness and the hopes of this beloved country, committed to the issue and the auspices of this day, I shrink from the contemplation, and humble myself before the magnitude of the undertaking. Utterly, indeed, should I despair, did not the presence of many, whom I here see, remind me, that in the other high authorities, provided by our Constitution, I shall find resources of wisdom, of virtue, and of zeal, on which to rely under all difficulties. To you, then, gentlemen, who are charged with the sovereign functions of legislation, and to those associated with you, I look with encouragement for that guidance and support which may enable us to steer with safety the vessel in which we are all embarked, amidst the conflicting elements of a troubled world.

During the contest of opinion through which we have passed, the animation of discussions and of exertions has sometimes worn an aspect which might impose on strangers unused to think freely, and to speak and to write what they think ; but this being now decided by the voice of the nation, announced according to the rules of the Constitution, all will, of course, arrange themselves under the will of the law, and unite in common efforts for the common good. All too will bear in mind this sacred principle, that though the will of the majority is in all cases to prevail, that will to be rightful must be reasonable ; that the minority possess their equal rights, which equal laws must protect, and to violate would be oppression. Let us then, fellow-citizens, unite with one heart and one mind, let us restore to social intercourse that harmony and affection, without which liberty, and even life itself, are but dreary things. And let us reflect that having banished from our land that religious intolerance, under which mankind so long bled and suffered, we have yet gained little, if we countenance a political intolerance, as despotic, as wicked, and capable of as bitter and bloody persecutions. During the throes and convulsions of the ancient world, during the agonizing spasms of infuriated man, seeking through blood and slaughter his long lost liberty, it was not wonderful that the agitation of the billows should each even this distant and peaceful shore ; that this should be more felt and feared by some, and less by others ; and should divide opinions as to measures of safety ; but every difference of opinion is not a difference of principle. We have called by different names brethren of the same principle.—*We are* ALL *Republicans—We are* ALL *Federalists.* If there be any among us who would dissolve this union, or change its republican form, let them stand undisturbed as monuments of the safety with which error of opinion may be tolerated, where reason is left free to combat it. I know indeed that some honest men fear that a republican government cannot be strong ; that this government is not strong enough. But would the honest patriot, in the full tide of successful experiment, abandon a government which has so far kept us free and firm, on the theoretic and visionary fear, that this government, the world's best hope, may, by possibility, want energy to preserve itself? I trust not. I believe this, on the contrary, the strongest government on earth. I believe it the only one,

Fig. 2-7. *The Baltimore Weekly Magazine,* May 13, 1801. Duke University Library.

Mathew Carey's prints could be purchased in cities distant from Philadelphia. In April the Richmond *Virginia Argus* advertised the broadside at twenty-five cents, copying Carey's description of it as "elegantly printed on superfine paper, with a Miniature Likeness at the top."[8] Carey also published the inaugural speech in a pamphlet with Jefferson's portrait as a frontispiece (fig. 2-9). After an initial run of 500 copies, the printer provided an additional 550 prints of Jefferson's portrait for the pamphlet during April and May 1801.[9]

The image of Jefferson that adorned both the broadside and the pamphlet published by Carey was engraved by Benjamin Tanner from the life portrait of Jefferson painted by Rembrandt Peale in 1800 (fig. 2-1). Although not the best example of Peale's widely copied image, Tanner's engraving was superior to the image of Jefferson used as the frontispiece to Jefferson's inaugural address as printed by William Durell in New York in 1801 (fig. 2-10). Derived from a portrait painted by Edward Savage in 1800, that engraving—even though embellished with the national eagle and stars for the sixteen states—must surely have been among those that Jefferson referred to as "miserable caricatures."[10]

The earliest printings of Jefferson's inaugural address in newspapers outside Washington were commonly copied from the text published in the *National Intelligencer,* which had been printed directly from Jefferson's manuscript. As texts appeared in broadsides and leaflets, however, some printers called attention to words that Jefferson had not marked for emphasis in his text. In a passage that became widely quoted, Jefferson had written: "We have called by different names brethren of the same principle. We are

all republicans: we are all federalists." In not capitalizing the words *republicans* and *federalists,* Jefferson referred to common principles, not to political parties. At the same time, when he read this orally, he would have expected his listeners to draw a broader meaning that embraced both parties and principles. Although Smith copied Jefferson's text exactly in the first printing of the manuscript, later printings often gave this passage increased emphasis by using capital letters, italics, or a bolder font.

In an editorial published in the *Washington Federalist* on March 7, 1801, editor William A. Rind wrote:

> The inauguration Speech of Mr. Jefferson, is replete with wisdom and moderation. It has imparted new rays to the "Sun of Federalism" which will therefore continue to illumine our political hemisphere. It is worthy of a President of the United States. "WE ARE ALL REPUBLICANS—WE ARE ALL FEDERALISTS! We have called by *different names,* Brethren of the *same principle.*" . . . We are then all Republicans—we are all Federalists! We are all Federal Republicans—all, Republican Federalists![11]

A week after Jefferson's inaugural, the broadside published in Philadelphia by Mathew Carey called attention to Jefferson's words by capitalizing: "WE ARE ALL REPUBLICANS; WE ARE ALL FEDERALISTS" (fig. 2-8). In another broadside of the speech, John Barber, printer of the *Albany Register,* set the type to read "We are all REPUBLICANS: We are all FEDERALISTS" (fig. 2-11). The same emphasis appeared in the silk print *Speech of Mr. Jefferson at his Inauguration* (fig. 2-12), preserved in the Library of Congress. The *Baltimore Weekly Magazine,* May 13, 1801,

---

8. *Virginia Argus* (Richmond), April 10, 28, 1801.
9. Cunningham, *Image of Jefferson in the Public Eye,* 35–36.
10. Jefferson to Martha Jefferson Randolph, April 3, 1802, Edwin M. Betts and James A. Bear, Jr., eds., *Family Letters of Thomas Jefferson,* 221.

11. This editorial was reprinted in the Charleston, S.C., *Times,* March 21, 1801; the Rhode Island *Providence Gazette,* March 24, 1801; and the Lexington, Ky., *Stewart's Kentucky Herald,* May 5, 1801.

SPEECH

OF

THOMAS JEFFERSON, PRESIDENT OF THE UNITED STATES,

DELIVERED

AT HIS INSTALMENT,

MARCH 4, 1801,

AT THE CITY OF WASHINGTON.

FRIENDS, AND FELLOW-CITIZENS,

CALLED upon to undertake the duties of the first executive office of our country, I avail myself of the presence of that portion of my fellow-citizens, which is here assembled, to express my grateful thanks, for the favour with which they have been pleased to look towards me; to declare a sincere consciousness, that the task is above my talents, and that I approach it with those anxious and awful presentiments, which the greatness of the charge, and the weakness of my powers, so justly inspire. A rising nation, spread over a wide and fruitful land....traversing all the seas with the rich productions of their industry....engaged in commerce with nations who feel power and forget right....advancing rapidly to destinies beyond the reach of mortal eye....when I contemplate these transcendent objects, and see the honour, the happiness, and the hopes of this beloved country, committed to the issue and the auspices of this day, I shrink from the contemplation, and humble myself before the magnitude of the undertaking. Utterly, indeed, should I despair, did not the presence of many, whom I here see, remind me, that, in the other high authorities, provided by our constitution, I shall find resources of wisdom, of virtue, and of zeal, on which to rely under all difficulties. To you, then, gentlemen, who are charged with the sovereign functions of legislation, and to those associated with you, I look with encouragement for that guidance and support, which may enable us to steer, with safety, the vessel in which we are all embarked, amidst the conflicting elements of a troubled world.

During the contest of opinion, through which we have past, the animation of discussions and of exertions, has sometimes worn an aspect which might impose on strangers, unused to think freely, and to speak and to write what they think: but this being now decided by the voice of the nation, announced according to the rules of the constitution, all will, of course, arrange themselves under the will of the law, and unite in common efforts, for the common good. All, too, will bear in mind this sacred principle.... that though the will of the majority is, in all cases, to prevail, that will, to be rightful, must be reasonable....that the minority possess their equal rights, which equal laws must protect, and to violate would be oppression. Let us then, fellow-citizens, unite with one heart, and one mind. Let us restore to social intercourse, that harmony and affection, without which, liberty, and even life itself, are but dreary things. And let us reflect, that, having banished from our land, that religious intolerance, under which mankind so long bled and suffered, we have yet gained little, if we countenance a political intolerance, as despotic, as wicked, and capable of as bitter and bloody persecutions.

During the throes and convulsions of the ancient world....during the agonizing spasms of infuriated man, seeking, through blood and slaughter, his long-lost liberty ....it was not wonderful that the agitation of the billows should reach even this distant and peaceful shore,...that this should be more felt and feared by some, and less by others....and should divide opinions, as to measures of safety. But every difference of opinion is not a difference of principle. We have called by different names, brethren of the same principle. WE ARE ALL REPUBLICANS; WE ARE ALL FEDERALISTS. If there be any among us, who would wish to dissolve this union, or to change its republican form, let them stand undisturbed, as monuments of the safety with which error of opinion may be tolerated, where reason is left free to combat it. I know, indeed, that some honest men fear that a republican government cannot be strong....that this government is not strong enough. But would the honest patriot, in the full tide of successful experiment, abandon a government which has so far kept us free and firm, on the theoretic and visionary fear, that this government, the world's best hope, may, by possibility, want energy to preserve itself?....I trust not....I believe this, on the contrary, the strongest government on earth....I believe it the only one, where every man, at the call of the law, would fly to the standard of the law, and would meet invasions of the public order as his own personal concern. Sometimes it is said, that man cannot be trusted with the government of himself. Can he then be trusted with the government of others? Or have we found angels, in the form of kings, to govern him? Let history answer this question.

Let us, then, with courage and confidence, pursue our own federal and republican principles....our attachment to union and representative government. Kindly separated, by nature and a wide ocean, from the exterminating havoc of one quarter of the globe....too high-minded to endure the degradations of the others....possessing a chosen country, with room enough for our descendents to the thousandth and thousandth generation....entertaining a due sense of our equal right to the use of our own faculties....to the acquisitions of our own industry....to honour and confidence from our fellow-citizens; resulting not from birth, but from our actions, and their sense of them....enlightened by a benign religion, professed, indeed, and practised in various forms, yet all of them inculcating honesty, truth, temperance, gratitude, and the love of man....acknowledging and adoring an over-ruling Providence, which, by all its dispensations, proves that it delights in the happiness of man here, and his greater happiness hereafter....with all these blessings, what more is necessary to make us a happy and a prosperous people?....Still one thing more, fellow-citizens, a wise and frugal government, which shall restrain men from injuring one another; shall leave them otherwise free to regulate their own pursuits of industry and improvement; and shall not take from the mouth of labor the bread it has earned. This is the sum of good government; and this is necessary to close the circle of our felicities.

About to enter, fellow-citizens, on the exercise of duties, which comprehend every thing dear and valuable to you, it is proper you should understand what I deem the essential principles of our government, and consequently those which ought to shape its administration. I will compress them within the narrowest compass they will bear, stating the general principle, but not all its limitations. Equal and exact justice to all men, of whatever state or persuasion, religious or political....peace, commerce, and honest friendship with all nations....entangling alliances with none....the support of the state governments in all their rights, as the most competent administrations for our domestic concerns, and the surest bulwarks against anti-republican tendencies....the preservation of the general government in its whole constitutional vigor, as the sheet anchor of our peace at home, and safety abroad.....a jealous care of the right of election by the people....a mild and safe corrective of abuses, which are lopped by the sword of revolution, where peaceable remedies are unprovided.... absolute acquiescence in the decisions of the majority, the vital principle of republics, from which is no appeal but to force, the vital principle and immediate parent of despotism....a well-disciplined militia, our best reliance in peace, and for the first moments of war, till regulars may relieve them....the supremacy of the civil over the military authority....economy in the public expence, that labor may be lightly burdened....the honest payment of our debts, and sacred preservation of public faith....encouragement of agriculture, and of commerce, as its handmaid....the diffusion of information, and arraignment of all abuses at the bar of the public reason....freedom of religion....freedom of the press....and freedom of person, under the protection of the habeas corpus, and trial by juries impartially selected. These principles form the bright constellation, which has gone before us, and guided our steps through an age of revolution and reformation. The wisdom of our sages, and blood of our heroes, have been devoted to their attainment. They should be the creed of our political faith....the text of civic instruction....the touchstone by which to try the services of those we trust: and should we wander from them, in moments of error or alarm, let us hasten to retrace our steps, and to regain the road which alone leads to peace, liberty, and safety.

I repair, then, fellow citizens, to the post you have assigned me. With experience enough in subordinate offices, to have seen the difficulties of this, the greatest of all, I have learned to expect, that it will rarely fall to the lot of imperfect man, to retire from this station, with the reputation, and the favor, which bring him into it. Without pretensions to that high confidence you reposed in our first and greatest revolutionary character, whose pre-eminent services had entitled him to the first place in his country's love, and destined for him the fairest page in the volume of faithful history, I ask so much confidence only, as may give firmness and effect to the legal administration of your affairs. I shall often go wrong, through defect of judgment. When right, I shall often be thought wrong, by those whose positions will not command a view of the whole ground. I ask your indulgence for my own errors, which will never be intentional; and your support against the errors of others, who may condemn what they would not, if seen in all its parts. The approbation implied by your suffrage, is a great consolation to me for the past: and my future solicitude will be, to retain the good opinion of those who have bestowed it in advance, to conciliate that of others by doing them all the good in my power, and to be instrumental to the happiness and freedom of all.

Relying, then, on the patronage of your good will, I advance with obedience to the work, ready to retire from it whenever you become sensible how much better choices it is in your power to make. And may that infinite Power, which rules the destinies of the universe, lead our councils to what is best, and give them a favourable issue, for our peace and prosperity.

THOMAS JEFFERSON.

THIRD EDITION.

PHILADELPHIA, PUBLISHED BY MATHEW CAREY.

H. MAXWELL, PRINTER.

Fig. 2-8. *Speech of Thomas Jefferson, President of the United States, Delivered at His Instalment, March 4, 1801, at the City of Washington.* 3d ed. Philadelphia: Published by Mathew Carey, Hugh Maxwell, Printer, [1801]. Massachusetts Historical Society.

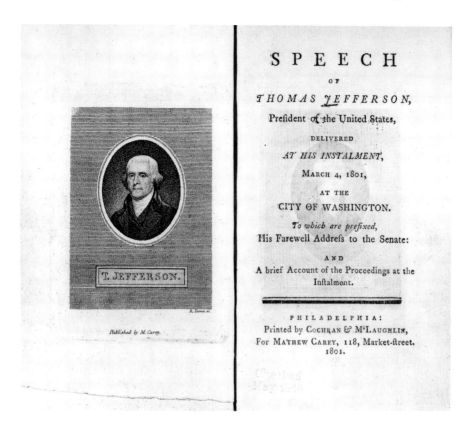

Fig. 2-9. *Speech of Thomas Jefferson, President of the United States, Delivered at His Instalment, March 4, 1801, at the City of Washington.* Philadelphia: Printed by Cochran and McLaughlin, for Mathew Carey, 1801. Portrait engraved by Benjamin Tanner. Rare Book Division, New York Public Library.

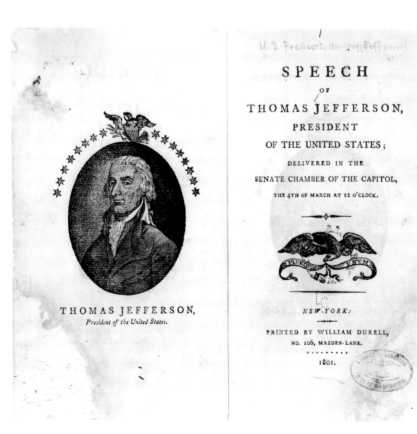

Fig. 2-10. *Speech of Thomas Jefferson, President of the United States; Delivered in the Senate Chamber of the Capitol, the 4th of March at 12 O'Clock.* New York: Printed by William Durell, 1801. Engraving of Jefferson from a portrait by Edward Savage. Library of Congress.

rendered the line as *We are ALL Republicans—We are ALL Federalists* (fig. 2-7). Similar emphasis appeared in the broadside published in Baltimore by William Pechin (fig. 2-13). In advertising this print in the Baltimore *American* on March 17, 1801, Pechin described it glowingly:

> It is handsomely printed on a large size type, and in a form which will not only be convenient for perusal, but will give it a chance of durability beyond what its insertion in a daily paper can ensure.
>
> In this address, Columbia's venerated patriot and sage, presents to our view, sentiments, congenial with those which inspired the revolutionary worthies of our country; and which (if adhered to) will secure to him immortal honor—they are such as ought to be impressed on the minds of every American—and our children should be taught to lisp them from the cradle of infancy. As we may safely calculate, that it will form the *ground-work* of the present administration, its importance to every individual is sufficiently obvious. It is presumed that its beauty and grandeur has never been surpassed by the pen of man.

Pechin advertised the print for sale on first-quality paper for twelve and a half cents and on inferior paper for six cents. To admirers who sought a more striking print, he also offered "a whole sheet impression, elegantly designed, for framing . . . on wove paper or satin." Jefferson preserved one of the satin prints among his own papers.[12] Pechin also printed and sold a pamphlet edition of Jefferson's inaugural address (fig. 2-14).

In Hagerstown, Maryland, John J. May produced an impressive print of Jefferson's first inaugural address (fig. 2-15). The large, handsome print with decorative borders was clearly designed for display, and it was one of the most attractive pieces produced in the nation. But Hagerstown was not a large city, and May still had copies on hand four years later, when he sent five of the prints to Jefferson. "The goddess of fortune has not been over liberal in bestowing her gifts upon me," he explained to Jefferson, suggesting that if the president was pleased with the prints he might send May a five-dollar note.[13]

In Chillicothe, in the Northwestern Territory, Nathaniel Willis, who printed the text of Jefferson's inaugural address in the *Scioto Gazette,* advertised in the issue of May 7, 1801:

> A few copies of the Speech of THOMAS JEFFERSON, President of the United State, delivered at his inauguration, elegantly printed with a new type on white sattin, may be had at the Printing Office.[14]

A well-preserved example of this print (fig. 2-16) is in the collection of the Chicago Historical Society.

Other reproductions of Jefferson's first inaugural speech include the text printed in three columns on silk by Samuel Nutting and John Whitelock, publishers of the Portsmouth, New Hampshire, *Republican Ledger* (fig. 2-17).

However printed, Jefferson's words "We are republicans: we are all federalists" became the most widely publicized declaration of his first inaugural address, and they quickly became imbedded in American popular culture. In celebration of the Fourth of July in New York in 1801, Waldron's Museum illuminated an eight-by-five-foot, full-length, transparent painting of Jefferson, picturing the president (according to

---

12. Pechin also promised prints gratis to clients who had subscribed to the recent edition he had published of Jefferson's *Notes on the State of Virginia.* Jefferson's copy is in the Thomas Jefferson Papers, Library of Congress.

13. May to Jefferson, October 29, 1805, Jefferson Papers, Library of Congress.

14. The prints were also advertised in the issues of May 14 and 21, 1801.

SPEECH

Of Mr. JEFFERSON, on his Inauguration as President of the United States.

WASHINGTON, *March* 4.

THIS day at 12 o'clock THOMAS JEFFERSON, President of the United States, took the oath of office required by the Constitution, in the Senate Chamber, in the presence of the Senate, the Members of the House of Representatives, the Public Officers, and a large concourse of Citizens. Previously to which he delivered the following

ADDRESS.

Friends and Fellow-Citizens,

Called upon to undertake the duties of the first executive office of our country, I avail myself of the presence of that portion of my fellow-citizens which is here assembled, to express my grateful thanks for the favour with which they have been pleased to look towards me; to declare a sincere consciousness that the task is above my talents; and that I approach it with those anxious and awful presentiments which the greatness of the charge, and the weakness of my powers so justly inspire. A rising nation, spread over a wide and fruitful land, traversing all the seas with the rich productions of their industry, engaged in commerce with nations who feel power and forget right, advancing rapidly to destinies beyond the reach of mortal eye; when I contemplate these transcendant objects, and see the honour, the happiness, and the hopes of this beloved country committed to the issue and the auspices of this day, I shrink from the contemplation, and humble myself before the magnitude of the undertaking. Utterly indeed should I despair, did not the presence of many, whom I here see, remind me, that in the other high authorities provided by our Constitution, I shall find resources of wisdom, of virtue, and of zeal, on which to rely under all difficulties. To you, then, gentlemen, who are charged with the sovereign functions of legislation, and to those associated with you, I look with encouragement for that guidance and support which may enable us to steer with safety the vessel in which we are all embarked, amidst the conflicting elements of a troubled world.

During the contest of opinion through which we have past, the animation of discussions and of exertions has sometimes worn an aspect which might impose on strangers unused to think freely, and to speak and to write what they think: but this being now decided by the voice of the nation, announced according to the rules of the constitution, all will of course arrange themselves under the will of the law, and unite in common efforts for the common good. All too will bear in mind this sacred principle, that though the will of the majority is in all cases to prevail, that will, to be rightful, must be reasonable; that the minority possess their equal rights which equal laws must protect, and to violate would be oppression. Let us then, fellow-citizens, unite with one heart and mind, let us restore to social intercourse that harmony and affection, without which liberty and even life itself are but dreary things. And let us reflect, that having banished from our land that religious intolerance under which mankind so long bled and suffered, we have yet gained little, if we countenance a political intolerance as despotic, as wicked, and capable of as bitter and bloody persecutions. During the throes and convulsions of the ancient world; during the agonizing spasms of infuriate man, seeking through blood and slaughter his long lost liberty, it was not wonderful that the agitation of the billows should reach even this distant and peaceful shore; that this should be more felt and feared by some and less by others; and should divide opinions as to measures of safety; but every difference of opinion is not a difference of principle. We have called by different names brethren of the same principle. We are all REPUBLICANS: We are all FEDERALISTS. If there be any among us who would wish to dissolve this union, or to change its Republican form, let them stand undisturbed as monuments of the safety with which error of opinion may be tolerated, where reason is left free to combat it. I know indeed that some honest men fear that a Republican government cannot be strong; that this government is not strong enough. But would the honest patriot, in the full tide of successful experiment, abandon a government which has so far kept us free and firm, on the theoretic and visionary fear that this government, the world's best hope, may, by possibility, want energy to preserve itself? I trust not. I believe this, on the contrary, the strongest government on earth. I believe it the only one, where every man, at the call of the law, would fly to the standard of the law, and would meet invasions of the public order as his own personal concern. Sometimes it is said that man cannot be trusted with the government of himself. Can he then be trusted with the government of others? Or have we found angels in the form of Kings to govern him? Let history answer this question.

Let us then, with courage and confidence, pursue our own federal and republican principles, our attachment to union and representative government. Kindly separated by nature and a wide ocean from the exterminating havoc of one quarter of the globe; too high minded to endure the degradations of the others; possessing a chosen country, with room enough for our descendants to the thousandth and thousandth generation; entertaining a due sense of our equal right to the use of our own faculties, to the acquisitions of our own industry, to honor and confidence from our fellow-citizens, resulting not from birth, but from our actions and their sense of them; enlightened by a benign religion, professed indeed and practised in various forms, yet all of them inculcating honesty, truth, temperance, gratitude and the love of man; acknowledging & adoring an overruling Providence, which by all its dispensations proves that it delights in the happiness of man here, and his greatest happiness hereafter: with all these blessings, what more is necessary to make us a happy and prosperous people? Still one thing more, fellow-citizens, a wise and frugal government, which shall restrain men from injuring one another, shall leave them otherwise free to regulate their own pursuits of industry and improvement, and shall not take from the mouth of labor the bread it has earned. This is the sum of good government; and this is necessary to close the circle of our felicities.

About to enter, fellow-citizens, on the exercise of duties which comprehend every thing dear and valuable to you, it is proper you should understand what I deem the essential principles of our government, and consequently those which ought to shape its administration. I will compress them within the narrowest compass they will bear, stating the general principle, but not all its limitations. Equal and exact justice to all men, of whatever state or persuasion, religious or political:—peace, commerce and honest friendship with all nations; entangling alliances with none:—the support of the State governments in all their rights, as the most competent administrations for our domestic concerns, and the surest bulwarks against anti-republican tendencies:—the preservation of the general government in its whole constitutional vigor, as the sheet-anchor of our peace at home, and safety abroad:—a jealous care of the right of election by the people, a mild and safe corrective of abuses which are lopped by the sword of revolution where peaceable remedies are unprovided:—absolute acquiescence in the decisions of the majority, the vital principle of Republics, from which is no appeal but to force, the vital principle and immediate parent of Despotism:—a well disciplined militia, our best reliance in peace, and for the first moments of war, till regulars may relieve them:—the supremacy of the civil over the military authority:—economy in the public expence, that labour may be lightly burthened:—the honest payment of our debts and sacred preservation of the public faith:—encouragement of agriculture, and of commerce as its hand-maid:—the diffusion of information, and arraignment of all abuses at the bar of the public reason:—freedom of religion; freedom of the press; and freedom of person, under the protection of the Habeas Corpus, and trial by juries impartially selected. These principles form the bright constellation which has gone before us, and guided our steps through an age of revolution and reformation. The wisdom of our sages, and the blood of our heroes, have been devoted to their attainment. They should be the creed of our political faith; the text of civic instruction, the touch-stone by which to try the services of those we trust; and should we wander from them in moments of error or of alarm, let us hasten to retrace our steps, and to regain the road which alone leads to peace, liberty and safety.

I repair, then, fellow-citizens, to the post you have assigned me. With experience enough in subordinate offices to have seen the difficulties of this, the greatest of all; I have learnt to expect that it will rarely fall to the lot of imperfect man to retire from this station with the reputation and the favor which bring him into it. Without pretensions to that confidence which you reposed in our first and greatest revolutionary character, whose pre-eminent services had entitled him to the first place in his country's love, and destined for him the fairest page in the volume of faithful history; I ask so much confidence only, as may give firmness and effect to the legal administration of your affairs. I shall often go wrong thro' defect of judgment: When right, I shall be thought wrong by those whose positions will not command a view of the whole ground. I ask your indulgence for my own errors, which will never be intentional; and your support against the errors of others, who may condemn what they would not, if seen in all its parts. The approbation implied by your suffrage, is a great consolation to me for the past; and my future solicitude will be, to retain the good opinion of those who have bestowed it in advance; to conciliate that of others, by doing them all the good in my power; and to be instrumental to the happiness and freedom of all.

Relying then on the patronage of your good will, I advance with obedience to the work, ready to retire from it whenever you become sensible how much better choices it is in your power to make: And may that infinite power which rules the destinies of the universe, lead our councils to what is best, and give them a favourable issue for your peace and prosperity.

THOMAS JEFFERSON.

ALBANY:—Printed and sold by JOHN BARBER, at the Sign of *Faust's* Statue, State-Street.—*P*rice, 3 *Cents.*

1801

Fig. 2-11. *Speech of Mr. Jefferson, on his Inauguration as President of the United States.* Broadside, printed and sold by John Barber, Albany, New York, [1801]. New-York Historical Society.

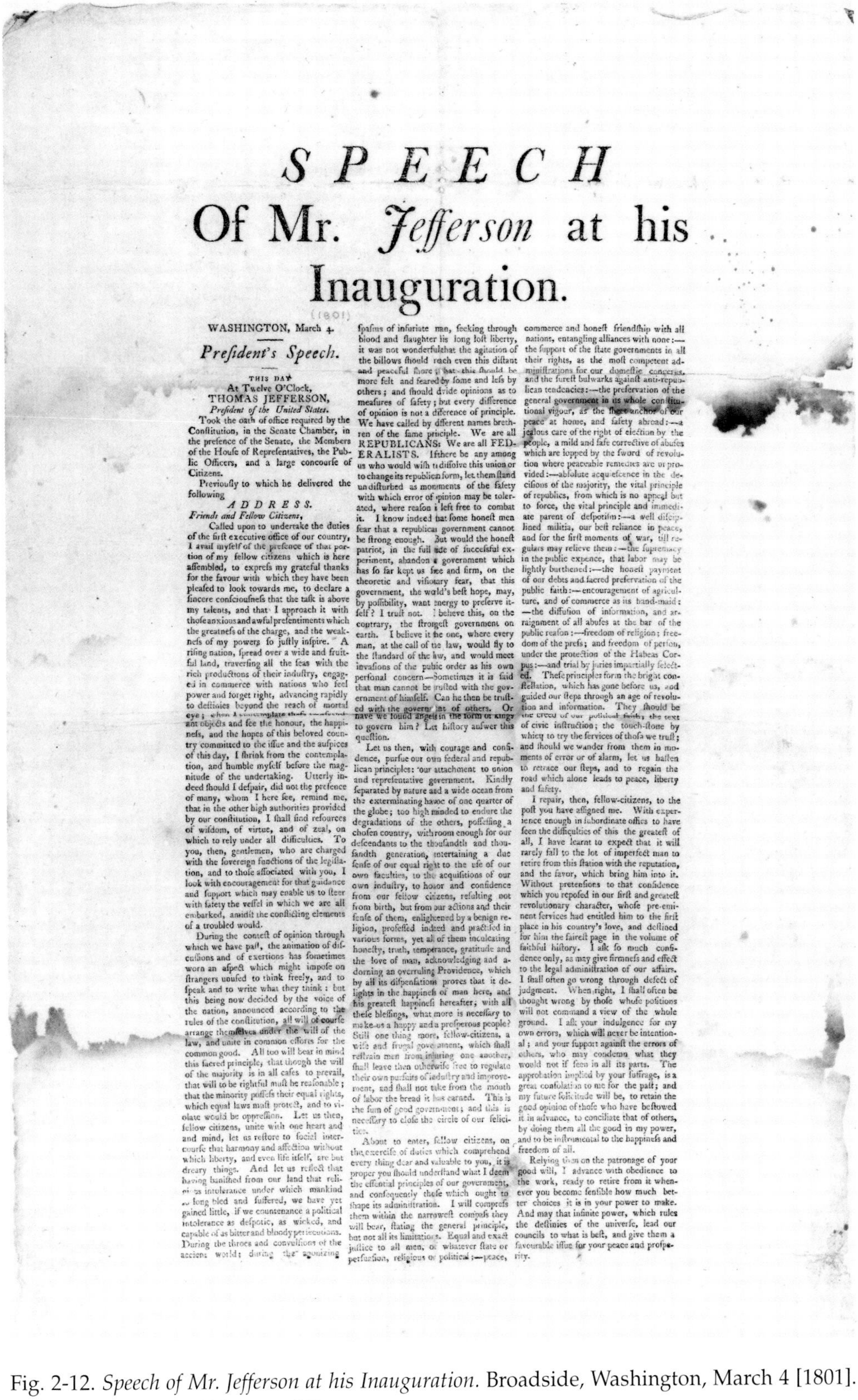

Fig. 2-12. *Speech of Mr. Jefferson at his Inauguration.* Broadside, Washington, March 4 [1801]. Rare Book Division, Library of Congress.

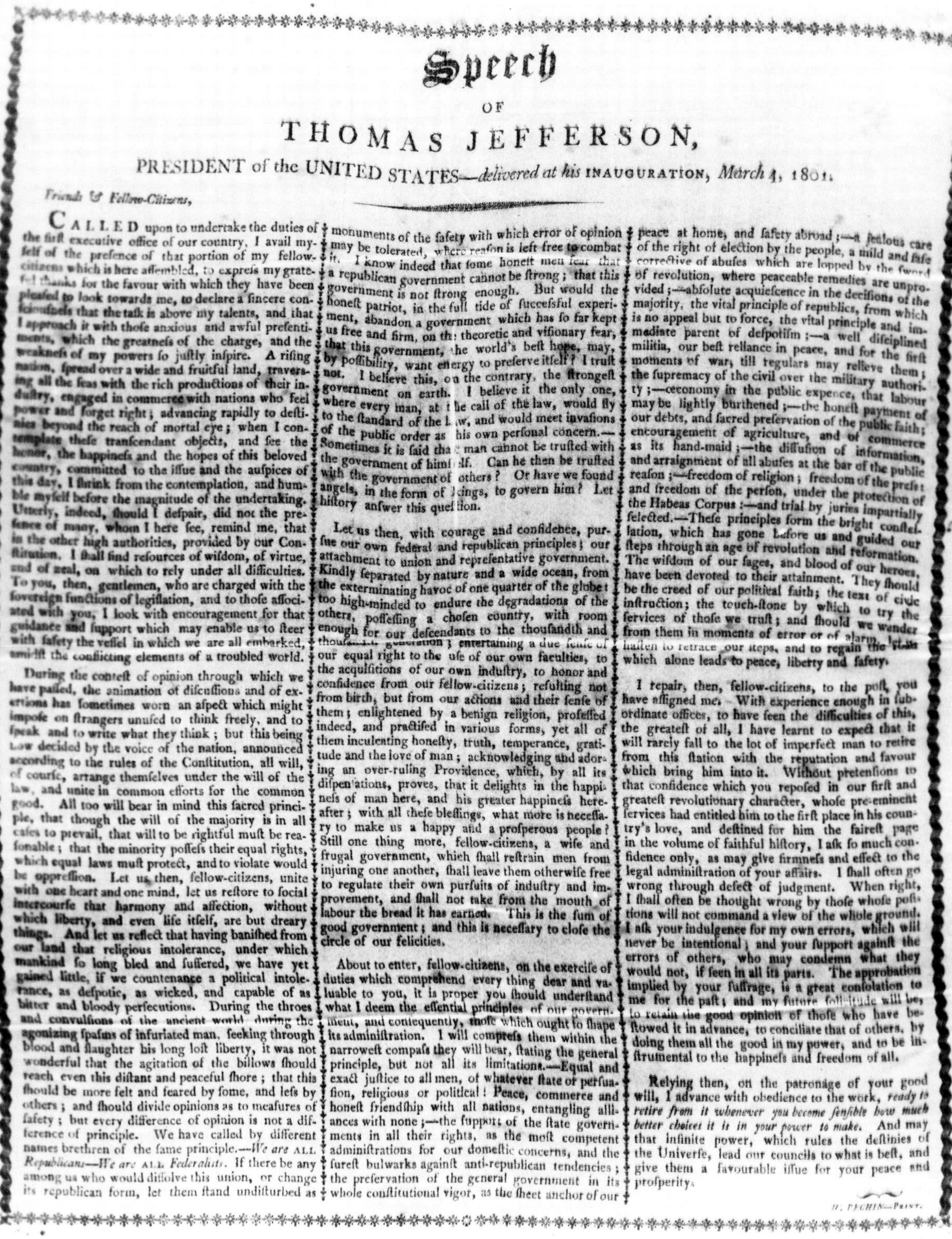

Fig. 2-13. *Speech of Thomas Jefferson, President of the United States—delivered at his Inauguration, March 4, 1801.* Printed on silk by W. Pechin [Baltimore, 1801]. College of William and Mary.

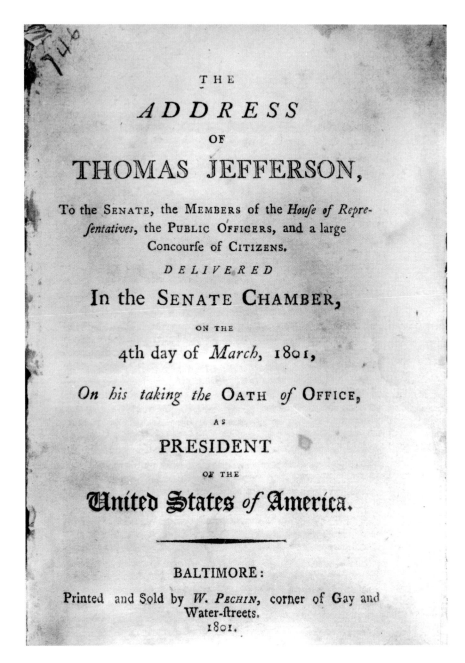

Fig. 2-14. *The Address of Thomas Jefferson, To the Senate, the Members of the House of Representatives, the Public Officers, and a large Concourse of Citizens. Delivered In the Senate Chamber on the 4th day of March, 1801, On his taking the Oath of Office, as President of the United States of America.* Baltimore: Printed and Sold by W. Pechin, 1801. American Antiquarian Society.

Fig. 2-15. *Speech of Thomas Jefferson, President of the United States, Delivered in the Senate Chamber, March 4th, 1801.* Broadside, Hagerstown, Maryland, J. J. May, Printer, [1801]. Rare Book Division, Library of Congress.

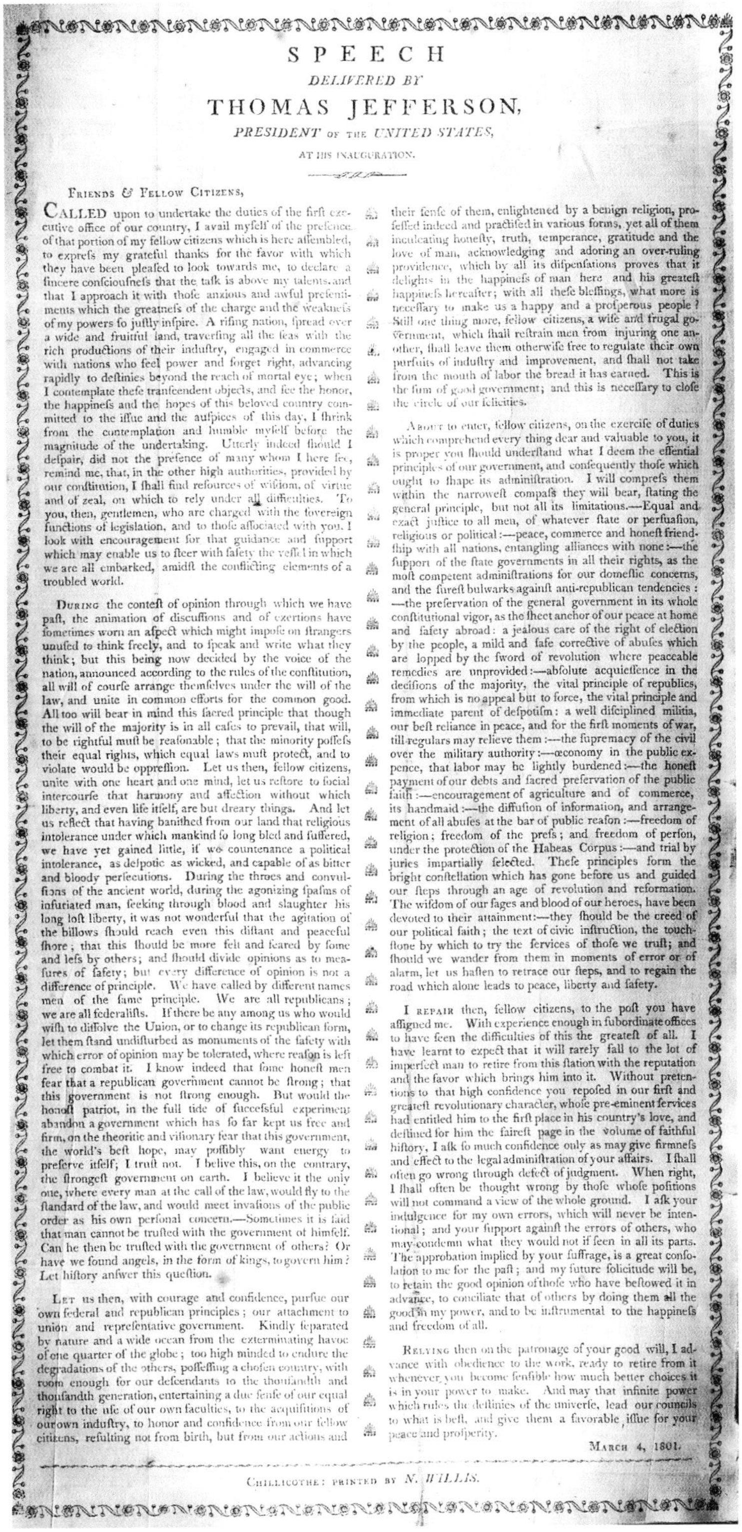

SPEECH

DELIVERED BY

THOMAS JEFFERSON,

PRESIDENT OF THE UNITED STATES,

AT HIS INAUGURATION.

FRIENDS & FELLOW CITIZENS,

CALLED upon to undertake the duties of the first executive office of our country, I avail myself of the presence of that portion of my fellow citizens which is here assembled, to express my grateful thanks for the favor with which they have been pleased to look towards me, to declare a sincere consciousness that the task is above my talents, and that I approach it with those anxious and awful presentiments which the greatness of the charge and the weakness of my powers so justly inspire. A rising nation, spread over a wide and fruitful land, traversing all the seas with the rich productions of their industry, engaged in commerce with nations who feel power and forget right, advancing rapidly to destinies beyond the reach of mortal eye; when I contemplate these transcendent objects, and see the honor, the happiness and the hopes of this beloved country committed to the issue and the auspices of this day, I shrink from the contemplation and humble myself before the magnitude of the undertaking. Utterly indeed should I despair, did not the presence of many whom I here see, remind me, that, in the other high authorities, provided by our constitution, I shall find resources of wisdom, of virtue and of zeal, on which to rely under all difficulties. To you, then, gentlemen, who are charged with the sovereign functions of legislation, and to those associated with you, I look with encouragement for that guidance and support which may enable us to steer with safety the vessel in which we are all embarked, amidst the conflicting elements of a troubled world.

DURING the contest of opinion through which we have past, the animation of discussions and of exertions have sometimes worn an aspect which might impose on strangers unused to think freely, and to speak and write what they think; but this being now decided by the voice of the nation, announced according to the rules of the constitution, all will of course arrange themselves under the will of the law, and unite in common efforts for the common good. All too will bear in mind this sacred principle that though the will of the majority is in all cases to prevail, that will, to be rightful must be reasonable; that the minority possess their equal rights, which equal laws must protect, and to violate would be oppression. Let us then, fellow citizens, unite with one heart and one mind, let us restore to social intercourse that harmony and affection without which liberty, and even life itself, are but dreary things. And let us reflect that having banished from our land that religious intolerance under which mankind so long bled and suffered, we have yet gained little, if we countenance a political intolerance, as despotic as wicked, and capable of as bitter and bloody persecutions. During the throes and convulsions of the ancient world, during the agonizing spasms of infuriated man, seeking through blood and slaughter his long lost liberty, it was not wonderful that the agitation of the billows should reach even this distant and peaceful shore; that this should be more felt and feared by some and less by others; and should divide opinions as to measures of safety; but every difference of opinion is not a difference of principle. We have called by different names men of the same principle. We are all republicans; we are all federalists. If there be any among us who would wish to dissolve the Union, or to change its republican form, let them stand undisturbed as monuments of the safety with which error of opinion may be tolerated, where reason is left free to combat it. I know indeed that some honest men fear that a republican government cannot be strong; that this government is not strong enough. But would the honest patriot, in the full tide of successful experiment abandon a government which has so far kept us free and firm, on the theoretic and visionary fear that this government, the world's best hope, may possibly want energy to preserve itself? I trust not. I believe this, on the contrary, the strongest government on earth. I believe it the only one, where every man at the call of the law, would fly to the standard of the law, and would meet invasions of the public order as his own personal concern.—Sometimes it is said that man cannot be trusted with the government of himself. Can he then be trusted with the government of others? Or have we found angels, in the form of kings, to govern him? Let history answer this question.

LET us then, with courage and confidence, pursue our own federal and republican principles; our attachment to union and representative government. Kindly separated by nature and a wide ocean from the exterminating havoc of one quarter of the globe; too high minded to endure the degradations of the others, possessing a chosen country, with room enough for our descendants to the thousandth and thousandth generation, entertaining a due sense of our equal right to the use of our own faculties, to the acquisitions of our own industry, to honor and confidence from our fellow citizens, resulting not from birth, but from our actions and their sense of them, enlightened by a benign religion, professed indeed and practised in various forms, yet all of them inculcating honesty, truth, temperance, gratitude and the love of man, acknowledging and adoring an over-ruling providence, which by all its dispensations proves that it delights in the happiness of man here and his greatest happiness hereafter; with all these blessings, what more is necessary to make us a happy and a prosperous people? Still one thing more, fellow citizens, a wise and frugal government, which shall restrain men from injuring one another, shall leave them otherwise free to regulate their own pursuits of industry and improvement, and shall not take from the mouth of labor the bread it has earned. This is the sum of good government; and this is necessary to close the circle of our felicities.

ABOUT to enter, fellow citizens, on the exercise of duties which comprehend every thing dear and valuable to you, it is proper you should understand what I deem the essential principles of our government, and consequently those which ought to shape its administration. I will compress them within the narrowest compass they will bear, stating the general principle, but not all its limitations.—Equal and exact justice to all men, of whatever state or persuasion, religious or political:—peace, commerce and honest friendship with all nations, entangling alliances with none:—the support of the state governments in all their rights, as the most competent administrations for our domestic concerns, and the surest bulwarks against anti-republican tendencies: —the preservation of the general government in its whole constitutional vigor, as the sheet anchor of our peace at home and safety abroad: a jealous care of the right of election by the people, a mild and safe corrective of abuses which are lopped by the sword of revolution where peaceable remedies are unprovided:—absolute acquiescence in the decisions of the majority, the vital principle of republics, from which is no appeal but to force, the vital principle and immediate parent of despotism: a well disciplined militia, our best reliance in peace, and for the first moments of war, till regulars may relieve them:—the supremacy of the civil over the military authority:—economy in the public expence, that labor may be lightly burdened:—the honest payment of our debts and sacred preservation of the public faith:—encouragement of agriculture and of commerce, its handmaid:—the diffusion of information, and arrangement of all abuses at the bar of public reason:—freedom of religion; freedom of the press, and freedom of person, under the protection of the Habeas Corpus:—and trial by juries impartially selected. These principles form the bright constellation which has gone before us and guided our steps through an age of revolution and reformation. The wisdom of our sages and blood of our heroes, have been devoted to their attainment:—they should be the creed of our political faith; the text of civic instruction, the touchstone by which to try the services of those we trust; and should we wander from them in moments of error or of alarm, let us hasten to retrace our steps, and to regain the road which alone leads to peace, liberty and safety.

I REPAIR then, fellow citizens, to the post you have assigned me. With experience enough in subordinate offices to have seen the difficulties of this the greatest of all. I have learnt to expect that it will rarely fall to the lot of imperfect man to retire from this station with the reputation and the favor which brings him into it. Without pretentions to that high confidence you reposed in our first and greatest revolutionary character, whose pre-eminent services had entitled him to the first place in his country's love, and destined for him the fairest page in the volume of faithful history, I ask so much confidence only as may give firmness and effect to the legal administration of your affairs. I shall often go wrong through defect of judgment. When right, I shall often be thought wrong by those whose positions will not command a view of the whole ground. I ask your indulgence for my own errors, which will never be intentional; and your support against the errors of others, who may condemn what they would not if seen in all its parts. The approbation implied by your suffrage, is a great consolation to me for the past; and my future solicitude will be, to retain the good opinion of those who have bestowed it in advance, to conciliate that of others by doing them all the good in my power, and to be instrumental to the happiness and freedom of all.

RELYING then on the patronage of your good will, I advance with obedience to the work, ready to retire from it whenever you become sensible how much better choices it is in your power to make. And may that infinite power which rules the destinies of the universe, lead our councils to what is best, and give them a favorable issue for your peace and prosperity.

MARCH 4, 1801.

CHILLICOTHE: PRINTED BY N. WILLIS.

Fig. 2-16. *Speech Delivered by Thomas Jefferson, President of the United States, at His Inauguration,* March 4, 1801. Chillicothe, Ohio, printed on silk by Nathaniel Willis, [1801]. Chicago Historical Society.

Prefident JEFFERSON's SPEECH,

DELIVERED ON THE FOURTH OF MARCH, 1801,

PREVIOUS TO HIS INAUGURATION TO THE

PRESIDENCY OF THE UNITED STATES.

FRIENDS & FELLOW CITIZENS,

CALLED upon to undertake the duties of the firft Executive office of our country, I avail myfelf of the prefence of that portion of my fellow citizens which is here affembled, to exprefs my grateful thanks for the favor with which they have been pleafed to look towards me, to declare a fincere confcioufnefs that the tafk is above my talents, and that I approach it with thofe anxious and awful prefentiments which the greatnefs of the charge, and the weaknefs of my powers fo juftly infpire. A rifing nation, fpread over a wide and fruitful land, traverfing all the feas with the rich productions of their induftry, engaged in commerce with nations who feel power and forget right, advancing rapidly to deftinies beyond the reach of mortal eye ; when I contemplate thefe tranfcendent objects, and fee the honor, the happinefs, and the hopes of this beloved country committed to the iffue and the aufpices of this day, I fhrink from the contemplation, and humble myfelf before the magnitude of the undertaking. Utterly indeed fhould I defpair, did not the prefence of many, whom I here fee, remind me, that in the other high authorities provided by our conftitution, I fhall find refources of wifdom, of virtue and of zeal, on which to rely under all difficulties. To you, then, gentlemen, who are charged with the fovereign functions of legiflation, and to thofe affociated with you, I look with encouragement for that guidance and fupport which may enable us to fteer with fafety the veffel in which we are all embarked, amidft the conflicting elements of a troubled world.

During the conteft of opinion thro' which we have paft, the animation of difcuffions and of exertions has fometimes worn an afpect which might impofe on ftrangers unufed to think freely, and to fpeak and to write what they think ; but this being now decided by the voice of the nation, announced according to the rules of the conftitution, all will of courfe arrange themfelves under the will of the law, and unite in common efforts for the common good. All too, will bear in mind this facred principle, that though the will of the majority is in all cafes to prevail, that will, to be rightful, muft be reafonable ; that the minority poffefs their equal rights, which equal laws muft protect, and to violate would be oppreffion. Let us, then, fellow citizens, unite with one heart and one mind, let us reftore to focial intercourfe that harmony and affection without which liberty, and even life itfelf, are but dreary things. And let us reflect that having banifhed from our land that religious intolerance under which mankind fo long bled and fuffered ; we have yet gained little, if we countenance a political intolerance, as defpotic, as wicked, and capable of of as bitter and bloody perfecutions. During the throes and convulfions of the ancient world, during the agonizing fpafms of infuriated man, feeking thro' blood and flaughter his long loft liberty, it was not wonderful that the agitation of the billows fhould reach even this diftant and peaceful fhore ; that this fhould be more felt and feared by fome and lefs by others ; and fhould divide opinions as to meafures of fafety ; but every difference of opinion is not a difference of principle. We have called by different names brethren of the fame principle. We are all republicans ; we are all federalifts. If there be any among us who would wifh to diffolve this Union, or to change its republican form,

let them ftand undifturbed as monuments of the fafety with which error of opinion may be tolerated, where reafon is left free to combat it. I know indeed that fome honeft men fear that a republican government cannot be ftrong ; that this government is not ftrong enough. But would the honeft patriot, in the full tide of fuccefsful experiment, abandon a government which has fo far kept us free and firm, on the theoretic and vifionary fear, that this government, the world's beft hope, may, by poffibility, want energy to preferve itfelf ? I truft not. I believe this on the contrary, the ftrongeft government on earth. I believe it the only one, where every man at the call of the law, would fly to the ftandard of the law, and would meet invafions of the public order as his own perfonal concern.— Sometimes it is faid that man cannot be trufted with the government of himfelf. Can he then be trufted with the government of others? Or have we found angels in the form of kings to govern him ? Let hiftory anfwer this queftion.

Let us then, with courage and confidence, purfue our own federal and republican principles ; our attachment to union and reprefentative government. Kindly feparated by nature and a wide ocean from the exterminating havoc of one quarter of the globe ; too high minded to endure the degradations of the others, poffeffing a chofen country, with room enough for our defcendants to the hundredth and thoufandth generation, entertaining a due fenfe of our equal right to the of our own faculties, [...] acquifitions of our own induftry, to honor and confidence from our fellow citizens, refulting not from birth, but from our actions and their fenfe of them, enlightened by a benign religion, profeffed indeed and practifed in various forms, yet all of them inculcating honefty, truth, temperance, gratitude & the love of man, acknowledging and adoring an overruling providence, which by all its difpenfations proves that it delights in the happinefs of man here, and his greater happinefs hereafter ; with all thefe bleffings, what more is neceffary to make us a happy and a profperous people ? Still one thing more, fellow-citizens, a wife and prudent government, which fhall reftrain men from injuring one another, fhall leave them otherwife free to regulate their own purfuits of induftry and improvement, and fhall not take from the mouth of labor the bread it has earned. This is the fum of good Government ; and this is neceffary to clofe the circle of our felicities.

About to enter, fellow citizens, on the exercife of duties which comprehend every thing dear and valuable to you, it is proper you fhould underftand what I deem the effential principles of our government, and confequently thofe which ought to fhape its adminiftration. I will comprefs them within the narroweft compafs they will bear, ftating the general principle, but not all its limitations. Equal and exact juftice to all men, of whatever ftate or perfuafion, religious or political : peace, commerce & honeft friendfhip with all nations, entangling alliances with none : the fupport of the ftate governments in all their rights, as the moft competent adminiftrations for our domeftic concerns, and the fureft bulwarks againft antirepublican tendencies : the prefervation of the general government in its whole conftitutional vigor, as the fheet anchor of our peace at home, and fafety abroad : a jealous

care of the right of election by the people, a mild and fafe corrective of abufes which are lopped by the fword of revolution where peaceable remedies are unprovided : abfolute acquiefcence in the decifions of the majority, the vital principle of republics, from which is no appeal but to force, the vital principle and immediate parent of defpotifm : a well difciplined militia, our beft reliance in peace, and for the firft moments of war, until regulars may relieve them : the fupremacy of the civil over the military authority : economy in the public expenfe, that labor may be lightly burthened : the honeft payment of our debts and facred prefervation of the public faith : encouragement of agriculture, and of commerce as its handmaid : the diffufion of information, and arraignment of all abufes at the bar of the public reafon ; freedom of religion ; freedom of the prefs ; and freedom of perfon, under the protection of the Habeas Corpus : and trial by juries impartially felected. Thefe principles form the bright conftellation, which has gone before us, and guided our fteps through an age of revolution and reformation. The wifdom of our fages, and blood of our heroes, have been devoted to their attainment : they fhould be the creed of our political faith : the text of civic inftruction, the touchftone by which [...] try the fervices of thofe we truft ; and [...] we [...] from them in moments [...] or of alarm, let us haften to retrace our [...] s, and to regain the road which alone [...] to peace, liberty [...]

I repair then, fellow citizens, to the poft you have affigned me. With experience [...] nough in fubordinate offices to have feen the difficulties of this the greateft of all ; I have learnt to expect that it will rarely fall to the lot of imperfect man to retire from this ftation with the reputation and favor, which bring him into it. Without pretenfions to that high confidence you repofed in our firft and greateft revolutionary character, whofe pre-eminent fervices had entitled him to the firft place in his country's love, and deftined for him the faireft page in the volume of faithful hiftory, I afk fo much confidence only as may give firmnefs and effect to the legal adminiftration of your affairs. I fhall often go wrong through defect of judgment. When right, I fhall often be thought wrong by thofe whofe pofitions will not command a view of the whole ground. I afk your indulgence for my own errors, which will never be intentional ; and your fupport againft the errors of others, who may condemn what they would not, if feen in all its parts. The approbation implied by your fuffrage, is a great confolation to me for the paft ; and my future folicitude will be, to retain the good opinion of thofe who have beftowed it in advance, to conciliate that of others by doing them all the good in my power, and to be inftrumental in the happinefs and freedom of all.

Relying then on the patronage of your good will, I advance with obedience to the work, ready to retire from it whenever you become fenfible how much better choices it is in your power to make. And may that infinite Power, which rules the deftinies of the univerfe, lead our councils to what is beft, and give them a favorable iffue for your peace and profperity.

THOMAS JEFFERSON.

Printed by NUTTING & WHITELOCK.

Fig. 2-17. *President Jefferson's Speech, Delivered on the Fourth of March, 1801, Previous to His Inauguration to the Presidency of the United States.* Printed on silk by Nutting and Whitelock [1801]. American Antiquarian Society.

the press announcement) "in the attitude in which he expressed that never to be forgotten sentence 'We are all Republicans we are all Federalists.'" In a July Fourth oration in Worcester, Massachusetts, Isaac Story, citing "the luminous language of President Jefferson," repeated the same increasingly notable passage.[15]

Jefferson's entire inaugural address continued to be reprinted well beyond its time as current news. The *National Magazine; or, Cabinet of the United States*, published in Washington, D.C., began publication in November 1801 by reprinting the address, which would receive additional recognition as time passed.[16]

15. *American Citizen* (New York), June 30, 1801; *New York Evening Post*, December 21, 1801, in Rita Susswein Gottesman, *The Arts and Crafts in New York, 1800–1804: Advertisements and News Items from New York City Newspapers* (New York, 1965), 44–45; Isaac Story, *An Oration, on the Anniversary of the Independence of the United States of America,* pronounced at Worcester, July 4, 1801 (Worcester, Mass: The Press of Isaiah Thomas, June, July, 1801), 30–31.

16. The first issue of *National Magazine* is in the Rare Book Division, Library of Congress. As early as 1802 the publication of *The Inaugural Speeches of Washington, Adams, and Jefferson* (Boston: H. Sprague) initiated the collective printing of presidential inaugural addresses. Presidential inaugural addresses also would be later reprinted together with annual messages of the presidents to Congress. For examples see Noble E. Cunningham, Jr., *Popular Images of the Presidency: From Washington to Lincoln,* 246, 248–49.

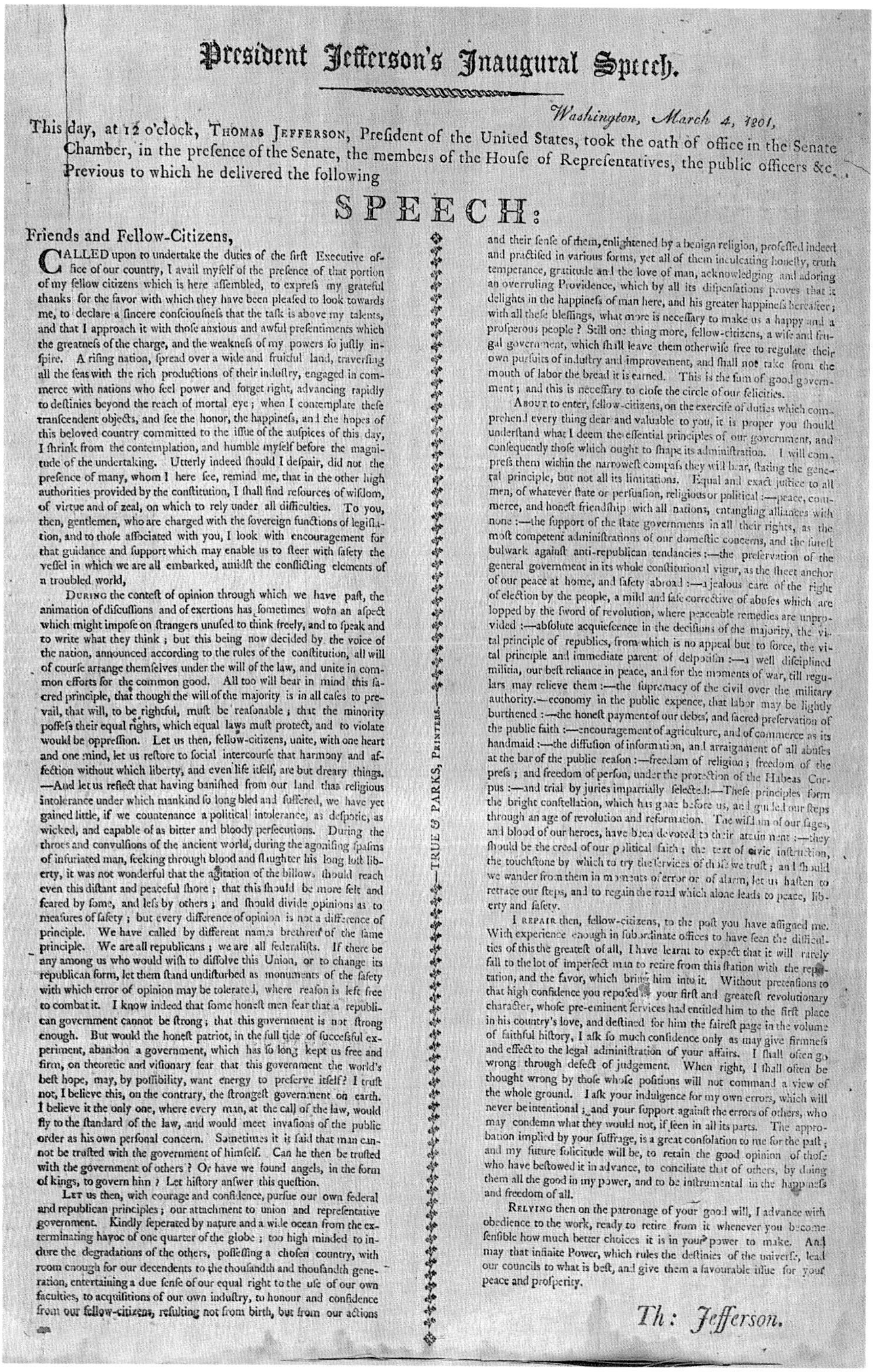

Fig. 3-1. *President Jefferson's Inaugural Speech.* Broadside, Washington, D.C., March 4, 1801, True and Parks, Printers, [1801]. Library of Virginia.

Chapter III

Reactions: Public and Private

Thomas Jefferson's inaugural address was the subject of widespread comment not only in the press but also in private letters and personal diaries. The reactions of some of Jefferson's contemporaries can best be sensed from their own words.

Chief Justice John Marshall, Washington, D.C., to Charles Cotesworth Pinckney, March 4, 1801:

> I have administered the oath to the President. You will before this reaches you see his inauguration speech. It is in general well judged and conciliatory. It is in direct terms giving the lie to the violent party declamation which has elected him; but it is strongly characteristic of the general cast of his political theory.[1]

Diary of Gouverneur Morris, Washington, D.C., March 4, [1801]:

> Our new President makes his inaugural Speech—Too long by Half and so he will find it himself before he is three Years older.[2]

Margaret Bayard Smith, Washington, D.C., to Mary Ann Smith, March 7, 1801:

> The Speech of Mr. Jefferson has raised him even in the opinion of his friends, and from appearances has gone far to diminish his enemies.[3]

Congressman James A. Bayard, Wilmington, Delaware, to Alexander Hamilton, March 8, 1801:

> I remained in Washington on the 4th, through necessity though not without some curiosity to see the inauguration and to hear the speech. The scene was the same as exhibited upon former occasions and the speech in political substance better than we expected; and not answerable to the expectations of the Partizans of the other side.[4]

Diary of Thomas Rodney, [Delaware], March 10, 1801:

1. Herbert A. Johnson, Charles T. Cullen, and Charles F. Hobson, eds., *The Papers of John Marshall,* 6:89–90. Pinckney, of South Carolina, was the Federalist candidate for vice president in 1800, favored by some Federalists over John Adams.

2. Papers of Gouverneur Morris, Library of Congress. Morris, a Federalist, was a United States senator from New York.

3. Papers of Margaret Bayard (Mrs. Samuel H.) Smith, Library of Congress. Mary Ann Smith was the sister of Samuel Harrison Smith.

4. Harold C. Syrett et al., eds., *The Papers of Alexander Hamilton,* 25:344.

Jefferson's Inauguration Speech came by the Mail. It is Mild Conciliatory and Philosophic. He pours out oil on the Pot that has been boiling over so long. It is such as I expected from him. Intended to soften and attract the minds of all, but where parties are so inveterate . . . as in America, perhaps he will fail, and by Endeavouring to gain his adversaries, loose his friends.[5]

Governor James Monroe, Richmond, Virginia, to James Madison, March 11, 1801:

Mr. Jefferson's address delivered on taking the oath gives general satisfaction, as it ought to do. It avows principles which are perfectly sound, and commands the unqualified approbation of the republicans, while it conciliates the opposite party.[6]

Dr. Benjamin Rush, Philadelphia, Pennsylvania, to Thomas Jefferson, March 12, 1801:

You have opened a new era by your speech on the 4th of March in the history of the United States. Never have I seen the public mind more generally or more agreeably affected by any publication. Old friends who had been separated by party names and a *supposed* difference of *principle* in politics for many years shook hands with each other immediately after reading it, and discovered, for the first time, that they had differed in *opinion* only, about the best means of promoting the interests of their common country. It would require a page to contain the names of all the citizens (formerly called Federalists) who have spoken in the highest terms of your speech. . . . I need hardly tell you how much every sentiment and even word in it accord with my feelings and principles.[7]

Diary of Dr. Nathaniel Ames, Dedham, Massachusetts, March 15, 1801:

New President's speech pleases all parties, yet some try to carp at it.[8]

Congressman William Branch Giles, Amelia, Virginia, to Thomas Jefferson, March 16, 1801:

I have seen your inauguration speech, and am highly gratified with its contents. . . . In fact it contains the only American language, I ever heard from the Presidential chair.[9]

General Henry Knox, Boston, Massachusetts, to Thomas Jefferson, March 16, 1801:

I cannot refrain from expressing to you, the heartfelt satisfaction I have experienced in perusing your address of the 4th of the present month. The just manner in which you appreciate the motives of the two parties, which have divided the opinions, and which sometimes have seemed to threaten to divide the territory and government of the Country; and the strong incitements you display for cementing more closely our union, the essential principle of our prosperity, evince conspicuously, at one view, your intelligence patriotism and magnanimity.

I rejoice at the early occasion you have taken to give publicity to your sentiments, which in their operation, cannot but produce the just support of all true Americans.[10]

Senator James Gunn, Washington, D.C., to John Rutledge, March 16, 1801:

---

5. Thomas Rodney Papers, Library of Congress. Rodney, a Federalist, had been speaker of the Delaware Assembly in 1787.

6. Robert Rutland et al., eds., *The Papers of James Madison: Secretary of State Series*, 1:11.

7. L. H. Butterfield, ed., *Letters of Benjamin Rush*, 2:831. A signer of the Declaration of Independence, Rush, in 1801, was treasurer of the United States Mint in Philadelphia.

8. Charles Warren, *Jacobin and Junto, or Early American Politics as Viewed in the Diary of Dr. Nathaniel Ames, 1758–1822*, 159.

9. Thomas Jefferson Papers, Library of Congress.

10. Knox to Jefferson, March 16, 1801, ibid. Knox's comments would have been especially appreciated by Jefferson, for Knox—who as secretary of war had served with Jefferson in Washington's cabinet—admitted in his letter that he had favored the reelection of John Adams.

I apprize you of Jeffersons beginning.—*His Speech,* or rather his Essay, gave great pleasure to all the *Trimmers* among the Federalists, who were to a man willing to Cut in with the new administration; But their hopes are already blasted, and the work of the Revolution is progressing Rapidly.[11]

Dr. William Thornton, Washington, D.C., to James Madison, March 16, 1801:

> We have now a philosopher also at our head, whose heart appears in every action. His late speech is full of wisdom, and is a model of conciliation. It is admired by all good men, and he will find them the firmest supporters of his administration.[12]

Governor James Monroe, Richmond, Virginia, to Thomas Jefferson, March 18, 1801:

> Your address has been approved by every description of persons here. It is sound and strong in principle, and grateful to the opposite party. With your judgment, views and principles it is hardly possible you should go wrong.[13]

Alexander Hamilton, *An Address to the Electors of the State of New-York* (March 21, 1801):

> In the speech of the new President upon assuming the exercise of his office, we find among the articles of his creed: "The honest payment of our debt, and sacred preservation of the public faith. . . ."
>
> In referring to this speech, we think it proper to make a public declaration of our approbation of its contents. We view it as virtually a candid

retraction of past misapprehensions, and a pledge to the community that the new President will not lend himself to dangerous innovations, but in essential points will tread in the steps of his predecessors.[14]

William Lee, Boston, Massachusetts, to James Monroe, March 24, 1801:

> The Presidents incomparable Speech, has disarmed his vile calumniators in this State, and strengthened his friends.—From the 'mad foamings' of Fisher Ames and his coadjutors, down to the 'punny whinings' of Dr. [Jedidiah] Morse, not a syllable has been uttered against it.[15]

Ralph Bowie, lawyer, York, Pennsylvania, to James Madison, March 24, 1801:

> I happened to be lately in Philadelphia for some days, at and since the time of the Presidents Speech was published, and had occasion to hear the Sentiments of a considerable number of persons, (professional men and others,) of as much respectability as any in this State, respecting this elegant address, and they all agreed in the most unequivocal and warm approbation of it. It might indeed naturally be expected that candid men of all descriptions, would cordially approve of Principles so pure and Sentiments so just and liberal, delivered in Language so elegant and impressive. But the most important information I wish to convey is, that I have heard it expressed by a very considerable number of what is called the Federal party 'that they will most cordially Support Mr. Jefferson's Administration if it is found to correspond with the principles in his Address.'[16]

11. John Rutledge Papers, University of North Carolina, Chapel Hill. Gunn was a Federalist senator from Georgia.

12. C. M. Harris, ed., *Papers of William Thornton,* 1:555. Thornton was head of the United States Patent Office.

13. Stanislaus M. Hamilton, ed., *The Writings of James Monroe,* 3:269.

14. Syrett et al., eds., *Hamilton Papers,* 25:365.

15. Papers of James Monroe, Library of Congress. Lee was recommended to Jefferson for appointment by Monroe, who judged him to be "a sensible deserving man, sound in his principles and amiable in his manners." Monroe to Jefferson, March 23, 1801, in Hamilton, ed., *Writings of Monroe,* 3:274–75.

16. Rutland et al., eds., *Papers of Madison,* 1:39.

William Bingham, Philadelphia, Pennsylvania, to Wilson Cary Nicholas, March 28, 1801:

> It gives me pleasure to observe the happy impression which has been made by the President's eloquent and dignified Speech at the Time of his Inauguration. The correct Principles which he advocated have reconciled many of his political opponents, who are disposed to give him considerable Credit, by anticipation, for the Measures of his future administration.[17]

John Hunter, Huntvill, South Carolina, to Madison, April 16, 1801:

> I Like the Sentiment in the President Speech, as Coming from him—(we are all Republicans, we are all Federalists) I would to God it were so.[18]

Writing from Washington to his father, British financier Sir Francis Baring, in London, Alexander Baring concluded:

> The accession of Mr. Jefferson may have excited apprehension, but you may depend on it that they are unfounded. . . .
>
> I recommend your reading [Jefferson's speech] as it is the manifesto of the party and a declaration (I believe a just one) of his political creed. It is here much admired though I confess it confirms my invariable opinion of the man, that he is a visionary theorist. The expressions of moderation have conciliated many of the Federalists and he appears disposed to act conformably to them.[19]

Returning to Harrisburg, Pennsylvania, after the inauguration, Congressman John Hanna observed on his way home that "the Speech of the President was well received by People of every political description. The Federalists knowing their past conduct and deserts expected to be more roughly treated." He predicted, however, that the calm would not last long. "If Mr. Jefferson were an Angel sent of God, they will never heartily be reconciled to his administration," he concluded.[20] In a similar vein, Gideon Granger of Connecticut—soon to become postmaster general—wrote to Jefferson:

> The inaugural Speech was read by the body of the people with delight and Satisfaction. The deceitful appearance of a spirit of Accommodation is assumed. This will soon be cast off, if the temper of the people will allow it. But in that the Monarchists will be disappointed. . . . Yet from what I see and hear I am fully persuaded that in the Course of a few weeks the opposition will begin to show itself.[21]

Another New Englander, Elbridge Gerry, wrote to the president from Cambridge, Massachusetts, on April 19, 1801:

> Your inaugural speech was in my mind, the best I had ever met with. No reasonable mind, however, could have supposed that you were pledged by it, to a disgraceful inattention to demerit; and yet by the *friends of order,* you are not allowed to judge of this, altho obliged to do it, by the obligations of law, of an oath, and of honor.[22]

As Jefferson's inaugural address appeared in newspapers throughout the country, it attracted

---

17. Wilson Cary Nicholas Papers, Library of Congress. Bingham had served as a United States senator from Pennsylvania from 1794 to 1801.

18. Rutland et al., eds., *Papers of Madison,* 1:97. Spelling of "Spech" in original corrected to "Speech." Hunter, a former Federalist representative in Congress, was a Jefferson-Burr elector in 1800.

19. Alexander Baring to Sir Francis Baring, March 29, 1801, quoted in Robert C. Alberts, *The Golden Voyage: The Life and Times of William Bingham, 1752–1804,* 410–11.

20. Hanna to Albert Gallatin, March 22, 1801, Albert Gallatin Papers, New-York Historical Society.

21. Granger to Jefferson, March 25, 1801, Jefferson Papers, Library of Congress.

22. Gerry to Jefferson, April 28, 1801, ibid.

considerable editorial comment. One friendly editor called it "a pleasant contrast to the exterminating war-whoops of John Adams," that "infuriated partisan."[23] In an age when newspaper editors were openly politically partisan, their editorials commonly displayed that partisanship. Two days after publishing the text of the address in the *National Intelligencer*, editor Samuel Harrison Smith reflected on the document in a lengthy commentary in which he declared:

> It is the Address of the Chief Magistrate of a People, who have shewn themselves amidst the storm of war and the calm of peace equally competent to protect their rights and establish their common happiness; and who in the enjoyment of sovereign unlimited power, have betrayed neither the intoxication of prosperity, or the depressions of fear.
>
> To such a People, it became the man of the people to speak with respectful truth. It became him, without reserve, to declare the general principles by which he was actuated, and by an adherence to which he was willing to be judged.
>
> In making this declaration we perceive no studied sacrifice of truth to ideal delicacy; no avoidance of subjects respecting which public opinion has been divided: On the contrary we are presented with an open avowal of the most important political principles, and a conclusive, though concise illustration of their truth.[24]

Some Republican editors reprinted Smith's commentary in their newspapers.[25] Others added their own opinion. In publishing Jefferson's address in the New York *American Citizen*, editor James Cheetham inserted the following paragraph preceding the text:

> Republicans Read!
> *A Speech*
>
> Of your President, which cannot fail to excite joyful emotions in your hearts—Let the sentiments expressed therein make a deep and lasting impression, and your liberties are secured forever. While the slanderers of its author, the enemies of freedom are covered with shame for their past crimes, may they learn from this speech, to rise above their former errors and to become men and republicans.

The next day Cheetham published the following lengthy editorial:

> Mr. Jefferson, the President of the United States, has delivered a Speech consoling to every friend of liberty, and which is calculated to strike terror into the hearts of those who oppose it.
>
> The federal aristocrats, or monarchists of America, have frequently declared that a change of administration would be the ruin of the country and form the blackest features in the political arrangements of republicanism. This has been done however for the purpose of exciting alarm, and encreasing anti-republican influence. Without particular comment upon former administrations—without reverting to executive speeches, which perhaps may have been modified by causes which do not now exist—without any departure from the principles of political truth, it is conceived and affirmed, that the present speech of Thomas Jefferson has not been equalled in the political history of mankind. He speaks the language of republican firmness—he rises above all parties—he comprehends the welfare of nations—he cements the sentiments of Americans by declaring that we are all republicans, and all federalists; and that the essential and important existence of American liberty depends upon a faithful adherence to this idea. The elevation of sentiment, correctness of principle, extention of political view—in short, the general idea of philanthropic temper of mind therein displayed, shews that the American people have not laboured under a mistake in regard

---

23. Washington, Pa., *Herald of Liberty*, March 23, 1801, cited in Donald H. Stewart, *The Opposition Press of the Federalist Period*, 538, 832.

24. *National Intelligencer* (Washington), March 6, 1801.

25. For example, the *American Mercury* (Hartford), published by Elisha Babcock, March 26, 1801.

to the true character of Mr. Jefferson. He has now proved to the free citizens of this country, that his wishes have been sincerely devoted to the republican cause—to the union of the states, to the order, peace, freedom, and the civil and religious toleration of the country. It will be difficult for any person disposed to favour aristocratic opinions, to point out any part of this speech which exhibits any kind of departure from the best interests and the real happiness which the people of the U[nited] States had a reasonable right to expect from the result of the revolution. It has been declared by the anti-republicans of the country, that we should be disappointed—that democracy would be appalled, and distressed even in the favourable issue of the election of the favourite Jefferson; but these malignant predictions are essentially destroyed, and the first speech of the first magistrate of a free and enlightened people; or in other words, the solemn declaration of the first republican officer of an executive capacity that ever adorned the annals of history, furnishes a fruitful source of expectation that our hopes have been realized, and more than realized; so far as the experiment has gone; and that the anglo-federal faction have reason to blush and be confounded.[26]

Federalist newspaper editors were not so admiring of the new pres
speech to the nation, but ma
the moderate commentarie
alists. The *Gazette of the Un*
piece from a Federalist con
that Jefferson's "benevolen
manly address, delivered to
bled at his initiation into o
instant, composed the ferm
tion had excited, and gave u
pation of the wisdom, with which he intends to govern;—pleasing in the highest degree as it

frustrates the Democrats in their unjust, extravagant, and mercenary views, and pleasing too as it relieves the Federalists from their unfounded apprehensions."[27]

A Federalist editorial published in Georgetown on March 9, 1801, and reprinted in distant newspapers, observed:

> Without concurring in every political opinion expressed in the speech of the 4th, it must be acknowledged to promise such an administration, as may be acquiesced in with satisfaction, by federalists themselves. . . . If the principles announced in the address are adhered to in practice, *the public debts will be honestly paid, and the public faith preserved; peace, commerce and honest friendship with all nations will be sought, and entangling alliances formed with none:* in short, what is inestimable in the view of every genuine federalist, *the general government will be preserved in its whole constitutional vigor, as the sheet anchor of our peace at home and safety abroad.*[28]

Jefferson's address was so widely published as to arouse detractors, as well as admirers, to respond. One reviewer in a lengthy criticism for the *Port Folio*, published in Philadelphia, began by noting: "The friends and admirers of Mr. Jefferson, have not only extolled him as a great statesman, but also, as a finished scholar. His writings, therefore, may be justly made the subject of criticism." This critic gave more attention to style than to content. He pronounced the president "passionately fond of soft language and flowing periods" and pointed out discrepancies in grammar, such as using "past" when he should have written "passed." He protested that there were "some nominatives without verbs, which is a violation of concord, and gives an affected air to composition." The reviewer also

---

26. *American Citizen* (New York), March 10, 11, 1801.

27. *Gazette of the United States* (Philadelphia), March 12, 1801.
28. *City Gazette* (Charleston, S.C.), March 24, 1801.

devoted considerable space to criticizing Jefferson's use of metaphors. "It sometimes happens, that authors, who are fond of figurative language, fail in its management," he noted. "But I have met with few instances, in writers of reputation where so many high-sounding expressions were used with so bad effect." He quoted one of the most notable passages of the speech—in which Jefferson affirmed, "But every difference of opinion is not a difference of principle. We are all republicans: we are all federalists"—and added his assessment: "Here there is too much artful colouring to comport with the dignity of a presidential speech." Closing with a reference to "this celebrated speech," the writer confirmed how widely Jefferson's address was publicized in the weeks following his inauguration.[29]

It is not known whether Jefferson read the criticism in the *Port Folio*, but it seems certain that he read James Cheetham's glowing praise in the *American Citizen*, for that New York paper was one of a number of newspapers nationwide to which Jefferson subscribed.[30] Before the end of March, Jefferson wrote to Henry Knox that "it is with the greatest satisfaction I learn from all quarters that my inaugural address is considered as holding out a ground for conciliation and union. . . . I was always satisfied that the great body of those called Federalists were real republicans as well as Federalists."[31]

Besides newspapers and private letters, several public commendations reached Jefferson. More than two hundred inhabitants of Newbury Township in York County, Pennsylvania, sent the new president a short address, declaring themselves "highly gratified with the sentiments you have announced as the governing principles of your administration" and expressing their "sincere attachment and steady support."[32]

From Rhode Island's governor, Arthur Fenner, Jefferson received an address from the legislators of that state passed unanimously on May 9 "to express their entire approbation of the principles which, in your address to a portion of our fellow Citizens, on the fourth of March last, you declared would be the basis of your administration." Jefferson replied, thanking the General Assembly of Rhode Island for its approbation of the "principles which flowed sincerely from the heart and judgment, and which, with sincerity, will be pursued." Among the newspapers in Rhode Island and elsewhere that printed both the Rhode Island address and the president's reply was the *Scioto Gazette* in Chillicothe in the Northwestern Territory.[33]

In private letters Federalists expressed satisfaction, but also caution and sometimes contempt. Two weeks after the inauguration, George ading Massachusetts Federalist, wrote, rson's conciliatory speech is better r party than his own: how he will act be proved, but hopes are entertained could not have existed if his speech en of the temper of his party." Some took credit for the moderation of ddress. Theodore Sedgwick, Federalist the House of Representatives at the rson's inauguration, argued that the new president's speech resulted from the strong

29. *Port Folio* (Philadelphia), May 16, 1801.

30. For a list see Noble E. Cunningham, Jr., *The Jeffersonian Republicans in Power: Party Operation, 1801–1809*, 253–54.

31. Jefferson to Knox, March 27, 1801, in Ford, ed., *Works of Thomas Jefferson*, 9:236.

32. "Address of a meeting consisting of over two hundred of the inhabitants of Newbury Township in York County, Pennsylvania," [May 2, 1801], signed by Henry Krieger, James Todd, Jesse Glancy, Eli Lewis, and R. Hamersly, Jr., Jefferson Papers, Library of Congress.

33. Fenner to Jefferson, May 12, 1801, enclosing address of Rhode Island legislature, May 9, 1801; Jefferson to the General Assembly of the State of Rhode Island and Providence Plantations, May 26, 1801, Jefferson Papers, Library of Congress. *Scioto Gazette* (Chillicothe), July 23, 1801.

opposition of the Federalists to his election. Shortly after Jefferson's address appeared in the newspapers, New York Federalist Robert Troup wrote: "Jefferson's inaugural speech is particularly worthy of notice. It has displeased the most violent of the party attached to him. The federalists, in general, are taken with it and hope better things than they were led to expect from him." Two months later, Troup suggested, "Jefferson's inaugural speech has had a wonderful lullaby effect. I do not apprehend the serious mischiefs from his administration that have been foretold; but my opinion is, that it will be the little contemptible thing that grows of a trimming system and a studied adherence to popular notions."[34]

As time passed, some Federalist critics became more contemptuous of the wording of Jefferson's address. In a parody published in 1804, Josiah Quincy sought to discredit both the president and the Enlightenment philosophy of natural rights.[35] But the popularity of the president and the words he had voiced would be confirmed by his sweeping reelection in the presidential election of 1804.

Years later, after the War of 1812, when Jefferson gathered together miscellaneous papers of earlier years, he recalled the now famous words of his inaugural address, adding: "I fondly hope we may now truly say 'we are all republicans, all federalists,' and that the motto of the standard to which our country will forever rally, will be 'federal union, and republican government.'"[36]

34. Cabot to Rufus King, March 20, 1801; Sedgwick to King, May 24, 1801; and Troup to King, March 23, May 25, 1801, in Charles R. King, ed., *The Life and Correspondence of Rufus King*, 3:408, 456, 409, 461.

35. Linda K. Kerber, *Federalists in Dissent: Imagery and Ideology in Jeffersonian America*, 131–32.

36. Jefferson, "The Anas," February 4, 1818, in Ford, ed., *Works of Thomas Jefferson*, 1:182.

Fig. 3-2. Silver medal, [Philadelphia, 1802], executed by Jacob Reich to commemorate Jefferson's inauguration as president of the United States. Jefferson's image was taken from Jean-Antoine Houdon's bust of Jefferson (1789). The medal is inscribed "Th. Jefferson President of the U.S. 4 March 1801." American Numismatic Society, New York.

Fig. 4-1. *Thomas Jefferson, President des Etats Unis de L'Amerique an 1801.* Engraving by Auguste-Gaspard-Louis Boucher Desnoyers, [Paris, 1801]. Manuscripts and Archives Division, New York Public Library.

Chapter IV

Impact Abroad

"I count on the good effects of your administration being felt in favor of republican government abroad as well as at home," Virginia Governor James Monroe wrote to President Thomas Jefferson in March 1801, soon after reading the new president's inaugural address. In more soaring language, Dr. Benjamin Rush wrote to the president praising his speech as "a solemn and affecting address to your fellow citizens, to the nations of Europe, to all inhabitants of the globe, and to posterity to the latest generations, upon the great subject of political order and happiness."[1]

Jefferson's inaugural address of March 4, 1801, was far more widely republished outside the United States than has been generally recognized. The complete speech was published in the *Montreal Gazette* in both English and French on April 6, the texts being printed in parallel columns. The *Royal Gazette, and New-Brunswick Advertiser* printed the full English text on April 7.

A week after the Canadian printings, *The Times* of London reported: "We yesterday received the *American Papers* to the 9th of March. In a Paper of that day there is a Copy of the Speech of Mr.

Jefferson to the Legislature, on taking the oaths of his new office, which cannot fail to be read with great attention and interest." The London *Times* printed the full text on April 14. Three days later, the *Courier de Londres*—a French-language newspaper published in London—began printing the address (fig. 4-2), concluding the text in the next issue the following week.[2]

Among British magazines publishing Jefferson's inaugural address in London were the *Universal Magazine*, which printed the complete address in the April issue; the *European Magazine*, in which the address appeared in the May issue; and the London *Monthly Magazine*, which published the address in its issue of May 1. The London *Annual Register of History, Politics, and Literature* for 1801 included the text of Jefferson's speech among the major public papers for the year.[3]

In reporting the speech, the London *Monthly Magazine* described it as

an animated, but cautious speech, upon the internal disputes which have lately prevailed

---

1. Monroe to Jefferson, March 18, 1801, in Hamilton, ed., *Writings of Monroe*, 3:269; Rush to Jefferson, March 12, 1801, in Butterfield, ed., *Letters of Rush*, 2:831.

2. *The Times* (London), April 14, 1801; *Courier de Londres*, April 17, 24, 1801.

3. *Universal Magazine* (London) 108 (April 1801): 275–77; *The New Annual Register, or General Repository of History, Politics, and Literature, for the Year 1801* (London, 1802), 201–4.

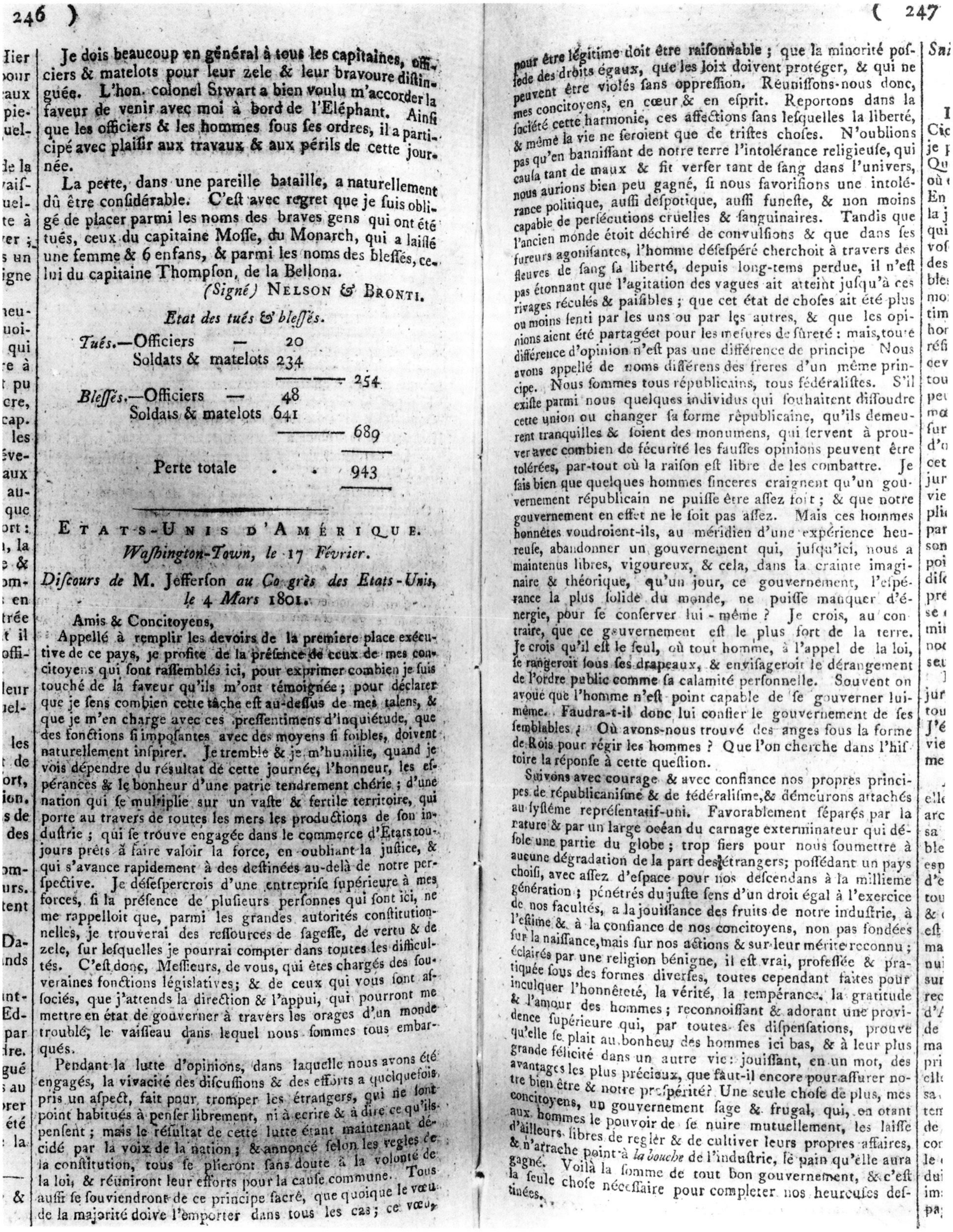

246)

Je dois beaucoup en général à tous les capitaines, officiers & matelots pour leur zele & leur bravoure distinguée. L'hon. colonel Stwart a bien voulu m'accorder la faveur de venir avec moi à bord de l'Eléphant. Ainsi que les officiers & les hommes sous ses ordres, il a participé avec plaisir aux travaux & aux périls de cette journée.

La perte, dans une pareille bataille, a naturellement dû être considérable. C'est avec regret que je suis obligé de placer parmi les noms des braves gens qui ont été tués, ceux du capitaine Mosse, du Monarch, qui a laissé une femme & 6 enfans, & parmi les noms des blessés, celui du capitaine Thompson, de la Bellona.

(Signé) NELSON & BRONTI.

Etat des tués & blessés.

Tués.—Officiers   20
    Soldats & matelots   234
                         ———— 254

Blessés.—Officiers   48
    Soldats & matelots   641
                         ———— 689

Perte totale   .   943

ETATS-UNIS D'AMÉRIQUE.

Washington-Town, le 17 Février.

Discours de M. Jefferson au Congrès des Etats-Unis, le 4 Mars 1801.

Amis & Concitoyens,

Appellé à remplir les devoirs de la première place exécutive de ce pays, je profite de la présence de ceux de mes concitoyens qui sont rassemblés ici, pour exprimer combien je suis touché de la faveur qu'ils m'ont témoignée; pour déclarer que je sens combien cette tâche est au-dessus de mes talens, & que je m'en charge avec ces pressentimens d'inquiétude, que des fonctions si imposantes avec des moyens si foibles, doivent naturellement inspirer. Je tremble & je m'humilie, quand je vois dépendre du résultat de cette journée, l'honneur, les espérances & le bonheur d'une patrie tendrement chérie; d'une nation qui se multiplie sur un vaste & fertile territoire, qui porte au travers de toutes les mers les productions de son industrie; qui se trouve engagée dans le commerce d'Etats toujours prêts à faire valoir la force, en oubliant la justice, & qui s'avance rapidement à des destinées au-delà de notre perspective. Je désespercrois d'une entreprise supérieure à mes forces, si la présence de plusieurs personnes qui sont ici, ne me rappelloit pas, parmi les grandes autorités constitutionnelles, je trouverai des ressources de sagesse, de vertu & de zele, sur lesquelles je pourrai compter dans toutes les difficultés. C'est donc, Messieurs, de vous, qui êtes chargés des souveraines fonctions législatives; & de ceux qui vous sont associés, que j'attends la direction & l'appui, qui pourront me mettre en état de gouverner à travers les orages d'un monde troublé, le vaisseau dans lequel nous sommes tous embarqués.

Pendant la lutte d'opinions, dans laquelle nous avons été engagés, la vivacité des discussions & des efforts a quelquefois pris un aspect, fait pour tromper les étrangers, qui ne sont point habitués à penser librement, ni à écrire & à dire ce qu'ils pensent; mais le résultat de cette lutte étant maintenant décidé par la voix de la nation; & annoncé selon les regles de la constitution, tous se plieront sans doute à la volonté de la loi, & réuniront leurs efforts pour la cause commune. Tous aussi se souviendront de ce principe sacré, que quoique le vœu de la majorité doive l'emporter dans tous les cas; ce vœu

(247

pour être légitime doit être raisonnable; que la minorité possede des droits égaux, que les loix doivent protéger, & qui ne peuvent être violés sans oppression. Réunissons-nous donc, mes concitoyens, en cœur & en esprit. Reportons dans la société cette harmonie, ces affections sans lesquelles la liberté, & même la vie ne seroient que de tristes choses. N'oublions pas qu'en bannissant de notre terre l'intolérance religieuse, qui causa tant de maux & fit verser tant de sang dans l'univers, nous aurions bien peu gagné, si nous favorisions une intolérance politique, aussi despotique, aussi funeste, & non moins capable de persécutions cruelles & sanguinaires. Tandis que l'ancien monde étoit déchiré de convulsions & que dans les fureurs agonisantes, l'homme désespéré cherchoit à travers des fleuves de sang sa liberté, depuis long-tems perdue, il n'est pas étonnant que l'agitation des vagues ait atteint jusqu'à ces rivages réculés & paisibles; que cet état de choses ait été plus ou moins senti par les uns ou par les autres, & que les opinions aient été partagées pour les mesures de sûreté: mais, toute différence d'opinion n'est pas une différence de principe. Nous avons appellé de noms différens des freres d'un même principe. Nous sommes tous républicains, tous fédéralistes. S'il existe parmi nous quelques individus qui souhaitent dissoudre cette union ou changer sa forme républicaine, qu'ils demeurent tranquilles & soient des monumens, qui servent à prouver avec combien les fausses opinions peuvent être tolérées, par-tout où la raison est libre de les combattre. Je sais bien que quelques hommes sinceres craignent qu'un gouvernement républicain ne puisse être assez fort; & que notre gouvernement en effet ne le soit pas assez. Mais ces hommes honnêtes voudroient-ils, au méridien d'une expérience heureuse, abandonner un gouvernement qui, jusqu'ici, nous a maintenus libres, vigoureux, & cela, dans la crainte imaginaire & théorique, qu'un jour, ce gouvernement, l'espérance la plus solide du monde, ne puisse manquer d'énergie, pour se conserver lui-même? Je crois, au contraire, que ce gouvernement est le plus fort de la terre. Je crois qu'il est le seul, où tout homme, à l'appel de la loi, se rangeroit sous ses drapeaux, & envisageroit le dérangement de l'ordre public comme sa calamité personnelle. Souvent on avoué que l'homme n'est point capable de se gouverner lui-même. Faudra-t-il donc lui confier le gouvernement de ses semblables? Où avons-nous trouvé des anges sous la forme de Rois pour régir les hommes? Que l'on cherche dans l'histoire la réponse à cette question.

Suivons avec courage & avec confiance nos propres principes de républicanisme & de fédéralisme, & démeurons attachés au système représentatif-uni. Favorablement séparés par la nature & par un large océan du carnage exterminateur qui désole une partie du globe; trop fiers pour nous soumettre à aucune dégradation de la part des étrangers; possédant un pays choisi, avec assez d'espace pour nos descendans à la millieme génération; pénétrés du juste sens d'un droit égal à l'exercice de nos facultés, à la jouissance des fruits de notre industrie, à l'estime & à la confiance de nos concitoyens, non pas fondées sur la naissance, mais sur nos actions & sur leur mérite reconnu; éclairés par une religion bénigne, il est vrai, professée & pratiquée sous des formes diverses, toutes cependant faites pour inculquer l'honnêteté, la vérité, la tempérance, la gratitude & l'amour des hommes; reconnoissant & adorant une providence supérieure qui, par toutes ses dispensations, prouve qu'elle se plait au bonheur des hommes ici bas, & à leur plus grande félicité dans un autre vie: jouissant, en un mot, des avantages les plus précieux, que faut-il encore pour assurer notre bien être & notre prospérité? Une seule chose de plus, mes concitoyens, un gouvernement sage & frugal, qui, en ôtant aux hommes le pouvoir de se nuire mutuellement, les laisse d'ailleurs libres de régler & de cultiver leurs propres affaires, & n'arrache point à *la bouche* de l'industrie, le pain qu'elle aura gagné. Voilà la somme de tout bon gouvernement, & c'est la seule chose nécessaire pour compléter nos heureuses destinées.

Fig. 4-2. *Courier de Londres,* London, April 17, 1801. American Antiquarian Society.

throughout many of the Provinces, and upon the alliances of America with the different nations of Europe. This speech, as we have already observed, is cautious, though spirited: but it is obvious, nevertheless, that the new President is more inclined to French than to English politics. The expression, that 'during the throes and convulsions of the ancient world, infuriate man has been seeking through blood and slaughter his *long-lost liberty*,' is language which the members of Congress have not been accustomed to hear from the Chair, and fully unfolds a difference between the political bias of the present President and his predecessor.[4]

It is likely that the British foreign secretary, Lord Grenville, first read the text of Jefferson's address in an American newspaper or in the London *Times* long before he received the dispatch from the British chargé d'affaires in Washington, Edward Thornton. On the day of the inauguration Thornton had transmitted a copy of Jefferson's speech to Grenville, commenting, "The same republican spirit which runs through this performance, and which in many passages discovers some bitterness through all the sentiments of conciliation and philanthropy with which it is overcharged, Mr. Jefferson affected to display in performing the customary ceremonies."[5]

It is also likely that Rufus King—the U.S. minister to Great Britain—first read Jefferson's inaugural address in the London *Times*. On May 9,

King wrote to a New York Federalist friend, Robert Troup, that it had been "nearly two months since we have received any political news from America: indeed we scarcely know anything which has passed since the completion of the Presidential election." But he also wrote in the same letter that in Great Britain "the speech of Mr. Jefferson has been very generally well received."[6] King had surely read the text before opening a letter, dated March 20, from his Boston friend and fellow Federalist George Cabot, who wrote:

> All our newspapers have copied the inauguration speech of Mr. Jefferson, you cannot fail therefore of having seen it before this will reach you. It is so conciliatory that much hope is derived from it by the Federalists; it certainly contains *some foolish and some pernicious* as well as *many good* ideas. On the whole however its temper entitles it to respect and whatever may be the sincerity of its professions, good policy requires that they be trusted till contradicted by actions.[7]

The New York papers of March 9 reached Paris about the same time that they arrived in London. Jefferson's address was translated into French, and the complete text appeared on the front page of the *Gazette Nationale ou Le Moniteur Universel* on April 20 (fig. 4-3). The address was published in The Hague in *Binnenlandsche Bataafsche Courant* on April 28 (fig. 4-4).

Napoleon's armies were already redrawing the boundaries of central Europe before Jefferson's election as president of the United States. On June 2, 1800, French troops in Italy occupied Milan. At the time of Jefferson's inauguration in March 1801, the Milan newspaper *Il Redattore Cisalpino* included in its masthead the words "Liberty" and "Equality" and used the dates of the French Revolutionary calendar. On

---

4. *Monthly Magazine* (London) 2 (May 1, 1801): 354. The same commentary was printed in *Walker's Hibernian Magazine* (Dublin) for May 1801, pp. 313–14.

5. Thornton to Grenville, March 4, 1801, Dispatch No. 15, Dispatches of British Ministers to the United States to the Foreign Office, transcripts at the Library of Congress, 50:53. Thornton's dispatch did not reach the Foreign Office until after Jefferson's inaugural address was published in the *Times* of London on April 14. On April 13, the British foreign secretary reported to Thornton that his dispatches through number 11 had been received (Bernard Mayo, ed., "Instructions to British Ministers to the United States, 1791–1812," *Annual Report of the American Historical Association for 1936*, 3:188).

6. King to Troup, London, May 9, 1801, in King, ed., *Life and Correspondence of Rufus King*, 3:444.

7. Cabot to King, March 20, 1801, in ibid., 3:407.

GAZETTE NATIONALE ou LE MONITEUR UNIVERSEL.

N° 211. *Primedi*, 1er *floréal an 9 de la république française, une et indivisible.*

Nous sommes autorisés à prévenir nos souscripteurs, qu'à dater du 7 nivôse, an 8 le MONITEUR est le *seul journal officiel.*

EXTÉRIEUR.

ÉTATS-UNIS D'AMÉRIQUE.

Newyork, 9 *mars* (18 *ventôse.*)

MERCREDI dernier, le nouveau président des Etats-Unis, M. Jefferson, a prêté le serment prescrit par la constitution, dans la chambre du sénat, en présence du sénat, des membres de la chambre des représentans, des officiers publics et d'un grand concours de citoyens. Voici le discours qu'il a prononcé à cette occasion:

Amis et concitoyens,

Appellé à remplir les fonctions du premier emploi exécutif de notre pays, je profite de la présence de cette portion de mes concitoyens, réunis dans cette chambre, pour exprimer la reconnaissance dont je suis pénétré pour la faveur dont on a bien voulu m'honorer; pour déclarer la conviction sincere où je suis que la tâche est au-dessus de mes talens, et que je ne l'entreprends qu'avec un pressentiment inquiet que m'inspire si justement la grandeur du fardeau et la faiblesse de mes moyens. Quand je vois une nation qui commence, répandue sur une terre vaste et fertile, traversant toutes les mers avec les riches productions de son industrie, en relation de commerce avec les nations qui connaissent la puissance et oublient le droit, élevant avec rapidité ses destinées au-delà de la portée de l'œil des mortels; quand je considere ces grands objets, que je vois l'honneur, le bonheur, les espérances de cette contrée chérie, confiés au résultat et aux auspices de ce jour, je tremble et je m'humilie devant la grandeur de l'entreprise. Je serais, en effet, entiérement sans espoir de succès, si la présence d'un grand nombre de personnes que j'apperçois dans cette assemblée, ne me rappelait que je trouverai dans nos premieres autorités constituées des ressources de sagesse, de vertu et de zele, sur lesquelles je pourrai compter dans toutes les occasions difficiles.

C'est de vous, messieurs, à qui sont remises les suprêmes fonctions de la législation, et de ceux qui sont associés à vos travaux, que j'attends avec confiance les conseils et l'appui dont nous avons besoin pour gouverner avec assurance, le vaisseau sur lequel nous sommes tous embarqués, au milieu du conflit des élémens d'un monde agité.

Durant la contestation d'opinion dans laquelle nous nous sommes trouvés engagés, la vivacité des discussions et de la lutte a présenté quelquefois un aspect qui pourrait en imposer à des étrangers qui ne sont point accoutumés à penser librement, et à dire ou écrire ce qu'ils pensent. Maintenant que la querelle est terminée, la voix de la nation s'étant fait entendre dans toutes les formes prescrites par la constitution, toutes les volontés doivent plier sous la volonté de la loi, et se réunir pour le bien général. Nous portons tous dans nos cœurs ce principe sacré, que, quoique la volonté de la majorité doive prévaloir dans tous les cas, cette volonté, pour être juste, doit être raisonnable; que la minorité possede des droits égaux que des lois égales doivent protéger, et qui ne peuvent être violés sans qu'il y ait oppression. Unissons-nous donc, concitoyens, de cœur et d'esprit, rendons à nos relations sociales cette harmonie, cette affection sans lesquelles la liberté, la vie même, seraient un pesant fardeau. Songez qu'en bannissant de notre pays cette intolérance religieuse sous laquelle le genre humain gémit depuis si long-tems, nous n'aurons rien gagné si nous laissons subsister parmi nous une intolérance politique, aussi tyrannique que criminelle, et qui peut engendrer des persécutions sanglantes.

Pendant que l'ancien monde était dans les convulsions, pendant les spasmes de l'agonie de l'homme furieux qui cherchait dans le sang et le carnage sa liberté, perdue depuis long-tems, il n'est pas étonnant que l'agitation des flots se soit fait sentir à une grande distance, jusque sur ces paisibles rivages; que le danger ait fait plus d'impression sur les uns que sur les autres; qu'il y ait eu partage d'opinion sur les mesures de salut; mais une diversité d'opinions n'est pas une diversité de principes. Nous sommes tous républicains: nous sommes tous fédéralistes. S'il existait quelqu'un parmi nous qui desirât de voir cette union dissoute, ou les formes républicaines changées, laissons-le vivre en paix; qu'il subsiste au milieu de nous comme un monument de la sécurité avec laquelle l'erreur d'opinion peut être tolérée dans un pays où l'on peut la combattre avec l'arme de la raison. Je sais en effet qu'il y a des hommes très-honnêtes qui pensent qu'un gouvernement républicain ne saurait être trop fort; que celui ci ne l'est pas assez; mais le patriote honnête voudrait-il, malgré l'expérience d'un succès complet, abandonner un gouvernement à qui nous devons notre liberté et notre vigueur, pour des théories, des visions enfantées par la crainte que ce gouvernement, le meilleur auquel le monde puisse prétendre, n'ait point assez d'énergie pour se défendre lui-même? Je ne le pense pas. Pour moi, je suis persuadé que notre gouvernement est le plus fort qui existe sur la terre. Je suis convaincu qu'il est le seul sous lequel chaque citoyen, obéissant à la loi qui l'appelle, sera toujours prêt à voler sous son étendart pour s'opposer à la violation de l'ordre public, comme il s'opposerait à celle de ses propriétés. On dit quelquefois que l'homme n'est pas en état de se gouverner lui-même. Comment pourrait-on lui confier le gouvernement des autres? A-t-on trouvé des anges, sous la forme de rois, pour gouverner les peuples? c'est à l'histoire à résoudre la question. Pour nous, persévérons avec courage et confiance dans nos principes fédéralistes et républicains, dans notre attachement pour l'union et le gouvernement représentatif. Séparés par le bienfait de la nature, et par un vaste océan du champ de carnage d'une partie du globe; trop fiers pour endurer des outrages de la part de l'étranger, maîtres d'une terre choisie, assez grande pour nous et pour nos descendans, jusqu'à la millieme et millieme génération; connaissant parfaitement le droit égal que nous avons tous à l'usage de nos propres facultés, aux profits de notre propre industrie; à l'estime, à la confiance de nos concitoyens; estime et confiance qu'ils accordent non à la naissance, cette distinction est inconnue parmi nous, mais aux actions; vivifiés par une religion douce, pratiquée sous des formes différentes, mais qui toutes sont propres à inculquer l'honneur, la bonne foi, la tempérance, la reconnaissance, l'amour des hommes; reconnaissant et adorant une Providence qui regle tout, qui nous prouve par ses bienfaits qu'elle se plaît à rendre heureux l'habitant de cette terre; comblés de toutes ces bénédictions, que nous faut-il de plus pour être un peuple fortuné et florissant? Un gouvernement sage et frugal, qui empêche les hommes de se nuire les uns aux autres; qui leur laisse d'ailleurs la liberté de conduire leurs affaires, et d'user de leur industrie comme ils le jugent convenable; qui n'arrache pas le pain de la bouche de celui qui travaille; voilà, mes concitoyens, le gouvernement le plus parfait, celui auquel il faut que nous bornions nos recherches.

Au moment d'entrer dans l'exercice des devoirs d'une place qui comprend tout ce qu'il y a de cher et de précieux pour vous, je vais essayer de vous exposer ce que j'entends par les principes essentiels de notre gouvernement, et conséquemment ceux sur lesquels il faut que se regle l'administration. Je me bornerai aux principes généraux: justice égale et exacte pour tous les hommes, quelles que soient leur condition et leur croyance politique ou religieuse: paix, commerce, et amitié honorable avec toutes les nations, sans violation de traités avec aucune; appui donné pour l'exercice de tous leurs droits aux gouvernemens des états, genre d'administration le plus convenable à nos intérêts domestiques, et le boulevard le plus sûr contre la tendance anti-républicaine; le maintien du gouvernement général dans toute sa vigueur constitutionnelle; la garantie la plus forte de notre tranquillité au-dedans, de notre sûreté au-dehors; zele jaloux pour le droit d'élection par le peuple, correctif doux et sûr des maux que cause le glaive de la révolution, dans les pays où l'on n'a pas su se pourvoir de remedes calmans; acquiescement absolu aux décisions de la majorité, principe vital des républiques, duquel il ne peut y avoir appel qu'à la force, principe vital du despotisme; milice bien disciplinée, notre plus ferme soutien pendant la paix et dans les premiers momens de la guerre, jusqu'à ce que des troupes réglées puissent défendre le pays; supériorité de l'autorité civile sur l'autorité militaire; économie dans les dépenses publiques, pour que l'homme qui travaille soit moins chargé; paiement de la dette, et respect pour la foi publique; encouragement de l'agriculture, et du commerce son frere; propagation des lumieres, et comparution de tous les abus à la barre de la raison publique; liberté du culte, liberté de la presse, liberté individuelle, sous la garantie de l'*habeas corpus;* jugement par jurys, choisis avec impartialité: ces principes forment la constellation brillante qui a marché devant nous, et a guidé nos pas dans un tems de révolution et de réforme: c'est à l'établissement de ces principes que nos sages ont consacré leurs veilles; c'est pour eux que nos héros ont répandu leur sang: ils sont notre *credo politique*, le texte de l'instruction civique; la pierre de touche avec laquelle nous essayons les services de ceux à la conduite desquels nous nous confions, et si dans des momens d'erreur et d'alarme nous avons le malheur de nous en écarter, hâtons-nous de revenir sur nos pas, et de regagner la route qui, seule, conduit à la paix, à la liberté, au salut.

Je me rends donc, mes concitoyens, au poste que vous m'avez marqué. Avec assez d'expérience dans les emplois subalternes, pour connaître toutes les difficultés de celui auquel je me vois appelé, et qui est le premier et le plus grand de tous, j'ai appris qu'un homme, créature imparfaite, doit rarement espérer de sortir de place avec la même réputation, la même faveur qui l'y ont porté. Sans prétendre à cette confiance absolue que vous aviez dans le premier et le plus grand génie dont s'honore notre révolution, ce grand homme auquel ses services prééminens avaient valu la premiere place dans l'amour de son pays, comme ils lui ont assuré une page brillante dans le livre véridique de l'histoire; je réclame de vous seulement le degré de confiance qui est nécessaire pour donner de la force et de l'effet à l'administration légale de vos affaires. Je pourrai pécher souvent par défaut de lumieres; le bien même que je ferai pourra passer pour du mal aux yeux de ceux qui ne sont pas obligés de porter leurs regards sur tout le pays à la fois; je réclame votre indulgence pour mes propres erreurs: elles ne seront jamais chez moi le résultat d'une mauvaise intention; et votre appui contre les erreurs des autres qui pourront blâmer ce qu'ils ne blâmeraient pas, s'ils voyaient les choses dans tout leur ensemble. En m'honorant de vos suffrages, vous avez donné une approbation implicite à ma conduite passée, et c'est pour moi une consolation puissante; toute mon inquiétude à l'avenir sera de conserver la bonne opinion de ceux qui me l'ont accordée, avant que j'eusse fait tout ce qu'il fallait pour la mériter, de me concilier celle des autres, en fesant tout le bien qui sera en mon pourvoir, et de me rendre l'instrument du bonheur et de la liberté de tous.

Ainsi, plein de confiance dans votre bonne volonté, je me mets avec soumission à l'ouvrage, disposé à le laisser dès que vous aurez reconnu que vous pouvez faire un meilleur choix. Je prie le tout-puissant, qui regle les destinées de l'univers, de présider à nos conseils, et de leur donner la direction la plus favorable à la paix et au bonheur de mon pays.

Aaron Burr, vice-président des Etats-Unis, a pris, mercredi dernier, séance au sénat comme président de ce corps.

Lundi dernier, la chambre des représentans des Etats-Unis a pris en considération les amendemens adressés par le sénat à la chambre, pour un monument à ériger à George Wasinghton. — Il a été proposé de consacrer à ce monument cent mille dollars, au lieu de cinquante qu'avait arrêté le sénat. — La proposition mise aux voix, 34 ont été pour; et 49 contre.

Le désordre à la barre de la chambre, occasionné par la grande affluence des étrangers et un grand nombre de dames, a presqu'empêché pendant plusieurs jours l'orateur de se faire entendre. On s'est vu obligé une fois de commander aux officiers de se répandre dans l'audience; plusieurs fois l'orateur a menacé de faire évacuer la gallerie. Vendredi, M. Harper qui avait la parole, fut si incommodé du bruit que fesait la multitude, qu'il déclara qu'il ne s'entendait pas lui-même parler. (*Extrait de l'Oracle.*)

TURQUIE.

Des frontieres de la Turquie, 15 *mars* (24 *ventôse.*)

ON apprend de Constantinople, que le ministre d'Angleterre ne pouvant communiquer avec le divan d'après un ordre formel du grand-seigneur, fait les préparatifs de son départ. Les mêmes lettres portent qu'une flotte russe de 16 vaisseaux de guerre était arrivée aux Dardanelles, et qu'on lui avait d'abord refusé le passage; mais que l'ambassadeur de Russie s'étant adressé directement au sultan, il en avait sur le champ obtenu l'ordre que le détroit fut ouvert en tous les tems aux vaisseaux russes.

ALLEMAGNE.

Wesel, 13 *avril* (23 *germinal.*)

EN conséquence de l'acte conclu à Hanovre, le 3 avril au soir, entre le ministre prussien de Schulembourg, la régence de l'électorat et le général Walmoden Gimborn, les troupes prussiennes sont entrées paisiblement dans ce pays; déjà une partie de l'armée hanovrienne a été

Fig. 4-3. *Gazette Nationale ou Le Moniteur Universel*, Paris, April 20, 1801. Ellis Library, University of Missouri–Columbia.

May 5, 1801, *Il Redattore Cisalpino* printed an extensive excerpt from Jefferson's inaugural address of March 4 (fig. 4-5). The excerpt ended with Jefferson's reference to "a wise and frugal government, which shall restrain men from injuring one another, shall leave them otherwise free to regulate their own pursuits of industry and improvement, and shall not take from the mouth of labor the bread it has earned. This is the sum of good government; and this is necessary to close the circle of our felicities." In parenthesis the editor added: "When may the same be said about Italy?"

German newspapers in 1801 widely reported Jefferson's election and his inauguration as the third president of the United States. The *Berlinische Zeitung* published a biographical summary of the Virginian's life on June 11, 1801. Other German newspaper editors gave special attention to the speech, in some instances printing the entire text. The Augsburg *Allgemeine Zeitung* required two issues (April 28 and 29) to print the full address (figs. 4-6 and 4-7).[8] In publishing most of the text on June 30, the editor of the *Hamburgische Neue Zeitung* omitted only the closing, largely personal, remarks of Jefferson (fig. 4-8).

By early May, David Humphreys, the U.S. minister to Spain, had read the address, and he wrote to the president from Madrid on May 8, expressing "how sensibly I was affected with your Speech, when you entered upon the execution of the office of President." Then he added: "I need not say it has been extremely applauded on this side of the Atlantic."[9]

Writing from Lisbon to Rufus King in London, where King remained as the U.S. minister to Great Britain, fellow Federalist William Loughton Smith, the U.S. minister to Portugal, confided:

The President's Speech contains in general very good principles; if he acts in conformity to them, I shall be content, but I trust little to professions in public men—actions must decide. He and Madison are able and experienced men and may do much good, if they pursue a proper system.— I don't like the language of the Speech—its too much of an oration and was more adapted to a 4th July Declaration by a young spouter hot from Princeton than to a solemn discourse delivered by the President to the Nation on such an occasion.[10]

In June, the Marquis de Lafayette wrote to Jefferson from Cirey: "Your speech has had among the friends of liberty, and the pretenders to be so, the great success it deserves. Every eyes are fixed upon you and from my rural retirements the heart goes with them."[11]

Some three months after Lafayette dispatched this letter to Jefferson, Joel Barlow wrote to Jefferson from Paris on October 4: "Your inaugural speech has had a general run in Europe and will have a good effect. I enclose you here a polyglotte or tetraglotte of it as printed here and distributed to all ambassadors and other persons from foreign countries, as likewise an American copy printed for the use of Americans here."[12] The publication that Barlow sent to Jefferson was surely the sixteen-page pamphlet *Speech of Thomas Jefferson, President of the United States, Delivered at His Instalment, March 4, 1801, at the City of Washington, with Translations into the French, Italian, and German Tongues*, printed at the English Press in Paris (figs. 4-9, 4-10, 4-11, 4-12).[13]

8. *Allgemeine Zeitung*, Augsburg, April 28, 29, 1801, pp. 471–72, 475–76.

9. Humphreys to Jefferson, May 8, 1801, in Frank L. Humphreys, *Life and Times of David Humphreys*, 294.

10. Smith to King, May 14, 1801, William Loughton Smith Papers, Library of Congress.

11. Lafayette to Jefferson, June 21, 1801, Thomas Jefferson Papers, Library of Congress.

12. Barlow to Jefferson, October 4, 1801, ibid. On Barlow and the English Press of Paris, see James Woodress, *A Yankee's Odyssey: The Life of Joel Barlow*, 215.

13. E. Millicent Sowerby, *Catalogue of the Library of Thomas Jefferson*, 3:326–27. The copy of the pamphlet from Jefferson's library, now in the Library of Congress, contains no title page, but the copy in the Beinecke Rare Book and Manuscript Library, Yale University, contains the cover-title page (fig. 4-9).

Fig. 4-4. *Binnenlandsche Bataafsche Courant*, The Hague, April 28, 1801. Library of Congress.

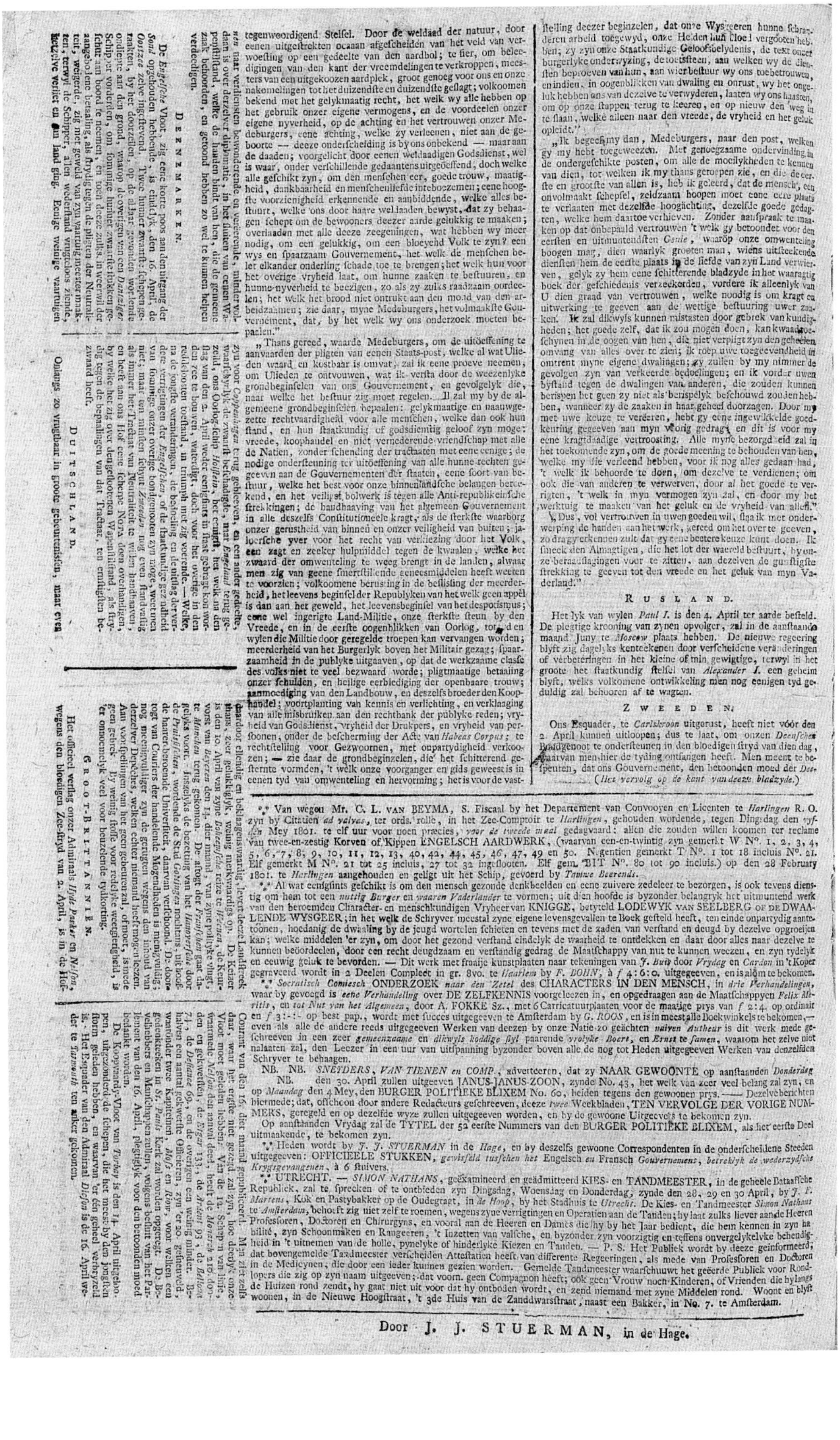

tegenwoordigend Stelsel. Door de weldaad der natuur, door eenen uitgestrekten ocaaan afgescheiden van het veld van verwoesting op een gedeelte van den aardbol; te fier, om beleedigingen van den kant der vreemdelingen te verkroppen, meesters van een uitgekoozen aardplek, groot genoeg voor ons en onze nakomelingen tot het duizendste en duizendste geslagt; volkoomen bekend met het gelykmaatig recht, het welk wy alle hebben op het gebruik onzer eigene vermogens, en de voordeelen onzer eigene nyverheid, op de achting en het vertrouwen onzer Medeburgers, eene achting, welke zy verleenen, niet aan de geboorte — deeze onderscheiding is by ons onbekend — maar aan de daaden; voorgelicht door eenen weldaadigen Godsdienst, wel is waar, onder verschillende gedaantens uitgeöeffend, doch welke alle geschikt zyn, om den menschen eer, goede trouw, maatigheid, dankbaarheid en menschenliefde inteboezemen; eene hoogste voorzienigheid erkennende en aanbiddende, welke alles bestuurt, welke ons door haare weldaaden bewyst, dat zy behaagen schept om de bewooners deezer aarde gelukkig te maaken; overlaaden met alle deeze zeegeningen, wat hebben wy meer nodig, om een gelukkig, om een bloeyend Volk te zyn? een wys en spaarzaam Gouvernement, het welk de menschen belet elkander onderling schade toe te brengen; het welk hun voor het overige vryheid laat, om hunne zaaken te bestuuren, en hunne nyverheid te beezigen, zo als zy zulks raadzaam oordeelen; het welk het brood niet ontrukt aan den mond van den arbeidzaamen; zie daar, myne Medeburgers, het volmaakste Gouvernement, dat, by het welk wy ons onderzoek moeten bepaalen."

„Thans gereed, waarde Medeburgers, om de uitöeffening te aanvaarden der pligten van eenen Staats-post, welke al wat Ulieden waard en kostbaar is omvat, zal ik eene proeve neemen, om Ulieden te ontvouwen, wat ik versta door de weezenlyke grondbeginselen van ons Gouvernement, en gevolgelyk die, naar welke het bestuur zig moet regelen. Il zal my by de algemeene grondbeginselen bepaalen: gelykmaatige en naauwgezette rechtvaardigheid voor alle menschen, welke dan ook hun stand, en hun staatkundig of godsdienstig geloof zyn moge: vreede, koophandel en niet vernederende vriendschap met alle de Natien, zonder schending der tractaaten met eene eenige; de nodige ondersteuning ter uitöeffening van alle hunne rechten gegeeven aan de Gouvernementen der staaten, eene soort van bestuur, welke het best voor onze binnenlandsche belangen berekend, en het veiligst bolwerk is tegen alle Anti-republikeinsche strekkingen; de handhaaving van het algemeen Gouvernement in alle deszelfs Constitutioneele kragt, als de sterkste waarborg onzer gerustheid van binnen en onzer veiligheid van buiten; jaloersche yver voor het recht van verkiezing door het Volk, een zagt en zeeker hulpmiddel tegen de kwaalen, welke het zwaard der omwenteling te weeg brengt in de landen, alwaar men zig van geene smertstillende geneesmiddelen heeft weeten te voorzien; volkoomene berusting in de beslissing der meerderheid, het leevens beginsel der Republyken van het welk geen appèl is dan aan het geweld, het leevensbeginsel van het despotismus; eene wel ingerigte Land-Militie, onze sterkste steun by den Vreede, en in de eerste oogenblikken van Oorlog, tot dat en wylen die Militie door geregelde troepen kan vervangen worden; meerderheid van het Burgerlyk boven het Militair gezag; spaarzaamheid in de publyke uitgaaven, op dat de werkzaame classe des volks niet te veel bezwaard worde; pligtmaatige betaaling onzer schulden, en heilige eerbiediging der openbaare trouw; aanmoediging van den Landbouw, en deszelfs broeder den Koophandel; voortplanting van kennis en verlichting, en verklaaging van alle misbruiken aan den rechtbank der publyke reden; vryheid van Godsdienst, vryheid der Drukpers, en vryheid van persoonen, onder de bescherming der Acte van *Habeas Corpus*; te rechtstelling voor Gezwoornen, met onpartydigheid verkoozen; — zie daar de grondbeginzelen, die het schitterend gesternte vormden, 't welk onze voorganger en gids geweest is in eenen tyd van omwenteling en hervorming; het is voor de vaststelling deezer beginzelen, dat onze Wysgeeren hunne schranderen arbeid toegewyd, onze Helden hun bloed vergooten hebben; zy zyn onze Staatkundige Geloofsbelydenis, de text onzer burgerlyke onderwyzing, de toetssteen, aan welken wy de diensten beproeven van hun, aan wier bestuur wy ons toebetrouwen, en indien, in oogenblikken van dwaling en onrust, wy het ongeluk hebben ons van dezelve te verwyderen, laaten wy ons haasten, om op onze stappen terug te keeren, en op nieuw den weg in te slaan, welke alleen naar den vreede, de vryheid en het geluk opleidt."

„Ik begeef my dan, Medeburgers, naar den post, welken gy my hebt toegeweezen. Met genoegzaame ondervinding in de ondergeschikte posten, om alle de moeilykheden te kennen van dien, tot welken ik my thans geroepen zie, en die de eerste en grootste van allen is, heb ik geleerd, dat de mensch, een onvolmaakt schepsel, zeldzaam hoopen moet eene eere plaats te verlaaten met dezelfde hoogächting, dezelfde goede gedagten, welke hem daartoe verhieven. Zonder aanspraak te maaken op dat onbepaald vertrouwen 't welk gy betoondet voor den eersten en uitmuntendsten *Genie*, waaröp onze omwenteling boogen mag, dien waarlyk grooten man, wiens uitsteekende diensten hem de eerste plaats in de liefde van zyn Land verwierven, gelyk zy hem eene schitterende bladzyde in het waaragtig boek der geschiedenis verzeekerden, vordere ik alleenlyk van U dien graad van vertrouwen, welke noodig is om kragt en uitwerking te geeven aan de wettige bestuuring uwer zaaken. Ik zal dikwyls kunnen mistasten door gebrek van kundigheden; het goede zelf, dat ik zou mogen doen, kan kwaad toeschynen in de oogen van hen, die niet verpligt zyn den geheelen omvang van alles over te zien; ik roep uwe toegeevendheid in omtrent myne eigene dwalingen; zy zullen by my nimmer de gevolgen zyn van verkeerde bedoelingen; en ik vorder uwen bystand tegen de dwalingen van anderen, die zouden kunnen berispen het geen zy niet als berispelyk beschouwd zouden hebben, wanneer zy de zaaken in haar geheel doorzagen. Door my met uwe keuze te veréeren, hebt gy eene ingewikkelde goedkeuring gegeeven aan myn vorig gedrag, en dit is voor my eene kragtdaadige vertroosting. Alle myne bezorgdheid zal in het toekomende zyn, om de goede meening te behouden van hen, welke my die verleend hebben, voor ik nog alles gedaan had, 't welk ik behoorde te doen, om dezelve te verdienen; om ook die van anderen te verwerven, door al het goede te verrigten, 't welk in myn vermogen zyn *zal*, en door my het werktuig te maaken van het geluk en de vryheid van allen."

„Dus, vol vertrouwen in uwen goeden wil, slaa ik met onderwerping de handen aan het werk, gereed om het over te geeven, zo dra gy erkennen zult dat gy eene beetere keuze kunt doen. Ik smeek den Almagtigen, die het lot der waereld bestuurt, by onze beraadslagingen voor te zitten, aan dezelven de gunstigste strekking te geeven tot den vreede en het geluk van myn Vaderland."

R U S L A N D.

Het lyk van wylen *Paul I.* is den 4. April ter aarde besteld. De plegtige krooning van zynen opvolger, zal in de aanstaande maand Juny te *Moscow* plaats hebben. De nieuwe regeering blyft zig dagelyks kenteekenen door verscheidene veranderingen of verbeteringen in het kleine of min gewigtige, terwyl in het groote het staatkundig stelsel van *Alexander I.* een geheim blyft, welks volkomene ontwikkeling men nog eenigen tyd geduldig zal behooren af te wagten.

Z W E E D E N.

Ons Esquader, te *Carlskroon* uitgerust, heeft niet vóór den 2. April kunnen uitloopen; dus te laat, om onzen *Deenschen* Bondgenoot te ondersteunen in den bloedigen stryd van dien dag, waarvan men hier de tyding ontfangen heeft. Men meent te bespeuren, dat ons Gouvernement, den betoonden moed der *Dee-*

(*Het vervolg op de kant van deeze bladzyde.*)

*** Van wegen Mr. C. L. VAN BEYMA, S. Fiscaal by het Departement van Convooyen en Licenten te *Harlingen* R. O. zyn by Citatien *ad valvas*, ter ords. rolle, in het Zee-Comptoir te *Harlingen*, gehouden wordende, tegen Dingsdag den *vyfden* Mey 1801. te elf uur voor noen præcies, *voor de tweede maal* gedagvaard: allen die zouden willen koomen ter reclame van twee-en-zestig Korven of Kippen ENGELSCH AARDWERK, (waarvan een-en-twintig zyn gemerkt W N°. 1, 2, 3, 4, 5, 6, 7, 8, 9, 10, 11, 12, 13, 40, 42, 44, 45, 46, 47, 49 en 50. Negentien gemerkt T N°. 1 tot 18 incluis N°. 21. Elf gemerkt M N°. 21 tot 25 incluis, 27 tot 32 ingesloten. Elf gem. BIT N°. 80 tot 90 incluis.) op den 28 February 1801. te *Harlingen* aangehouden en geligt uit het Schip, gevoerd by *Tamme Beerends*.

*** Al wat eenigsints geschikt is om den mensch gezonde denkbeelden en eene zuivere zedeleer te bezorgen, is ook tevens dienstig om hem tot een *nuttig Burger* en *waaren Vaderlander* te vormen; uit dien hoofde is byzonder belangryk het uitmuntend werk van den beroemden Character- en menschkundigen Vryheer van KNIGGE, betyteld LODEWYK VAN SEELBERG OF DE DWAALENDE WYSGEER; in het welk de Schryver meestal zyne eigene levensgevallen te Boek gesteld heeft, ten einde onpartydig aantetoonen, hoedanig de dwaaling by de jeugd wortelen schieten en tevens met de zaden van verstand en deugd by dezelve opgroeijen kan; welke middelen 'er zyn, om door het gezond verstand eindelyk de waarheid te ontdekken en daar door alles naar dezelve te kunnen beöordeelen, door een recht deugdzaam en verstandig gedrag de Maatschappy van nut te kunnen weezen, en zyn tydelyk en eeuwig geluk te bevorden. — Dit werk met fraaije kunstplaaten naar tekeningen van *J. Buis* door *Vrydag* en *Cardon* in 't Koper gegraveerd wordt in 2 Deelen Compleet in gr. 8vo. te *Haarlem* by *F. BOHN*, à *f* 4:6:0. uitgegeeven, en is alöm te bekomen.

*** *Socratisch Comiesch* ONDERZOEK *naar den Zetel* des CHARACTERS IN DEN MENSCH, in *drie Verhandelingen*, waar by gevoegd is *eene Verhandeling* over DE ZELFKENNIS voorgeleezen in, en opgedraagen aan de Maatschappyen *Felix Meritis*, en *tot Nut van het Algemeen*, door A. FOKKE Sz., met 6 Carricatuurplaaten voor de maatige prys van *f* 2:4. op ordinair en *f* 3:-:- op best pap., wordt met succes uitgegeeven te Amsterdam by *G. ROOS*, en is in meest alle Boekwinkels te bekomen, — even als alle de andere reeds uitgegeeven Werken van deezen by onze Natie zo geächten *naiven Autheur* is dit werk mede geschreeven in een zeer *gemeenzaame* en *dikwyls koddige styl* paarende *vrolyke Boert*, en *Ernst te samen*, waarom het zelve niet nalaaten zal, den Leezer in een uur van uitspanning byzonder boven alle de nog tot Heden uitgegeeven Werken van denzelfden Schryver te behaagen.

NB. NB. *SNEYDERS*, *VAN TIENEN en COMP.*, adverteeren, dat zy NAAR GEWOONTE op aanstaanden *Donderdag*
NB. den 30. April zullen uitgeeven JANUS-JANUS-ZOON, zynde No. 43, het welk van zeer veel belang zal zyn, en op *Maandag* den 4 Mey, den BURGER POLITIEKE BLIXEM No. 60, beiden tegens den gewoonen prys. —— Dezelve berichten hiermede; dat, offschoon door andere Redacteurs geschreeven, deeze *twee* Weekbladen, TEN VERVOLGE DER VORIGE NUMMERS, geregeld en op dezelfde wyze zullen uitgegeeven worden, en by de gewoone Uitgeevers te bekomen zyn.

Op aanstaanden Vrydag zal de TYTEL der 52 eerste Nummers van den BURGER POLITIEKE BLIXEM, als het eerste Deel uitmaakende, te bekomen zyn.

*** Heden wordt by *J. J. STUERMAN* in de *Hage*, en by deszelfs gewoone Correspondenten in de onderscheidene Steeden uitgegeeven: OFFICIEELE STUKKEN, *gewisseld tusschen het* Engelsch *en* Fransch *Gouvernement*, *betreklyk de wederzydsche Krygsgevangenen*, à 6 stuivers.

*** UTRECHT. — *SIMON NATHANS*, geëxamineerd en geädmitteerd KIES- en TANDMEESTER, in de geheele Bataafsche Republick, zal te spreeken of te ontbieden zyn Dingsdag, Woensdag en Donderdag, zynde den 28, 29 en 30 April, by *J. F. Martens*, Kok en Pastybakker op de Oudegragt, in *de Hoop*, by het Stadhuis te *Utrecht*. De Kies- en Tandmeester *Simon Nathans* te *Amsterdam*, behoeft zig niet zelf te roemen, wegens zyne verrigtingen en Operatien aan de Tanden; hy laat zulks liever aan de Heeren Professoren, Doctoren en Chirurgyns, en vooral aan de Heeren en Dames die hy by het Jaar bedient, die hem kennen in zyn habilité, zyn Schoonmaken en Rangeeren, 't Inzetten van valsche, en byzonder zyn voorzigtig en tessens onvergelykelyke behendigheid in 't uitnemen van de holle, pynelyke of hinderlyke Kiezen en Tanden. — P. S. Het Publiek wordt by deeze geinformeerd, dat bovengemelde Tandmeester verscheiden Attestatien heeft van differente Regeeringen, als mede van Professoren en Doctoren in de Medicynen, die door een ieder kunnen gezien worden. Gemelde Tandmeester waarschuuwt het geëerde Publiek voor Rondlopers die zig op zyn naam uitgeeven; dat voorn. geen Compagnon heeft; ook geen Vrouw noch Kinderen, of Vrienden die hy langs de Huizen rond zendt, hy gaat niet uit voor dat hy ontboden wordt, en zend niemand met zyne Middelen rond. Woont en blyft woonen, in de Nieuwe Hoogstraat, 't 3de Huis van de Zanddwarsstraat, naast een Bakker, in No. 7. te Amsterdam.

Door J. J. STUERMAN, in de Hage.

Libertà   (Num. XXV.)   Eguaglianza

IL REDATTORE CISALPINO.

Milano 15. Floreale anno IX. Repub. (5. Maggio 1801. v. s.)

Il presente foglio officiale esce il tridì, il quintidì ed il nonidì d' ogni Decade. Le associazioni si ricevono in Milano al Negozio di Federico Agnelli nella Contrada di S. Margarita Num. 1113. Il prezzo annuo è di lir. 12. e mezza di Milano, franco per tutta la Repubblica Cisalpina.

REPUBBLICA CISALPINA.

Estratto de' registri del comitato di Governo. Seduta del giorno 18. Germile anno IX. Repub. La Consulta Legislativa ha fatto deporre negli atti del Comitato di governo la seguente Legge. *Milano il 1. Ventoso anno IX. Rep.*

LA CONSULTA LEGISLATIVA

Considerando, che è della massima importanza di dar pronta esecuzione alla legge 9. nevoso p. p. anche nella parte che riguarda un corpo di Gendarmeria nazionale per tutto il territorio della repubblica, onde mantenere la tranquillità pubblica, la sicurezza delle persone, e delle proprietà;

Considerando, che è essenziale il riunire in un sol Codice le disposizioni legislative che devono determinare il servizio di questo corpo, li suoi rapporti verso le Autorità civili, la guardia nazionale, e la forza armata;

Dedotta l' urgenza dal messaggio del comitato di Governo del 4. frimale p. p.

DETERMINA.
TITOLO I.
Istituzione della Gendarmeria Nazionale.

1. Il corpo della gendarmeria nazionale è una forza istituita per assicurare il mantenimento dell' ordine, e l'esecuzione delle leggi nell' interno della repubblica.

Una vigilanza continua e repressiva costituisce l' essenza del servizio di questo corpo.

2. La forza armata specialmente istituita a difendere lo stato contro i nemici esterni è pure chiamata dalla legge, egualmente che la guardia nazionale sedentaria, a concorrere colla gendarmeria nazionale a reprimere i delitti, e a far cessare ogni resistenza all' esecuzione delle leggi.

3. Il servizio della gendarmeria nazionale è destinato specialmente alla sicurezza delle campagne, e delle strade.

TITOLO II.
Composizione della Gendarmeria Nazionale.

4. Il corpo della gendarmeria nazionale a piedi, ed a cavallo per il servizio di tutta la repubblica è stabilito dalla legge 9. nevoso anno IX. sul piano seguente.

Colonnello comandante	1.
Capi di squadrone	5.
Capitani	12.
Luogotenenti	24.
Marescialli d' alloggio capi facienti le funzioni di Quartier-mastri	12.
Tutti gli uffiziali, e sott-uffiziali qui sopra saranno montati.	
Marescialli d' alloggio, di cui 30. montati	60.
Brigadieri, di cui 60. montati	120.
Trombetti montati	12.
Gendarmi, di cui 540. montati	1080.

Forza tot. della Gendar. 1326.

Fig. 4-5. *Il Redattore Cisalpino,* Milan, May 5, 1801. Biblioteca Universitaria, Bologna, under concession of the Ministero per i Beni Culturali e Ambienteli.

New Jork 9. Marzo.

Squarcio del discorso pronunziato da Jefferson nel prestare il giuramento come presidente del congresso.

Il calore che ha animate le nostre discussioni nella crisi politica che abbiam sofferta potrebbe ingannar sulla nostra situazion: quegli uomini che non sanno nè pensare, nè parlare liberamente. Ma oggi che è finalmente noto il voto nazionale noi non avremo che la legge per guida, e la felicità della nostra patria sarà l'unico oggetto de' nostri voti comuni. Non obliamo giammai un principio sacro: il voto del maggior numero deve formar la legge, ma questo voto deve essere uniforme ai principj della giustizia e della ragione. Facciamo dunque regnare tra noi quell'armonia sociale senza di cui la libertà e la vita sarebbero un peso; pensiamo che in vano avressimo bandita dal nostro paese quell'intolleranza religiosa che tanto sangue e tante lagrime ha costato al genere umano, se in sua vece ora s'introducesse tra noi un'intolleranza politica non meno funesta.

Mentre l'antico mondo era, quasi direi, ne' dolori del parto; mentre si agitava furiosamente per ricuperare la libertà che da tanto tempo avea perduta, non deve far meraviglia che una simile scossa si sia fatta risentire fino a queste terre pacifiche e lontane, che abbia prodotti diversi effetti secondo i diversi caratteri, e che abbia divise le opinioni sulle misure da prendersi per garantirsi dagli effetti della scossa che si provava. Ma una differenza di opinioni non è differenza de' principj.

Noi siamo tutti repubblicani, tutti partigiani dell'unione. Se vi è taluno che desidera lo scioglimento di questa federazione, o un cangiamento nel nostro sistema di governo, lasciamolo pur vivere in pace; viva in mezzo di noi come un attestato della sicurezza colla quale l'errore di opinione può restare in un luogo ove può esser combattuto colla ragione. Io so in fatti che vi sono molti uomini onesti, i

quali pensano che un governo repubblicano federativo non sia abbastanza forte; ma un patriota onesto non vorrà mai, ad onta di ogni speranza contraria, abbandonare un governo a cui noi dobbiamo la nostra libertà e la nostra forza, mosso da vane teorie e da visioni. Io per me non lo credo. Son fermamente persuaso che il nostro governo sia il più forte che esista sulla terra; il solo in cui ogni cittadino, obedendo all'invito della legge, sarà sempre pronto a volare sotto i suoi stendardi per opporsi alla violazione dell'ordine pubblico coll'istesso zelo con cui si opporrebbe alla violazione delle sue proprietà. Si dice che l'uomo non è sempre capace di regolarsi da se stesso. Come dunque a quest'istesso uomo si affida il governo di tanti? Vi son forse degli angioli che sotto forma di re governano i popoli? Spetta all'istoria di risolvere questa controversia. In quanto a noi, persevereriamo con coraggio ne' nostri principj repubblicani, nel nostro attaccamento per l'unione e pe 'l governo rappresentativo. Separati per un mare immenso dal campo della strage che desola il rimanente del globo; troppo superbi per poter soffrire gli oltraggi de' stranieri, padroni di un terra fertile e grande abbastanza per contener noi ed i nostri discendenti fino alla millesima generazione; conoscendo i diritti che tutti eguali abbiamo al frutto delle nostre terre, al prodotto delle nostre industrie, ed alla stima e confidenza che i nostri concittadini accordano non alla nascita, ma alle azioni; diretti da una religione pacifica ed umana, esercitata sotto forme diverse, ma tutte inspiranti onore, buona fede, temperanza, riconoscenza, amore degli uomini; adoratori di una provvidenza che regola tutto e ci mostra co' beneficj suoi che essa vuol la felicità dell'uomo che abita questa terra, che ci manca mai per formare un popolo felice? Un governo saggio e felice che toglie agli uomini la sola libertà di farsi del male; ma che non

impone veruna legge ne' loro affari privati, che non strappa il pane dalla bocca di colui che travaglia; eccovi, cittadini, il migliore de' governi, quello a cui convien restringere tutte le nostre ricerche.

(Quando si potrà dire lo stesso dell'Italia?)

Fig. 4-6. *Allgemeine Zeitung,* Augsburg, April 28, 29, 1801. Institut fur Zweitungsforschung, Dortmund.

472

Blik der Sterblichen erheben sehe, wenn ich diese grosen Gegenstände betrachte, wenn ich die Ehre, das Glük, die Hofnungen dieses geliebten Landes, dem Erfolg und den Auspizien des heutigen Tages anvertraut sehe, so zittre ich, und demüthige mich vor der Gröse des Unternehmens. Ich würde wirklich ohne alle Hofnung seyn, wenn die Gegenwart so vieler Personen, die ich in dieser Versammlung erblike, mich nicht erinnerte, daß ich bei unsern obersten Behörden Hilfsmittel der Klugheit, der Tugend und des Eifers finden werde, auf welche ich unter allen schwierigen Umständen zählen kan.

Von Ihnen, meine Herren, denen das höchste Amt der Gesezgebung übertragen ist, und von Ihren Mitarbeitern, erwarte ich zutrauensvoll die Rathschläge und die Unterstüzung, deren wir bedürfen, um das Schif, auf welchem wir uns mitten unter dem Streit der Elemente einer vom Sturm bewegten Welt, sämtlich befinden, sicher zu regieren.

Während des Meinungs Zwistes, in welchem wir uns verwikelt gefunden haben, bot die Lebhaftigkeit der Erörterungen und des Kampfes zuweilen einen Anblik dar, durch welchen Fremde, die nicht gewohnt sind, frei zu denken, und was sie denken, zu sagen oder zu schreiben, getäuscht werden mochten. Nun der Zwist geendigt ist, indem die Stimme der Nation sich nach allen von der Verfassung vorgeschriebenen Formen hat vernehmen lassen, muß jeder Wille sich unter den Willen des Gesezes beugen, und alle müssen sich zum allgemeinen Besten vereinigen. In unsern Herzen tragen wir alle den heiligen Grundsaz: daß, wenn gleich der Wille der Mehrzahl in allen Fällen die Oberhand behalten muß, dieser Wille dennoch, um gerecht zu seyn, vernünftig seyn muß; daß die Minderzahl gleiche Rechte besizt, welche durch gleiche Geseze beschüzt werden müssen, und welche nicht verlezt werden können, ohne daß Unterdrükung vorhanden sey. Lasset uns also, Mitbürger, uns mit Herz und Geist an einander schliessen, unsern gesellschaftlichen Verhältnissen die Eintracht, die Liebe wiedergeben, ohne welche die Freiheit, ja das Leben selbst, nur eine schwere Bürde wäre. Bedenket, daß wir nichts dabei gewonnen haben würden, die religiöse Intoleranz, unter welcher das Menschen Geschlecht seit so langer Zeit schmachtet, von unserm Vaterland verbannt zu haben, wenn wir eine, eben so tyrannische als frevelhafte, politische Intoleranz, durch welche blutige Verfolgungen erzeugt werden können, unter uns bestehen liessen.

Während die alte Welt in Zukungen lag, während der furchtbaren Krisis, da der wüthende Mensch seine längst verlörne Freiheit in Blut und Mord wiedersuchte, war es natürlich genug, daß die stürmische Bewegung auch in einer grosen Entfernung, und selbst an diesen friedlichen Küsten, verspürt wurde, daß die Gefahr auf die einen mehr Eindruk machte als auf die andern, daß die Meinungen über die Maasregeln, welche das Beste des Staats erforderte, getheilt waren. Aber eine Verschiedenheit von Meinungen ist keine Verschiedenheit von Grundsäzen. Wir sind alle Republikaner, wir sind alle Föderalisten. Gäbe es jemanden unter uns, der die Auflösung dieses Bundes, oder eine Veränderung der republikanischen Formen wünschte, so lassen wir ihn in unserer Mitte in Frieden leben; er stehe in unserer Mitte als ein Denkmal der Zuversicht, mit welcher der Irrthum der Meinung in einem Lande, wo man ihn mit den Waffen der Vernunft zu bekämpfen weiß, geduldet werden kan. Es ist mir wirklich bekannt, daß es sehr rechtschaffene Männer gibt, welche der Meinung sind, daß eine republikanische Regierung nicht zu stark seyn könne, und daß die unsrige es nicht genug sey. Möchte aber der rechtschaffene Patriot, selbst wenn die Erfahrung eines vollkommenen Erfolgs da wäre, einer Regierung, der wir unsre Freiheit und unsre Lebenskraft verdanken, für Theorien, für Hirngespinste entsagen, welche die Furcht, daß eben diese Regierung, die beste, auf welche die Welt Anspruch machen kan, nicht Energie genug haben möchte, um sich selbst zu vertheidigen, erzeugen würde? Ich denke es nicht. Ich meines Theils bin überzeugt, daß unsre Regierung die stärkste ist, die es auf Erden gibt; ich bin überzeugt, daß sie die einzige ist, unter welcher jeder Bürger, dem Gesez das ihn ruft gehorchend, stets bereit seyn wird, unter ihr Panier zu treten, um sich der Verlezung der öffentlichen Ordnung zu widersezen, wie er sich der Verlezung seines Eigenthums widersezen würde. Man sagt zuweilen, der Mensch sey nicht im Stande, sich selbst zu regieren. Wie könnte man ihm also die Regierung anderer anvertrauen? Hat man etwa Engel, in der Gestalt von Königen, gefunden, um über die Völker zu herrschen? Diese Frage mag die Geschichte beantworten. Uns aber lasset mit Muth und Vertrauen auf unsern föderalistischen und republikanischen Grundsäzen, auf unsrer Liebe zur Bundes Einigkeit und zur repräsentativen Regierung beharren. Durch die Wohlthat der Natur, durch einen weiten Ozean von dem Schauplaz des Blut Vergiessens abgesondert; zu stolz, um von dem Ausland Schmach zu erdulden; Herren eines auserwählten Bodens, der Raum genug hat für uns und unsre Nachkommen, bis in das tausendste und aber tausendste Glied; wohl bekannt mit dem gleichen Rechte, das wir alle auf den Gebrauch unsrer eignen Kräfte, auf den Ertrag unsers eignen Fleisses, auf die Achtung und das Vertrauen unsrer Mitbürger haben — eine Achtung, ein Vertrauen, die sie nicht der Geburt, diese Auszeichnung ist unter uns fremd, sondern den Handlungen schenken — belebt durch eine milde Religion, die unter verschiednen Formen geübt wird, deren Formen aber alle geschikt sind, Ehre, Rechtschaffenheit, Mäsigkeit, Dankbarkeit, Menschenliebe einzuflössen; Anbeter einer Vorsehung, welche alles lenkt, und uns durch ihre Wohlthaten beweist, daß sie sich darin gefällt, den Bewohner dieses Landes zu beglüken; begabt mit allem diesem Segen — was brauchen wir mehr, um ein glükliches und blühendes Volk zu seyn? Eine weise und nüchterne Regierung, welche die Menschen verhindert, einander zu schaden, ihnen die Freiheit läßt, ihre Angelegenheiten zu führen, und ihren Fleiß wuchern zu lassen wie es ihnen gut dünkt, eine Regierung, welche dem, der arbeitet, das Brod nicht vom Munde reißt: das, meine Mitbürger, das ist die vollkommenste Regierung, und diejenige, auf welche wir unser Streben beschränken müssen."

(Die Fortsezung folgt.)

Verbesserungen.

Nro. 116. S. 463. Sp. 1. Z. 20. v. u. st. mit preussischen Sauvegarden versehen l. mit Sauvegarden oder preussischem Schuz versehen.

der sich als Kourier von London nach | den eine, für die gemeine Sache nützlichere, Bestimmung geben. Als die Nachricht vom Tode des Kaisers von Rußland eintraf, ... des KronPrinzen vorzüglich dahin, zu

Allgemeine Zeitung.

Mittwoch — Nro. 119. — 29 April 1801.

GrosBritannien. — Italien. — Teutschland. — Oestreich. — Preussen. — Dänemark. — Rußland. — Vereinigte Staaten von Amerika. (Beschluß der Rede des neuen Präsidenten.)

schwankend abgefaßten, ... der baltischen Flotte gegeben worden waren, aus eben dem ... eiligen Ehrgeiz, der ihn die Schlacht liefern ließ, einen Sinn beigelegt zu haben, mit welchem der dänische Hof, in Betracht der Umstände, weit zufriedener war, als der englische OberBefehlshaber. Noch am 5 Abends hatten die englischen Admirale erklärt, daß sie nur auf die Bedingung einer förmlichen Abtretung Dänemarks von dem nordischen Bündniß abschliessen würden; aber die Festigkeit, mit welcher der KronPrinz darauf beharrte, seinen Verbindungen getreu zu bleiben, nebst der persönlichen Stimmung Nelsons, gab der Sache den bekannten Ausschlag. Nelson verlangte lange einen 4monatlichen Waffenstillstand. Der KronPrinz wollte nur einen von 12 Wochen höchstens, und endlich verstand man sich von beiden Seiten zu 14 Wochen. „Der Kopenhagener Hof, sagt jener Artikel, sieht den zu Stande gekommenen Vergleich als eine Art von Triumph an, indem er durch denselben seinen Verpflichtungen keinen Abbruch thut, ohne irgend etwas Niedriges oder Schwaches in seinem Betragen an den Tag zu legen, seine HauptStadt, seine Flotte, seine Werften rettet, und die Engländer bei ihrer Expedition nichts gewonnen haben, als die Zerstörung von 11 Schiffen, die man im Voraus als aufgeopfert ansah. Europa's Sache wird es seyn, die Meinung vieler hiesigen Personen, daß der Sieger von Abukir seine Lorbeere vor der Rhede von Kopenhagen beflekt hat, zu würdigen. In Ansehung Norwegens und der Elbe läßt der Waffenstillstand einen vollkommenen status quo, so daß die Engländer frei sind, dort anzugreifen, und die Dänen fortfahren, Hamburg u. s. w. besezt zu halten. — Durch Beharrlichkeit allein ist eine für die Lage Dänemarks so ehrenvolle Kapitulation erlangt worden." — Derselbe Artikel behauptet, Nelson habe sich wieder eingeschift, ohne die während seiner lezten Anwesenheit in Kopenhagen dort eingetroffene Nachricht vom Tode Pauls I erfahren zu haben, und man glaube, daß sich das englische Geschwader entfernen werde, ohne von diesem Ereigniß Wissenschaft erhalten zu haben, (was jedoch schwerlich der Fall gewesen ist.) Die Ratifikationen geschahen am 9 durch den Admiral Parker auf englischer Seite, und auf dänischer durch den KronPrinzen, nicht aber in seiner politischen, sondern in seiner militairischen Eigenschaft als OberBefehlshaber. Die Dänen hatten auch erlangt, daß die Konvention französisch abgefaßt wurde, weshalb Nelson am 8 einen Priester, der diese Sprache konnte, mit an Land genommen hatte. Der KronPrinz hatte, noch ehe er einen solchen Vergleich hoffen konnte, dem König von Schweden sagen lassen, daß sein Geschwader zu spät ankommen würde, um Kopenhagen zu retten; er möchte also demsel-

der Stockholmer ... ten, und 6 Kutters stationirt, welche zum ... Befehl des Königs erwarteten; bereits war die AdmiralsFlagge aufgestekt.

Rußland.

Am 28 März ist folgende Ukase erschienen: „Da unsre Fabriken noch nicht die nöthige Vollkommenheit erreicht haben, und für die Bedürfnisse unsers Reiches nicht hinreichen: so verordnen wir, daß das Verbot der Einfuhr des Porcellans, der Fayence, der GlasWaaren, der Instrumente von Stahl, der Seiden-, Baumwollen- und LeinenWaaren aufgehoben, und für dieses Jahr der Tarif von 1797 giltig seyn soll."

Über die MinisterialVeränderungen in Rußland sind die öffentlichen Nachrichten zum Theil mit einander im Widerspruch. Nach einigen ist der Fürst Kurakin PremierMinister geworden, (oder vielmehr geblieben), nach andern hingegen hat er seinen Abschied verlangt und erhalten; der Graf Panin trat die Stelle, und H. v. Wassiliew die als ReichsSchazmeister wieder an. Der Fürst Subow sollte, hieß es, GrosKanzler werden, und der Graf Rasumowski wieder als ordentlicher Botschafter nach Wien gehen.

Am 4 April hatte das feierliche LeichenBegängniß des verstorbenen Kaisers Statt haben sollen; und im Junius wollte sich Alexander I zu Moskau krönen lassen. Der neue Kaiser hatte befohlen, daß nach Abnuzung der izigen Uniformen die ehemals üblichen wieder eingeführt werden sollten. In Ansehung Malta's werden die ersten Gerüchte nun dahin berichtigt, daß der Kaiser beim FriedensSchluß die Zurükgabe dieser Insel an den Orden, dessen Grosmeister dort residiren solle, verlange. Auch meldet ein Frankfurter Blatt vom 25, daß der Baron Pfirdt, Minister und GeneralEinnehmer des Malteser Ordens, Depeschen aus Petersburg erhalten hatte, laut deren der Kaiser erklärte, er nehme den Orden unter seinen unmittelbaren Schuz, und werde sich bestreben, ihn bei seinen Würden, Rechten und Besizungen zu erhalten.

Vereinigte Staaten von Amerika.

Beschluß der AntrittsRede des Präsidenten Jefferson.

„Im Begrif, die Pflichten einer Stelle zu übernehmen, welche alles in sich faßt, was Euch theuer und werth seyn kan, will ich versuchen, Euch meine Begriffe von den wesentlichen Grundsäzen unsrer Regierung, von den Grundsäzen also, nach

Fig. 4-7. *Allgemeine Zeitung*, Augsburg, April 29, 1801. Institut fur Zweitungsforschung, Dortmund.

476

denen der Staat verwaltet werden muß, darzulegen. Ich werde mich auf die allgemeinen Grundsäze beschränken — gleiche und genaue Gerechtigkeit für alle Menschen, welches auch ihr Stand, ihr religiöser oder politischer Glaube seyn möge; Friede, HandelsVerkehr, ehrenvolle Freundschaft mit allen Nationen, ohne VertragsVerlezung gegen irgend eine; Unterstüzung der Regierung der einzelnen Staaten in der Handhabung aller ihrer Rechte: denn diese Art Verwaltung ist die zuträglichste für unsre innern Angelegenheiten, und sie bildet das sicherste Bollwerk gegen die antirepublikanische Tendenz; Aufrechthaltung der allgemeinen Regierung in ihrer ganzen verfassungsmäßigen Lebenskraft: denn auf ihr beruht die stärkste Garantie unsrer Ruhe im Innern, und unsrer äußern Sicherheit; wachsamer Eifer für das WahlRecht des Volkes: ein mildes und sikres Korrektiv der Uibel, welche das Schwerdt der Revolution in Ländern, wo man sich nicht mit niederschlagenden Mitteln zu versehen wußte, hervorbringt; unbedingter Beitritt zu Entscheidung der Mehrzahl: das LebensPrinzip der Republiken, von welchem nur an die Gewalt, das LebensPrinzip des Despotismus, appellirt werden kan; wohl disziplinirte Miliz: unsre festeste Stüze während des Friedens, und in den ersten Augenbliken des Krieges, bis regulirte Truppen das Land vertheidigen können; Uiberlegenheit der CivilGewalt über die militairische; Haushältrigkeit in den StaatsAusgaben, damit der arbeitende Bürger weniger belastet sey; Zahlung der Schuld, und Achtung für Treu und Glauben des Staats; Aufmunterung des Akerbau's, und des mit ihm verbrüderten Handels; Verbreitung der Aufklärung, und Berufung aller Mißbräuche vor die Schranken der öffentlichen Vernunft; Freiheit des Gottesdienstes, Freiheit der Preß, persönliche Freiheit, verbürgt durch das HabeasCorpus; GeschwornenGerichte, mit unparteiischen Wahlen — aus diesen Grundsäzen besteht das glänzende Gestirn, welches in Revolutions- und ReformationsZeiten vor uns herging, und unsre Schritte leitete; der Stiftung dieser Grundsäze weihten unsre Denker ihre NachtWachen, und unsre Helden ihr Blut; sie sind unsre politische GlaubensFormel, der Text des bürgerlichen Unterrichts, der ProbierStein, an welchem wir die Dienste der Männer prüfen, denen wir uns anvertrauen; und wenn wir in Augenbliken von Irthum und unruhiger Besorgniß das Unglük haben, davon abzuweichen, so lasset uns zurück eilen, und den Weg wieder suchen, der allein zum Frieden, zur Freiheit, zum Heil führt.

Ich begebe mich also, meine Mitbürger, auf den Posten, den Ihr mir angewiesen habt. Ich erwarb genug Erfahrung in untergeordneten Aemtern, um alle Schwierigkeiten jenes Postens, des ersten und größten von allen, zu kennen. Ich lernte, daß ein Mensch, seiner Natur nach ein unvollkommenes Wesen, selten hoffen darf, seine Stelle mit eben dem Ruf, eben der Gunst zu verlassen, durch welche er zu derselben erhoben wurde. Ohne auf das unbedingte Vertrauen Anspruch zu machen, das Ihr in den ersten und größten Geist, dessen unsre Revolution sich rühmt, in jenen großen Mann seztet, dem seine hervorleuchtende Dienste den ersten Plaz in der Liebe seines Vaterlands eintrugen, so wie sie ihm eine glänzende Stelle im wahrheitliebenden Buche der Geschichte sicherten, verlange ich von Euch nur den Grad von Zutrauen, der zur Kraft und Wirksamkeit der gesezmäßigen Verwaltung Eurer Angelegenheiten erforderlich ist. Oft werde ich

aus Mangel an Einsicht fehlen können; selbst das Gute, was ich thun werde, wird in den Augen derer, welche nicht genöthigt sind, ihre Blike auf das gesamte Land zu werfen, wie Böses aussehen können — ich verlange Eure Nachsicht für meine eignen Irthümer, die bei mir nie aus schlimmer Absicht fließen werden, und Eure Unterstüzung gegen die Irthümer andrer, die etwa tadeln möchten, was sie nicht tadeln würden, wenn sie die Dinge in ihrem Zusammenhang erblikten. Indem Ihr mich mit Euern Stimmen beehrtet, gabet Ihr eben dadurch Euern Beifall in Ansehung meines vergangenen Betragens zu erkennen, und dis ist für mich ein mächtiger Trost. Meine ganze Sorge wird für die Zukunft dahin gehen, mir die gute Meinung derer, welche mir dieselbe schenkten, ehe ich noch alles gethan hatte, um sie zu verdienen, zu erhalten, und mir den Beifall der andern zu verschaffen, indem ich alles Gute thue, was in meiner Macht stehen wird, und mich zum Werkzeug des Glüks und der Freiheit Aller mache.

Voll Vertrauen auf Euern guten Willen, unterwerfe ich mich, und gehe an das Werk, von dem ich gern abstehen werde, sobald Ihr erkannt haben möget, daß Ihr eine bessere Wahl treffen könnt. Der Allmächtige, in dessen Hand die Schiksale des Weltalls sind, walte über unsre Rathschlage, und lenke sie zum Frieden und zum Glük meines Vaterlands!"

Am nemlichen Tage, wo H. Jefferson sein Amt als Präsident antrat, nahm H. Aaron Burr, als VizePräsident, den Siz im Senat.

Der Antrag des Senats auf ein Denkmal Washingtons 100,000 Dollars, statt 50,000, zu verwenden, wurde am 2 März im Haus der Repräsentanten mit 49 Stimmen gegen 34 verworfen.

Die mit den direkten Posten vom 10 und 14 April angekommenen englischen Blätter scheinen nun doch außer Zweifel zu sezen, daß bei der Ratifikation der Pariser Konvention Klauseln Statt gehabt haben: sie erwähnen einer Botschaft des vorigen Präsidenten, Adams, an den Senat, durch welche er unterm 2 März äußerte: er hätte gewünscht, daß die Konvention ohne Einschränkung ratifizirt worden wäre; da aber der Senat andrer Meinung gewesen wäre, so hätte er, aus Achtung für diese Behörde, dieselbe unter den von ihr beliebten Bedingungen ratifizirt; er hätte H. Bayard zum bevollmächtigten Minister bei der franz. Republik ernannt; da ihm aber H. Bayard die befriedigendsten Gründe, um diesen Auftrag abzulehnen, angeführt hätte, und diese Gründe ihn verhinderten, einen andern zu diesem Posten zu ernennen, so müßte er das Weitere seinem Nachfolger überlassen.

Verbesserung.

Nro. 118 S. 472 Sp. 2 Z. 3 statt: selbst wenn die Erfahrung eines vollkommenen Erfolgs da wäre, muß es nach dem englischen, in der franz. Uibersezung misverstandenen, Original heißen: gerade während des besten Erfolgs der Erfahrung.

Fig. 4-8. *Hamburgische Neue Zeitung,* Hamburg, June 3, 1801. Staats- und Universitatsbibliothek Carl von Ossietzky, Hamburg.

In addition to this publication, another Italian translation was made by Philip Mazzei, a longtime friend of Jefferson's. Mazzei had come to America in 1773, settled in Virginia near Monticello, and started a vineyard, which attracted Jefferson's great interest. Mazzei returned to Italy in 1779, but he remained in contact with Jefferson. In a letter to Jefferson dated July 2, 1801, Mazzei enclosed, as he later explained, "a copy of my Italian translation of your inaugural address, printed clandestinely." The courier bearing that letter and pamphlet, Mazzei later learned, was murdered in Provence. Meanwhile, Mazzei polished his translation, and on November 15 he wrote to Jefferson from Pisa enclosing a copy of his letter of July 2 with the additions made on July 30. He also enclosed a copy of what he described to Jefferson in a subsequent letter as "my translation into Italian of the divine address you delivered upon assuming the presidency of the United States." The revised translation, he wrote "was corrected and not full of error like the first, which I had been unable to proofread."[14] *Discorso del Signor Tommaso Jefferson* (fig. 4-13) was printed as a small pamphlet, measuring 4 1/2 x 6 1/4 inches. The pamphlet itself did not name the translator, but Jefferson wrote on his copy—treasured in the Library of Congress today—"translated by Philip Mazzei."

Jefferson's inaugural address was also reprinted in a larger pamphlet edition published in London in 1801 (fig. 4-14). It was introduced in a preface signed "An Englishman," who exclaimed:

14. Mazzei to Jefferson, November 15, 1801, and April 10, 1802, in Margherita Marchione, ed., *Philip Mazzei: Selected Writings and Correspondence*, 3:254–55, 259.

15. *The Speech of Thomas Jefferson, Esq., the Newly Elected President of the United States of America; to the Senate, House of Representatives, Public Officers, &c., on the 4th of March, 1801. With a Few Remarks on Its Probable Effects*, by an Englishman (London, 1801), 3–6. The Tarpeian Rock was a cliff of the Capitoline hill in Rome from which, in ancient times, condemned criminals were thrown to their deaths.

Hail Liberty! Ye Votaries or Victims in her cause; whether homaging at her profaned altars, or expiring in unwholesome dungeons, ALL HAIL!!!

The wished for event, in which philosophy and lovers of human kind are interested, has occurred. Jefferson has been elected President of the United States of America, but which is more, an inauguration Speech, by way of address to the Senate, the Members of the House of Representatives, the Public Officers, and a large concourse of Citizens assembled on the occasion, proclaims those sentiments and dispositions his friends and admirers have long observed him to cherish. Yes, ye lovers of freedom and justice, this well-timed promulgation will prove a denunciation to every abettor of tyranny, whether in America or Europe, and why may we not add Asia and Africa; for commerce resembling Pandora's box, which contains the evil as well as the good, like that too contains Hope, and its fruits at the bottom. It spreads knowledge, it diffuses reason, it promotes intercourse between nation and nation, and makes men (who alas, will, in some respects, resemble less rational animals) unwilling to live in strife with their fellow men, with whom they once had an intercourse. The Constitution of America is obviously the most free we know of; the Government of that New World is *stronger*, because *juster*, than any we witness in the Old. . . .

The language of the new Trans-Atlantic President may confirm the wavering patriot on this side of the ocean. It may have a good effect on the great Bonaparte himself. It may make him, whom we have no reason to doubt, honest in intention, still more sincere. The new confirmed Government of America will be perhaps, to the framers of constitutions, hence-forward, a normal school, a model for statesmen to work by. Let the countrymen of Jefferson then, who are a part of ourselves, give him the confidence he asks, there can be no danger in doing so; while his actions correspond with his declarations, continue to give him confidence, never forgetting (nor should he, and all men in similar situations, ever forget) that whatever country has a CAPITOL has also a TARPEIAN ROCK.[15]

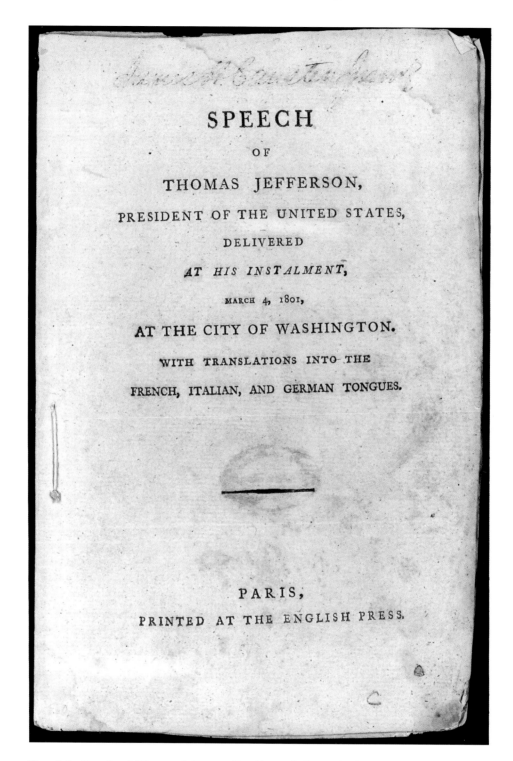

Fig. 4-9. *Speech of Thomas Jefferson, President of the United States, Delivered at His Instalment, March 4, 1801, at the City of Washington, with Translations into the French, Italian, and German Tongues.* Paris: Printed at the English Press, [1801]. Title-cover page of leaflet, Beinecke Rare Book and Manuscript Library, Yale University.

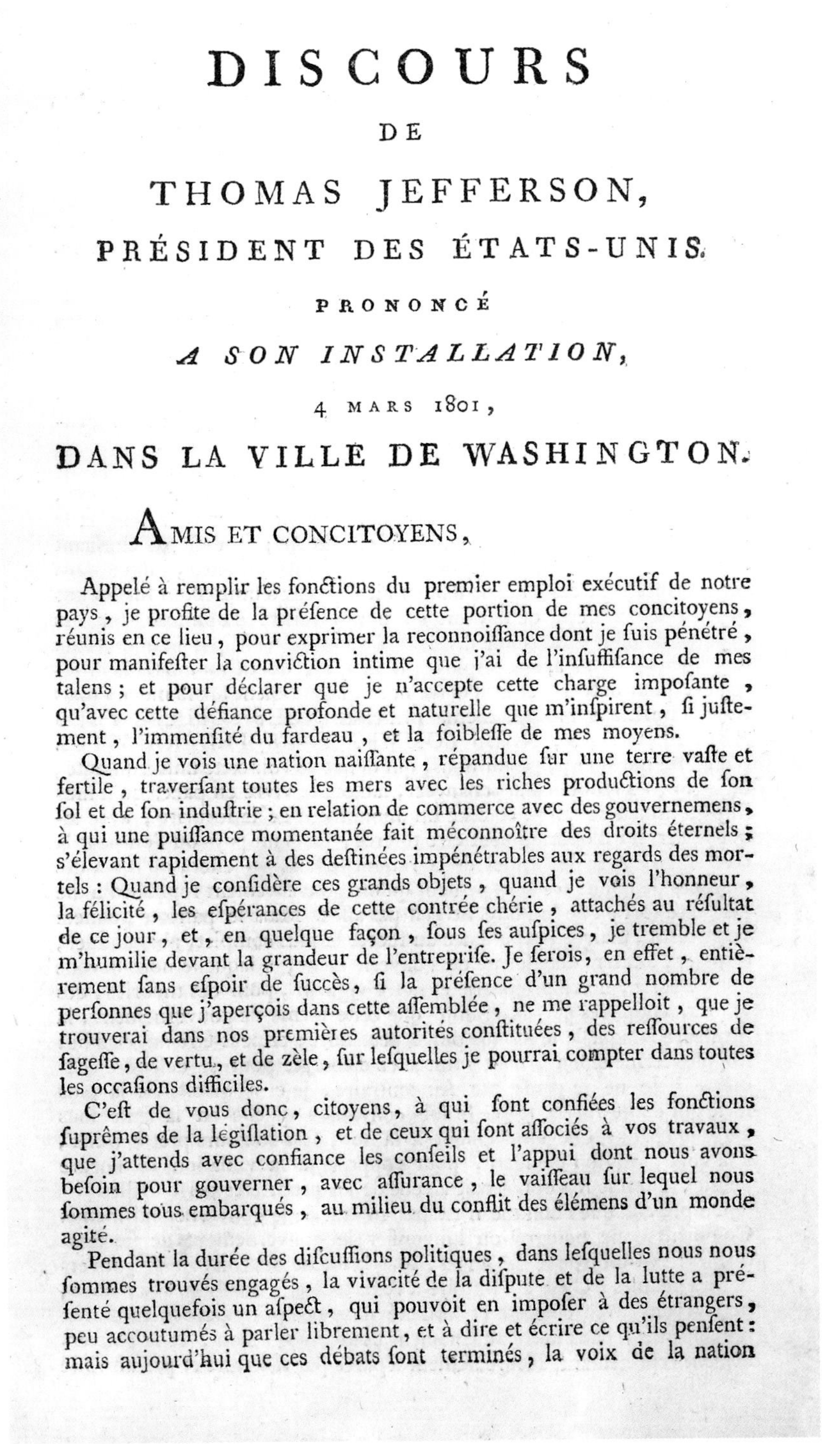

DISCOURS

DE

THOMAS JEFFERSON,

PRÉSIDENT DES ÉTATS-UNIS,

PRONONCÉ

A SON INSTALLATION,

4 MARS 1801,

DANS LA VILLE DE WASHINGTON.

Amis et concitoyens,

Appelé à remplir les fonctions du premier emploi exécutif de notre pays, je profite de la préfence de cette portion de mes concitoyens, réunis en ce lieu, pour exprimer la reconnoiffance dont je fuis pénétré, pour manifefter la conviction intime que j'ai de l'infuffifance de mes talens ; et pour déclarer que je n'accepte cette charge impofante, qu'avec cette défiance profonde et naturelle que m'infpirent, fi juftement, l'immenfité du fardeau, et la foibleffe de mes moyens.

Quand je vois une nation naiffante, répandue fur une terre vafte et fertile, traverfant toutes les mers avec les riches productions de fon fol et de fon induftrie ; en relation de commerce avec des gouvernemens, à qui une puiffance momentanée fait méconnoître des droits éternels ; s'élevant rapidement à des deftinées impénétrables aux regards des mortels : Quand je confidère ces grands objets, quand je vois l'honneur, la félicité, les efpérances de cette contrée chérie, attachés au réfultat de ce jour, et, en quelque façon, fous fes aufpices, je tremble et je m'humilie devant la grandeur de l'entreprife. Je ferois, en effet, entièrement fans efpoir de fuccès, fi la préfence d'un grand nombre de perfonnes que j'aperçois dans cette affemblée, ne me rappelloit, que je trouverai dans nos premières autorités conftituées, des reffources de fageffe, de vertu, et de zèle, fur lefquelles je pourrai compter dans toutes les occafions difficiles.

C'eft de vous donc, citoyens, à qui font confiées les fonctions fuprêmes de la légiflation, et de ceux qui font affociés à vos travaux, que j'attends avec confiance les confeils et l'appui dont nous avons befoin pour gouverner, avec affurance, le vaiffeau fur lequel nous fommes tous embarqués, au milieu du conflit des élémens d'un monde agité.

Pendant la durée des difcuffions politiques, dans lefquelles nous nous fommes trouvés engagés, la vivacité de la difpute et de la lutte a préfenté quelquefois un afpect, qui pouvoit en impofer à des étrangers, peu accoutumés à parler librement, et à dire et écrire ce qu'ils penfent : mais aujourd'hui que ces débats font terminés, la voix de la nation

Fig. 4-10. Opening page of French translation of Thomas Jefferson's Inaugural Address of March 4, 1801, printed at the English Press, Paris, [1801]. Rare Book Division, Library of Congress.

DISCORSO

DI

TOMMASO JEFFERSON

PRESIDENTE DEGLI STATI UNITI

RECITATO

NELLA OCCASIONE DEL SUO ISTALLAMENTO,

IL DI 4 MARZO 1801

NELLA CITTA DI WASHINGTON.

AMICI E CONCITTADINI,

Chiamato io ad efercitare le funzioni del primo Potere efecutivo del noftro paefe, profitto della prefenza di quefti miei concittadini qui adunati per efprimere i miei ringraziamenti pieni di riconofcenza per lo favore, col quale fi fono compiaciuti di porre gli occhi fopra di me, e per proteftare finceramente, effere io confcio, che la carica è fuperiore ai miei talenti, e che me le accofto con quell'inquieto e terribile prefentimento, che la grandezza del pefo e la tenuità delle mie forze tanto giustamente m'infpirano. Una nafcente nazione fparfa per vafte e fertili campagne, che attraverfa tutti i mari colle ricche produzioni della fua induftria, impegnata nel commercio con nazioni, che fentono la forza ed obbliano il diritto; che fi avanza a gran paffi verfo i fuoi deftini al di là dello fguardo umano : quando io contemplo quefti fublimi oggetti, e veggo l'onore la felicità e le fperanze di quefte dilette contrade dipendere dall'efito e dagli aufpici di quefto giorno, fbigottifco, mi umilio davanti alla grandezza della intraprefa. Anzi mi abbandonerei veramente alla difperazione, fe la prefenza di molti, che qui rimiro, non mi rammentaffe, che nelle altre autorità fuperiori ftabilite dalla noftra coftituzione, troverò mezzi di fapienza di virtù e di zelo, fu cui potrò confidare in tutte le difficoltà. A voi dunque, Cittadini, incaricati delle fovrane funzioni della legiflazione, ed a quelli che con voi fono affociati, mi rivolgo con corraggio, perchè mi fiate di fcorta e di foftegno, onde poffiamo guidare a falvamento il naviglio, nel quale fiamo tutti imbarcati, in mezzo al conflitto degli elementi di un mondo perturbato.

Durante il contrafto delle opinioni, che fi fono fuccedute, la vivacità delle difcuffioni, e dei fatti ha qualche volta prefo un afpetto capace di forprendere gli ftranieri non avvezzi al penfar libero, ed a dire e fcrivere quello, che penfano; ma questo effendo oggimai decifo dalla voce della

Fig. 4-11. Opening page of Italian translation of Thomas Jefferson's Inaugural Address of March 4, 1801, printed at the English Press, Paris, [1801]. Rare Book Division, Library of Congress.

REDE

DES PRÆSIDENTEN DER VEREINIGTEN STAATEN

THOMAS JEFFERSON,

GEHALTEN

BEY SEINER AMTSANTRETUNG

DEN 4.ten MARZ 1801,

IN DER STADT WASHINGTON.

F REÜNDE UND MITBRÜDER,

Indem ich ernannt bin die Pflichten der erften aufübenden Gewalt
unfres Landes zu übernehmen, benutze ich die Gegenwart des Theils
meiner Mitbrüder die hier verfammelt find, um meinen innigften Dank
für die Nachficht zu bezeugen mit welcher fie auf mich zu fehen die
Güte gehabt haben, und aufrichtigft zu erklären, dafs diefes Gefcheft
meine Fähigkeiten überfteigt, und dafs ichs mit der Bangigkeit, und
mit dem ehrfurchtsvollen Vorgefühl antrete, welches die Gröffe der
Obliegenheit und die Schwäche meiner Kräfte fo ernftlich einflösft. Eine
entftehende Nation über ein groffes fruchtbares Land verbreitet, welche
mit den reichen Producten ihres Fleiffes alle Seen durchchifft, und mit
Nationen in Handelsverbindungen tratt die Macht fühlen, und das
Recht vergeffen, und daher fchnell Schikfale ereilen deren Ende ein
fterbliches Auge nicht erreicht; wenn ich, fag ich, diefe weitauffehende
Gegenftände erblicke, und zugleich die Ehre, das Glück, un die
Hoffnungen diefes geliebten Landes betrachte, fo erftarre ich vor dem
Anblick, und beuge mich vor der Gröffe des Unternehmens. Ich
würde gänzlich verzweifeln, wenn die Gegenwart Vieler die ich hier
fehe mich nicht erinnerte, dafs ich in den andern hohen Autoritäten
die unfre Conftitution uns fchafft, die Quellen der Weifsheit, Tugend,
und des Eifers finden würde, auf welchen man unter allen Schwierigkeiten fich verlaffen kann. Auf Sie alfo, meine Herren, die fie
mit der hohen Function der Gefetzgebung bekleidet find, und auf
Alle, die mit Ihnen in Verbindung find, fehe ich mit Muth, nach
Leitung und Stütze die uns im Stande fezt, mit Sicherheit das Schiff
zu fteuern in welchem wir uns unter den ftreitenden Elementen einer
unruhigen Welt infgefammt befinden.

Wehrend den Streit der Meinungen den wir durchgegangen haben,
hat die Lebhaftigkeit der Difcuffion, und die Kraft mit der fie geführt
wurde, oft ein Anfehen erhalten, welches Freunde die ungewohnt find
frey zu denken, und das Gedachte frey zu fagen und zu fchreiben

Fig. 4-12. Opening page of German translation of Thomas Jefferson's
Inaugural Address of March 4, 1801, printed at the English Press, Paris,
[1801]. Rare Book Division, Library of Congress.

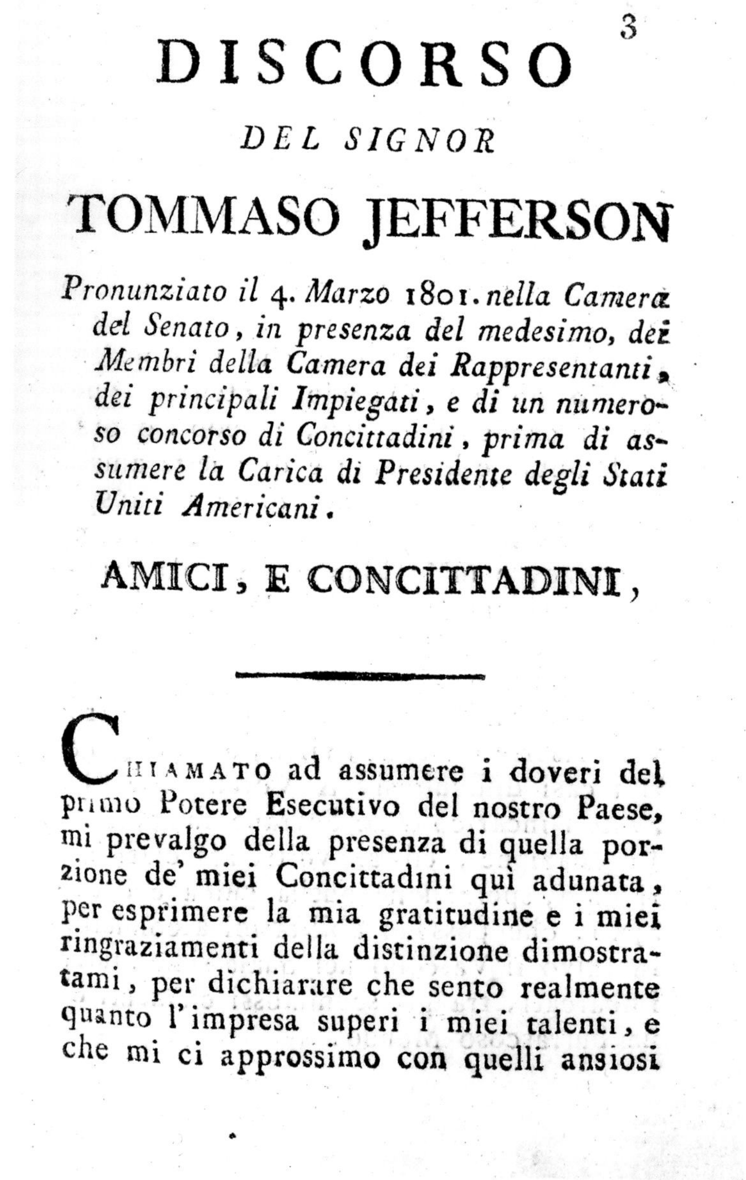

DISCORSO ³

DEL SIGNOR

TOMMASO JEFFERSON

Pronunziato il 4. Marzo 1801. nella Camera del Senato, in presenza del medesimo, dei Membri della Camera dei Rappresentanti, dei principali Impiegati, e di un numeroso concorso di Concittadini, prima di assumere la Carica di Presidente degli Stati Uniti Americani.

AMICI, E CONCITTADINI,

———

Cᴴɪᴀᴍᴀᴛᴏ ad assumere i doveri del primo Potere Esecutivo del nostro Paese, mi prevalgo della presenza di quella porzione de' miei Concittadini qui adunata, per esprimere la mia gratitudine e i miei ringraziamenti della distinzione dimostratami, per dichiarare che sento realmente quanto l'impresa superi i miei talenti, e che mi ci approssimo con quelli ansiosi

Fig. 4-13. *Discorso del Signor Tommaso Jefferson.* Translated by Philip Mazzei and printed in Italy, [1801]. Opening page. Rare Book Division, Library of Congress.

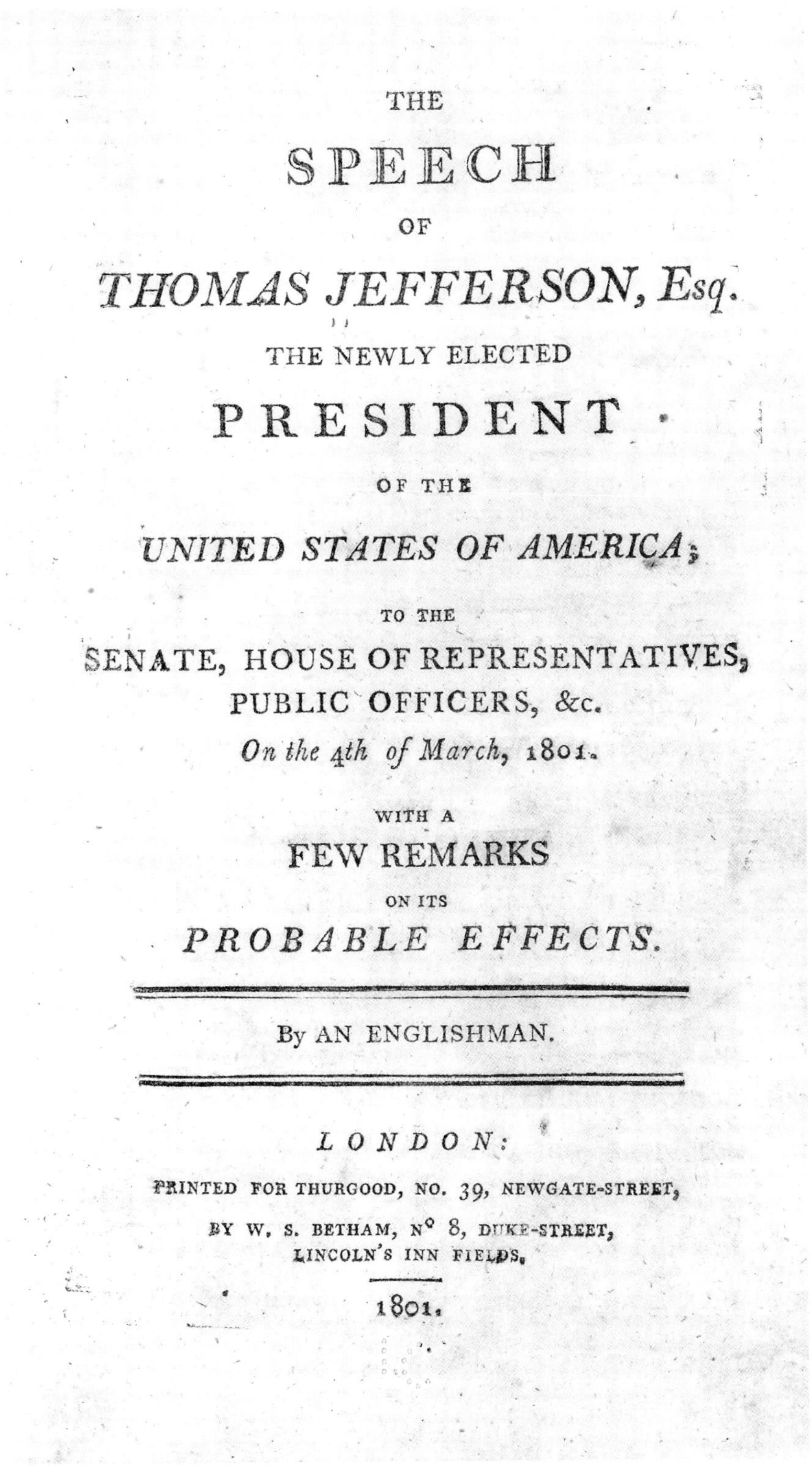

THE
SPEECH

OF

THOMAS JEFFERSON, Esq.

THE NEWLY ELECTED

PRESIDENT

OF THE

UNITED STATES OF AMERICA;

TO THE

SENATE, HOUSE OF REPRESENTATIVES,
PUBLIC OFFICERS, &c.

On the 4th of March, 1801.

WITH A

FEW REMARKS

ON ITS

PROBABLE EFFECTS.

By AN ENGLISHMAN.

LONDON:

PRINTED FOR THURGOOD, NO. 39, NEWGATE-STREET,

BY W. S. BETHAM, N° 8, DUKE-STREET,

LINCOLN'S INN FIELDS.

1801.

Fig. 4-14. Leaflet printing of Thomas Jefferson's Inaugural Address of March 4, 1801, with commentary by "An Englishman." London, 1801. Rare Book Division, Library of Congress.

Fig. 4-16. Liverpool pottery pitcher with quotation from Thomas Jefferson's inaugural address of 1801. National Museum of American History, Smithsonian Institution.

ommends conciliation and unanimity to all parties, and lays down the principles of the American Constitution, and the Administration which ought to flow from them, such as 'equal and exact justice to all men, of whatever state or persuasion, religious or political; peace, commerce, and honest friendship with all nations, and entangling alliances with none.'

The impact of Jefferson's first inaugural address persisted after its widespread republication in North America and Europe. A striking example of the continued influence of the address outside the United States was its republication more than a decade later in South America. In Santiago de Chile, Camilo Henriquez, the editor of the weekly *Aurora de Chile*, translated and published the entire address in his newspaper in November 1812 (fig. 4-15).[17]

Jefferson's election as president in 1801 prompted British pottery makers to place his portrait on Liverpool pottery pieces—mainly pitchers and mugs—produced primarily for the American market but also purchased by English admirers of Jefferson. A pitcher embellished with one of the better portraits of the new president added above his portrait an excerpt from his inaugural address: "We are all Republicans—all Federalists" (fig. 4-16). Another pitcher with Jefferson's portrait was embellished under the spout with a representation of the seal of the United States and the words "Peace, Commerce and honest Friendship with All Nations, Entangling Alliances with none"—taken from the inaugural address of 1801.[18]

Widespread enthusiasm for Jefferson was not shared by the editors of the London *Anti-Jacobin Review and Magazine,* which, during the election of 1800, had reported that "in America the cause of Jacobinism thrives" and predicted that "nothing is now wanting to complete the triumph of Jacobinism, but the elevation of Jefferson to the office of president."[16] His inaugural address was not reprinted in that magazine.

On the other hand, the *Edinburgh Weekly Journal* reported on April 22, after the receipt of American newspapers containing Jefferson's inaugural address:

We discover nothing of that spirit of hostility to this country which some of our intemperate journalists fancy they see in it. He strongly rec-

16. *Anti-Jacobin Review and Magazine* (London) 6 (June 1800): 236.

17. *Aurora de Chile* (Santiago), November 12, 1812, Staatsbibliothek zu Berlin–Preussischer Kulurbesitz, Zeitungsabteilung. I am grateful to Nicolò Russo Perez, University of Venice, for discovering this publication. See also Bernard Moses, *The Intellectual Background of the Revolution in South America, 1810–1824* (New York, 1926), 96–97, 104–5.

18. Cunningham, *Image of Thomas Jefferson in the Public Eye,* 108–9, 156, 98, 100, 156.

AURORA DE CHILE

¡LUCE BEET POPULOS, SOMNOS EXPELLAT, ET UMBRAS!

No. 40.   *Jueves* 12 *de Noviembre de* 1812.   Tomo 1.

ESPICIES FINAS.

ORACION INAUGURAL

DE TOMAS JEFFERSON, PRESIDENTE DE LOS ESTADOS
UNIDOS, AL PUEBLO.

Traducida del original por C. Hz.

AMIGOS, Y CONCIUDADANOS,

LLAMADO á tomar sobre mi las obligaciones del primer oficio executivo de nuestra patria, me aprovecho de la presencia de la porcion de mis conciudadanos que está aqui reunida, para expresarles mi profundo agradecimiento por el favor que se han dignado hacerme poniendo en mi los ojos: y para declararles que conosco intimamente que este cargo es muy superior á mis talentos; y que me acerco á el con aquel presentimiento timido y cuidadoso, que deben inspirarme la grandeza del empleo, y la debilidad de mis fuerzas.

Elevar una nacion esparsida sobre tierras extensas y fertiles—atravesar todos los mares con las ricas producciones de su industria—que tiene relaciones comerciales cen naciones, que imaginan derechos segun las fuerzas—que se avanza rapidamente à sus detinos, colocados mas alla de lo que alcanzan los jos mortales;—quando contemplo objetos de tanta trascendencia, y veo el honor, la prosperidad, y esperanzas de estas amadas regiones dependiendo del exito, y auspicios de estos dias, do puedo dexar de humillarme á vista de la magnitud del cargo, que me confiais. En verdad yo me abatiria, si la presencia de muchos de los asistentes no me recordase que en las otras autoridades establecidas por la Constitucion, he de encontrar recursos de sabiduria, virtud, y zelo à que ocurrir confiadamente en todas las dificultades. Vos y yo, hombres del Estado, hemos de dirigir con seguridad el vagel, en que nos hemos embarcado todos, entre el conflicto de los elementos y actual tempestad del mundo.

Durante la contienda de opiniones, al animarse y acalorarse las discusiones hemos ofrecido un aspecto no mui edificante á los extrangeros engañados, no acostumbrados á pensar libremente, ni á escribir con libertad lo que piensan. Pero habiendose decidido todo por la voz de la union, anunciada segun las leyes constitucionales, todas las voluntades se colocan por si mismas baxo la voluntad de la ley, y reuniràn sus efuerzos para el bien común. Asi todos debemos llevar gravado en el animo este sagrado principio: que aunque la voluntad de la mayoridad del pueblo debe prevalecer en todos los casos, esta voluntad para ser recta debe ser rasonable:—que la minoridad, que posee iguales derechos, debe ser protegida por leyes iguales, que no pueden violarse sin opresion. Unamos pues nuestros animos, y nuestros corazones.—Restablescase el comercio social, la harmonia, y el efecto, sin lo qual la libertad, y aun la vida misma son aborrecibles. Y reflexionemos que habiendo desterrado de nuestra patria aquella intolerancia que envolvio en sangre y en lagrimas al genero humano, habremos adelantado poco, si pjotegemos la intolerancia politica,* tan despotica como injusta, y capaz de producir unas persecuciones no menos sangrientas.

Mientras duran las convulsiones del antiguo mundo, y los mortales espasmos del hombre furioso, que busca entre la sangre, y los estragos, la libertad que ha perdido; no será extraño el que la agitacion de las olas se extienda hasta estas remotas, y pacificas orillas; que se dividan las opiniones, y las medidas de seguridad; pero la diferencia de opiniones no trahe siempre una diferencia de principios. Todos somos REPUBLICANOS todos somos FEDERALISTAS. Si hay alguno entre nosotros que opine que fuera mejor variar la forma republicana, quede tranquilo, como un monumento de la seguridad con que toleramos los errores de opinion: sean libres los errores, para que sean combatidos con libertad. Yo sè que algunos hombres honestos juzgan que el gobierno republicano no puede ser bastantemente vigoroso: que no es bastantemente fuerte para lo exterior. Pero querra un patriota honrado, despues de todo quanto nos dice la experiencia, abandonar un gobierno que nos ha conservado libres y firmes, por el theoretico y visionario temor de que esta forma de gobierno, que es la esperanza del mundo, pueda talvez no tener toda la energia necesa-

* Tirania contra la libertad de opinar en asuntos politicos.

Fig. 4-15. *Aurora de Chile,* Santiago, November 12, 1812. Staatsbibliothek zu Berlin–Preussischer Kulurbesitz, Zeitungsabteilung.

166   **AURORA DE CHILE.**

ria para conservarnos? Yo no soi de este parecer: al contrario, yo creo que esta forma de gobirno es la mas fuerte de la tierra. Yo creo que cada hombre al llamamiento de la ley corriera al estandarte de la ley, y miraria la invasion del orden publico como un daño propio y personal.—Se ha dicho, que los pueblos no se gobiernan bien à simismos. Pero ¿pueden ser bien gobernados por otros? Acaso decendieron alguna vez de los cielos angeles en forma de reyes para governarlos? Yo dexo à la historia que resuelva esta question.

Sigamos pues amigos, nuestros principios federativos y republicanos—nuestra adhesion à la union, y al govierno representativo. Separados felizmente por la naturaleza y por un inmenso occeano de las ruinas y desastres de una parte del globo—donde la ambicion ve con frialdad la degradacion de los mortales—poseyendo unos payses fecundos, con exelentes y dilatadas tierras y campos para nuestros decendientes hasta la milesima gene racion—conservando cada dia mas claro el conocimiento de nnestros derechos, y el exercicio libre de nuestras facultades—el honor y la confianza de nuestros conciudadanos, fundada no enel nacimiento, sino en nuestras acciones y en su gratitud—viviendo baxo una religion benigna, profesada, es verdad, y practicada en varias formas, pero que todas ellas inculcan, y predican la hosnestidad la buena fé, la templanza, el agradecimiento, y el amor del proximo*—reconociendo y adorando una Providencia universal, cuyos inefables beneficios y disposiciones prueban que se deleyta en la felicidad presente del hombre, y mucho mas en su felicidad futura:—Con estas bendiciones, ¿ que nos falta para ser el pueblo mas feliz y próspero de la tierra? Sí, amigos, nos falta otra cosa: necesitamos de un gobierno sabio, y economico, que impida que nos dañemos los unos à los tros,—que nos conserve libre el exercicio y uso de nuestro bienes é industria, y que no nos quite el pan de la boca. Esta es la suma de un buen gobierno, y esto es necesario para completar el circulo de nuestras felicidades.

Antes de entrar en el exercicio de mis nuevos deberes, juzgo conveniente exponer con brevedad los principios esenciales de nuestro gobierno, y que dirigen su administracion. Estos son pues:—justicia igual y exacta para con todo hombre, sea qual fueren su estado, y sus persuasiones—paz, comercio, buena amistad con todas las naciones—establecer alianzas con ninguna: conservar los gobiernos establecidos en todos su dere-

* Por un beneficio inestimable del cielo goza nuestro amado Chile de la moral pura, santisima, y amable de Jesu-Christo, unida à la fé incorrupta è inalterable de los ‘dogmas Apostolicos. Ventaja, que reunida à tcdos los dones mas preciosos de la naturaleza, lo constituyen una de las regiones mas recomendables del orbe.

chos como la administracion mas conveniente para los negocios domesticos, y como el firme baluarte contra las miras anti-republicanas—conservar el gobierno central en todo el vigor de la constitucion como la ancla de la paz domestica, y seguridad exterior—un zelo escrupuloso en conservar al pueblo el derecho de las elecciones: corregir los abusos tranquilamente, los quales se cortan con la espada de la revolucion, quando no tienen fuerza los remedios comunes y pacificos—obediencia á las decisiones de la mayoria principio vital de las republicas, del qnal no hay apelacion sino à la fuerza, origen del despotismo—una milicia bien diciplinada, nuestra confianza en la paz, y en los primeros movimientos de la guerra para dar tiempo á que se acerquen las tropas regulares—la supremacia de la autoridad civil sobre la militar—economia en los gastos publicos—pagar honradamente nuestras deudas–conservar como una cosa sacrosanta la fè publica—alentar la agricultura, la industria, y el comercio—proteger la educacion, difundir las luces, extirpar las preocupaciones, y perfeccionar la razon publica—libertad de opinion—libertad de la imprenta–libertad y seguridad individual baxo la proteccion del *habeas corpus*, y ser juzgados por jurados electos con imparcialidad. Estos principios forman la brillante constelacion, que hasta qui ha ido delante de nosotros, y ha guiado nuestros pasos en la edad de la revolucion y de la reforma. Al establecimiento y defensa de estos principios se consagraron la sabiduria de nuestros sabios, y la sangre de nuestros heroes. Ellos deben ser el catecismo y el credo de nuestra fè politica, el texto de la instruccion civil, y la piedra de toque de nuestros servicios y confianza. Si nos apartamos de ellos en los momentos de error, y de alrrma, volvamos á ellos nuestros pasos, y recobremos el camino de la paz, de la libertad, de la seguridad.

Me presento pues, amigos y conciudadanos, en el puesto que me destinais, con la experiencia adquirida en empleos subalternos, en que he palpado las dificultades de los unos, y la grandeza de todos: yo he conocido que es cosa mui rara el que un hombre, sér tan imperfecto, se retire de los cargos publicos con la misma reputacion con que entró en ellos. Sin pretender alcanzar aquella alta confianza, que justamente pusisteis en el mayor y primer caracter revolucionario, cuyos preeminentes servicios le han designado el primer lugar en el amor de estos pueblos, y la página mas bella, y brillante en el volumen de la fiel historia, solo os pido que confieis que administraré vuestros negocios con justicia, firmeza, y actividad. Yo pido indulgencia para mis hierros, que jamas sèran intencionales. La aprobacion, que envuelven vuestros sufragios, me consuela altamente en orden á mi pasada conducta; y

para lo fyturo será mi cuidado conservar la buena opinion con que me favoreceis, promoviendo por todos los medios posibles la prosperidad y libertad de todos.

Confiando pues en vuestro afecto y en el patrocinio de vuestra buena voluntad, avanzo con obediencia á estas nyevas fatigas, pronto á retirarme del empleo siempre que conoscais que podeis hacer una eleccion mas acertada. Entre tanto el Poder Infinito, que dirige los destinos del universo, guie nuestros consejos à lo mejor, y les de un exito favorable à vuestra paz y felicidad.

Tomas Jefferson.

Washington, 4 *de Marzo,* 1801.

Fig. 5-1. Oil portrait of Thomas Jefferson, taken from life by Gilbert Stuart, 1805. Owned jointly by the National Portrait Gallery, Smithsonian Institution, and the Thomas Jefferson Memorial Foundation, Monticello. Gift of Regents of the Smithsonian Institution, Thomas Jefferson Memorial Foundation, and Enid and Crosby Kemper Foundation.

Chapter V

Jefferson's Second Inaugural Address, March 4, 1805

Thomas Jefferson's second inaugural on March 4, 1805, did not attract so much attention as his first, but the press reported that "the concourse of spectators was immense." As in 1801, the president shunned ceremony. Dressed in black and wearing black silk stockings, Jefferson arrived at the Capitol in a carriage accompanied only by his private secretary and a groom. The Senate chamber, where he again took the oath of office at noon, was crowded, though many members of Congress had left Washington after Congress adjourned on the previous day. Chief Justice John Marshall once more administered the oath of office, and a reporter for the Philadelphia *Aurora* noticed that "the judge did not turn his back upon the president, whilst administering the oath, as he did this day four years." As in 1801, many listeners failed to hear the president's address in the crowded chamber, where echoes in the gallery compounded the weakness of Jefferson's voice. John Quincy Adams, who was present, wrote in his diary that Jefferson delivered his address "in so low a voice that not half of it was heard by any part of the crowded auditory."[1]

1. *Aurora* (Philadelphia), March 7, 8, 1805; Charles Francis Adams, ed., *The Memoirs of John Quincy Adams, Comprising Portions of His Diary from 1797 to 1848*, 1:373.

In drafting his second inaugural address, Jefferson prepared the following note, referring back to his first inaugural address and indicating the different focus of his second one:

The former one was an exposition of the principles of which I thought it my duty to administer the government. The second then should naturally be a *conte rendu*, or a statement of facts, showing that I have conformed to those principles. The former was *promise*: this is *performance*. Yet the nature of the occasion requires that details should be avoided, that, the most prominent heads only should be selected and these placed in a strong light but in as few words as possible. These heads are Foreign affairs; Domestic affairs, viz. Taxes, Debts, Louisiana, Religion, Indians, The Press. None of these heads need any commentary but that of the Indians. This is a proper topic not only to promote the work of humanizing our citizens towards these people, but to conciliate to us the good opinion of Europe on the subject of the Indians. This, however, might have been done in half the compass it here occupies. But every respector of science, every friend to political reformation must have observed with indignation the hue and cry raised against philosophy and the rights of man; and it really seems as if they would be overborne and barbarism, bigotry and despotism would recover the ground they have lost by the advance of the public understanding. I have thought the occasion justified some discountenance of these anti-social doctrines, some testimony against them, but not to commit myself in direct warfare on them, I have thought it best to say what is directly applied to the Indians only, but admits by inference a more general extension.[2]

The "more general extension" that Jefferson had in mind was to the Federalist opposition.[3]

Jefferson submitted drafts of his second inaugural address to the members of his cabinet for their comments and suggestions, as he routinely did in drafting his annual messages to Congress. Both James Madison and Albert Gallatin made substantial comments and suggestions, many of which Jefferson accepted, but the final draft was his own.[4] After making the revisions, Jefferson repeated the practice he had employed in 1801 and prepared a copy from which to read at the inauguration. This reading text filled two large sheets of papers written on both sides (fig. 5-2) and contained even more abbreviations than the reading copy he had used in 1801.

As he had done prior to his first inauguration, Jefferson wrote out in his own hand the full final text for publication (fig. 5-3) and gave it in advance to Samuel Harrison Smith, who published it in the *National Intelligencer* as a supplement to the March 4, 1805, issue. Smith also reprinted the address on the front page of the next number on March 6 (fig. 5-4) and in the *Universal Gazette*, the weekly edition of the *National Intelligencer*, on March 7.

A week before Jefferson's second inaugural, the artist Charles-Balthazar-Julien Fevret de Saint-Mémin advertised in the Washington *National Intelligencer* "a few likenesses of the President of the United States engraved by himself."[5] A talented French émigré, Saint Mémin, employing the physiognotrace, had taken Jefferson's image in November 1804 (frontispiece).

The Text of Jefferson's Address of March 4, 1805

Proceeding, fellow citizens, to that qualification which the constitution requires, before my entrance on the charge again conferred on me, it is my duty to express the deep sense I entertain of this new proof of confidence from my fellow citizens at large, and the zeal with which it inspires me so to conduct myself as may best satisfy their expectations.

On taking this station on a former occasion, I declared the principles on which I believed it my duty to administer the affairs of our commonwealth. My conscience tells me that I have on every occasion, acted up to that declaration, according to it's obvious import, and to the understanding of every candid mind.

In the transaction of your foreign affairs, we have endeavored to cultivate the friendship of all nations, and especially of those with which we have the most important relations. We have done them justice on all occasions, favor where favor was lawful, and cherished mutual interests and intercourse on fair and equal terms. We are firmly convinced, and we act on that conviction, that with nations, as with individuals, our interests,

2. Jefferson, "Notes of a draft for a second inaugural address," in Ford, ed., *Works of Thomas Jefferson,* 10:127–28.

3. Eugene R. Sheridan, *Jefferson and Religion,* 79.

4. Madison's comments, February 8 and 12, 1805, are published in James Morton Smith, ed., *The Republic of Letters: The Correspondence of Thomas Jefferson and James Madison, 1776–1826,* 3:1364–65. Gallatin's comments are in Henry Adams, ed., *The Writings of Albert Gallatin,* 1:227–28.

5. *National Intelligencer* (Washington, D.C.), Feb. 25, 27, 1805; Cunningham, *Image of Thomas Jefferson in the Public Eye,* 79–83.

soundly calculated, will ever be found inseparable from our moral duties. And history bears witness to the fact, that a just nation is trusted on it's
word, when recourse is had to armaments and
wars to bridle others.

At home, fellow-citizens, you best know
whether we have done well or ill. The suppression of unnecessary offices, of useless establishments and expences, enabled us to discontinue
our internal taxes. These, covering our land with
officers, and opening our doors to their intrusions, had already begun that process of domiciliary vexation, which, once entered, is scarcely to
be restrained from reaching successively every
article of produce and of property. If, among
these taxes, some minor ones fell, which had not
been inconvenient, it was because their amount
would not have paid the officers who collected
them, and because, if they had any merit, the
state authorities might adopt them, instead of
others less approved.

The remaining revenue on the consumption of
foreign articles, is paid chiefly by those who can
afford to add foreign luxuries to domestic comforts. Being collected on our seaboard and frontiers only, and incorporated with the transactions
of our mercantile citizens, it may be the pleasure
and the pride of an American to ask what farmer,
what mechanic, what labourer ever sees a tax-
gatherer of the U.S.? These contributions enable
us to support the current expences of the government, to fulfill contracts with foreign nations,
to extinguish the native right of soil within our
limits, to extend those limits, and to apply such a
surplus to our public debts, as places at a short
day their final redemption. And that redemption
once effected, the revenue thereby liberated may,
by a just repartition among the states, and a corresponding amendment of the constitution, be
applied, *in time of peace,* to rivers, canals, arts,
manufactures, education, and other great objects
within each state. *In time of war,* if injustice by
ourselves or others must sometimes produce

war, increased as the same revenue will be by
increased population and consumption, and
aided by other resources, reserved for that crisis,
it may meet within the year all the expences of
the year, without encroaching on the rights of
future generations, by burthening them with the
debts of the past. War will then be but a suspension of useful works, and a return to a state of
peace, a return to the progress of improvement.

I have said, fellow-citizens, that the income
reserved had enabled us to extend our limits. But
that extension may possibly pay for itself before
we are called on, and in the mean time may keep
down the accruing interest. In all events it will
replace the advances we shall have made. I know
that the acquisition of Louisiana, has been disapproved by some, from a candid apprehension
that the enlargement of our territory may endanger it's union. But who can limit the extent to
which the federative principle may operate effectively? The larger our association, the less will it
be shaken by local passions. And in any view, is
it not better that the opposite bank of the Mississippi should be settled by our own brethren and
children, than by strangers of another family?
With which shall we be most likely to live in
harmony and friendly intercourse?

In matters of Religion, I have considered that
it's free exercise is placed by the Constitution,
independant of the powers of the General government. I have therefore undertaken, on no
occasion, to prescribe the religious exercises suited to it, but have left them as the Constitution
found them, under the direction and discipline
of the state or church authorities acknoleged by
the several religious societies.

The aboriginal inhabitants of these countries I
have regarded with the commiseration their history inspires. Endowed with the faculties and the
rights of men, breathing an ardent love of liberty
and independence, and occupying a country
which left them no desire but to be undisturbed,
the stream of overflowing population from other

regions directed itself on these shores. Without power to divert, or habits to contend against it, they have been overwhelmed by the current, or driven before it. Now reduced within limits too narrow for the hunter state, humanity enjoins us to teach them agriculture and the domestic arts; to encourage them to that industry which can alone enable them to maintain their place in existence, and to prepare them in time for that state of society, which, to bodily comforts, adds the improvement of the mind and morals. We have therefore liberally furnished them with the instruments of husbandry and household use: we have placed among them instructors in the arts of first necessity; and they are covered with the aegis of the law against aggressors from among ourselves.

But the endeavours to enlighten them on the fate which awaits their present course of life, to induce them to exercise their reason, follow it's dictates, and change their pursuits with the change of circumstances, have powerful obstacles to encounter. They are combated by the habits of their bodies, prejudices of their minds, ignorance, pride, and the influence of interested and crafty individuals among them, who feel themselves something in the present order of things, and fear to become nothing in any other. These persons inculcate a sanctimonious reverence for the customs of their ancestors; that whatsoever they did must be done through all time; that reason is a false guide, and to advance under it's counsel in their physical, moral, or political condition, is a perilous innovation; that their duty is to remain as their creator made them, ignorance being safety, and knolege full of danger. In short, my friends, among them also is seen the action and counter-action of good sense and of bigotry. They, too, have their Anti-Philosophists, who find an interest in keeping things in their present state; who dread reformation, and exert all their faculties to maintain the ascendancy of habit over the duty of improving

our reason and obeying it's mandates.

In giving these outlines, I do not mean, fellow citizens, to arrogate to myself the merit of the measures. That is due, in the first place, to the reflecting character of our citizens at large, who, by the weight of public opinion, influence and strengthen the public measures. It is due to the sound discretion with which they select from among themselves those to whom they confide the legislative duties. It is due to the zeal and wisdom of the characters thus selected, who lay the foundations of public happiness in wholesome laws, the execution of which alone remains for others: and it is due to the able and faithful auxiliaries, whose patriotism has associated them with me in the executive functions.

During this course of administration, and in order to disturb it, the artillery of the Press has been levelled against us, charged with whatsoever it's licentiousness could devise or dare. These abuses of an institution so important to freedom and science, are deeply to be regretted, inasmuch as they tend to lessen it's usefulness, and to sap it's safety. They might, perhaps, have been corrected by the wholesome punishments reserved to, and provided by, the laws of the several states against falsehood and defamation. But public duties more urgent press on the time of public servants, and the offenders have therefore been left to find their own punishment in the public indignation.

Nor was it uninteresting to the world that an experiment should be fairly and fully made, whether freedom of discussion, unaided by power, is not sufficient for the propagation and protection of truth? whether a government, conducting itself in the true spirit of it's constitution, with zeal and purity, and doing no act which it would be unwilling the whole world should witness, can be written down by falsehood and defamation.—The experiment has been tried.—You have witnessed the scene.—Our fellow-citizens have looked on cool and collected. They saw the latent source from which these outrages proceeded. They gathered around their functionaries: and when the constitution called them to the decision by suffrage, they pronounced their verdict, honorable to those who had served them, and consolatory to the friend of man, who believes he may be entrusted with the controul of his own affairs.

No inference is here intended that the laws provided by the states against false and defamatory publications should not be enforced. He who has time renders a service to public morals and public tranquility, in reforming these abuses by the salutary coercions of the law. But the experiment is noted to prove that, since truth and reason have maintained the ground against false opinions in league with false facts, the Press confined to truth, needs no other legal restraint. The public judgment will correct false reasonings and opinions, on a full hearing of all parties, and no other definite line can be drawn between the inestimable liberty of the press, and its demoralizing licentiousness. If there be still improprieties which this rule would not restrain, it's Supplement must be sought in the Censorship of public opinion.

Contemplating the union of sentiment now manifested so generally, as arguing harmony and happiness to our future course, I offer to our country sincere congratulations. With those too not yet rallied to the same point, the disposition to do so is gaining strength. Facts are piercing through the veil drawn over them; and our doubting brethren will at length see that the mass of their fellow citizens, with whom they cannot yet resolve to act, as to principles and measures, think as they think, and desire what they desire. That our wish, as well as theirs, is that the public efforts may be directed honestly to the public good, that peace be cultivated, civil and religious liberty unassailed, law and order preserved, equality of rights maintained, and that state of property, equal or unequal, which

results to every man from his own industry or that of his fathers. When satisfied of these views, it is not in human nature that they should not approve and support them. In the meantime, let us cherish them with patient affection. Let us do them justice, and more than justice, in all competitions of interest: and we need not doubt that truth, reason, and their own interests will at length prevail, will gather them into the fold of their country, and will compleat that entire union of opinion which gives to a nation the blessings of harmony, and the benefit of all it's strength.

I shall now enter on the duties to which my fellow-citizens have again called me, and shall proceed in the spirit of those principles which they have approved. I fear not that any motives of interest may lead me astray: I am sensible of no passion which could seduce me knowingly from the path of justice. But the weakness of human nature, and limits of my own understanding, will produce errors of judgment sometimes injurious to your interests. I shall need therefore all the indulgence I have heretofore experienced; the want of it certainly will not lessen with increasing years. I shall need too the favour of that being in whose hands we are, who led our fathers, as Israel of old, from their native land, and planted them in a country flowing with all the necessaries and comforts of life: who has covered our infancy with his providence, and our riper years with his wisdom and power: and to whose goodness I ask you to join with me in supplications, that he will so enlighten the minds of your servants, guide their councils, and prosper their measures, that whatsoever they do, shall result in your good, and shall secure to you the peace, friendship, and approbation of all nations.[6]

---

6. Jefferson, inaugural address, March 4, 1805, manuscript (fig. 5-3) sent to Samuel Harrison Smith for publication in the *National Intelligencer,* Thomas Jefferson Papers, Library of Congress.

Fig. 5-2. First page of Thomas Jefferson's reading text of his inaugural address delivered in the Senate Chamber, March 4, 1805. Library of Congress.

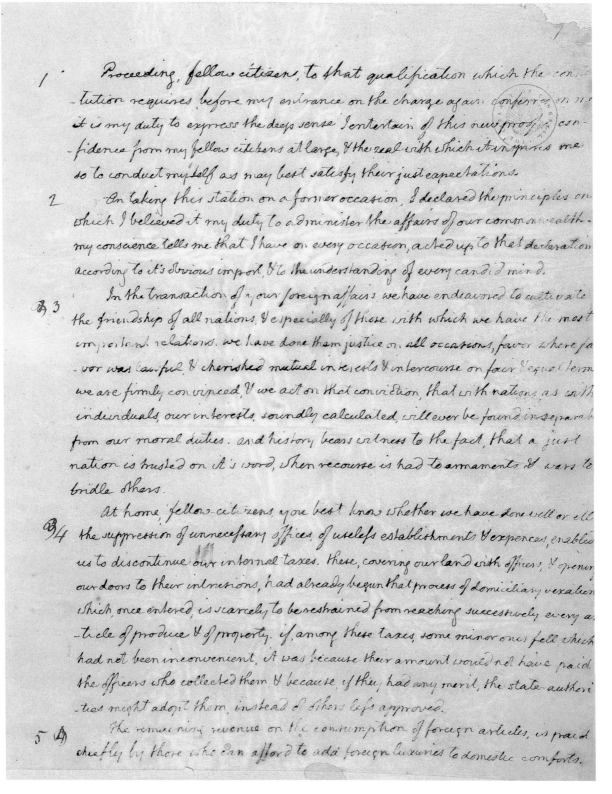

Fig. 5-3. Final text, in Thomas Jefferson's handwriting, of his inaugural address of March 4, 1805, given to Samuel Harrison Smith for publication in the Washington *National Intelligencer*. Library of Congress.

being collected on our seaboard & frontiers only. & incorporated with the transactions of our mercantile citizens, it may be the pleasure & the pride of an American to ask what farmer, what mechanic, what labourer, ever sees a tax-gatherer of the US? these contributions enable us to support the current expences of the government, to fulfill contracts with foreign nations, to extinguish the native right of soil within our limits, to extend those limits, & to apply such a surplus to our public debts, as places at a short day their final redemption. and that redemption once effected, the revenue thereby ~~liquated~~ liberated, may, by a just repartition among the states, & a corresponding amendment of the constitution, be applied, in time of peace, to rivers, canals, roads, arts, manufactures, education & other great objects within each state. in time of war, if injustice by ourselves or others must sometimes produce war, increased as the same revenue will be by increased population & consumption, & aided by other resources, reserved for that crisis, it may meet within the year all the expences of the year, without encroaching on the rights of future generations, by burthening them with the debts of the past. War will then be but a suspension of useful works, & a return to a state of peace, a return to the progress of improvement.

I have said, fellow citizens, that the income reserved had enabled us to extend our limits. but that extension may possibly pay for itself before we are called on, & in the mean time may keep down the accruing interest. in all events it will replace the advances we shall have made. I know that the acquisition of Louisiana has been disapproved by some, from a candid apprehension that the enlargement of our territory may endanger it's union. but who can limit the extent to which the federative principle may operate effectively? the larger our association, the less will it be shaken by local passions. and in any view, is it not better that the opposite bank of the Missisipi should be settled by our own brethren & children, than by strangers of another family? with which shall we be most likely to live in harmony & friendly intercourse?

In matters of Religion I have considered that it's free exercise is placed by the constitution independant of the powers of the General government. I have therefore

3

~~aristocratic~~ undertaken, on no occasion, to prescribe the religious exercises suited
to it. but have left them, as the Constitution found them, under the direction &
discipline of the state or church authorities acknoleged by the several religious societies.

8   The Aboriginal inhabitants of these countries, I have regarded with the com-
-miseration their history inspires. endowed with the faculties & the rights of men,
breathing an ardent love of liberty & independance, & occupying a country which
left them no desire but to be undisturbed, the stream of overflowing population
from other regions directed itself on these shores. without power to divert, or ha-
-bits to contend against it, they have been overwhelmed by the current, or driven
before it. now reduced within limits too narrow for the hunter state, humanity
enjoins us to teach them agriculture & the domestic arts; to encourage them to
that industry which alone can enable them to maintain their place in exist-
-ence, & to prepare them in time for that state of society, which, to bodily com-
-forts, adds the improvement of the mind & morals. we have therefore liberally
furnished them with the implements of husbandry & houshold use: we have
placed among them instructors in the arts of first necessity, & they are covered
with the Aegis of the law against ~~the extension coloured~~ aggressors from among ourselves.

9   But the endeavors to enlighten them on the fate which awaits their present
course of life, to induce them to exercise their reason follow it's dictates, & change their pur-
-suits with the change of circumstances. have powerful obstacles to encounter. they
are combated by the habits of their bodies, prejudices of their minds, ignorance, pride, &
the influence of interested & crafty individuals among them, who feel themselves some-
-thing in the present order of ~~things~~ & fear to become nothing in any other. these
persons inculcate a sanctimonious reverence for the customs of their ancestors;
that whatsoever they did must be done through all time; that reason is a false
guide, & to advance under it's counsel in their physical, moral, or political condi-
-tion, is perilous innovation: that their duty is to remain as their creator made
them, ignorance being safety, & knolege full of danger. in short, my friends, among
them also is seen the action & counter-action of good sense & of bigotry. they too
have their Anti-Philosophists, who find an interest in keeping things in their pre-

4

-sent state; who dread reformation, & exert all their faculties to maintain the ascendancy of habit over the duty of improving our reason & obeying it's mandates.

~~But the endeavors to enlighten them on the fate which awaits their present course of life,~~ In giving these outlines I do not mean, fellow citizens, to arrogate to myself the merit of the measures. that is due, in the first place, to the reflecting character of our citizens at large, who, by the weight of public opinion, influence & strengthen the public measures. it is due to the sound discretion with which they select from among themselves those to whom they confide the legislative duties. it is due to the zeal & wisdom of the characters thus selected, who lay the foundations of public happiness in wholsome laws, the execution of which alone remains for others: & it is due to the able & faithful auxiliaries, whose patriotism has associated them with me in the executive functions.

During this course of administration, & in order to disturb it, the artillery of the Press has been levelled against us, charged with whatsoever it's licentiousness could devise or dare. these abuses of an institution so important to freedom and science, are deeply to be regretted, inasmuch as they tend to lessen it's usefulness, & to sap it's safety. they might perhaps have been corrected by the wholsome punishments reserved to, & provided by, the laws of the several states against falsehood & defamation. but public duties more urgent press on the time of public servants, & the offenders have therefore been left to find their punishment in the public indignation.

[Nor was it uninteresting to the world that an experiment should be fairly and fully made, whether freedom of discussion, unaided by power, is not sufficient for the propagation & protection of truth? whether a government, conducting itself in the true spirit of it's constitution, with zeal & purity, & doing no act which it would be unwilling the whole world should witness, can be written down by falsehood and defamation. — the experiment has been tried. — you have witnessed the scene. — our fellow citizens have looked on cool & collected. they saw the latent source from which these outrages proceeded. they gathered around their public functionaries: & when the constitution called them to the decision by suffrage, they pronounced their verdict, honorable to those who had served them, & consolatory to the friend of man, who believes he may be entrusted with the controul of his own affairs.

13   no inference is here intended that the laws provided by the states against false & defamatory publications, should not be enforced. he who has time, renders a service to public morals & public tranquility, in reforming these abuses by the salutary coercions of the law. but the experiment is noted to prove that, since truth & reason have maintained their ground against false opinions in league with false facts, the press, confined to truth, needs no other legal restraint. the public judgment will correct false reasonings and opinions, on a full hearing of all parties; & no other definite line can be drawn between the inestimable liberty of the press, & it's demoralising licentiousness. if there be still improprieties which this rule would not restrain, it's supplement must be sought in the censorship of public opinion.

14   Contemplating the union of sentiment now manifested so generally, as auguring harmony & happiness to our future course, I offer to our country sincere congratulations. with those too not yet rallied to the same point, the disposition to do so is gaining strength. facts are piercing through the veil drawn over them; & our doubting brethren will at length see that the mass of their fellow citizens, with whom they cannot yet resolve to act, as to principles and measures, think as they think, & desire what they desire. that our wish, as well as theirs, is that the public efforts may be directed honestly to the public good, that peace be cultivated, civil & religious liberty unassailed, law and order preserved, equality of rights maintained, & that state of property equal or unequal, which results to every man from his own industry or that of his fathers. when satisfied of these views, it is not in human nature that they should not approve & support them. in the mean time let us cherish them with patient affection. let us do them justice, & more than justice, in all competitions of interest. & we need not doubt that truth, reason, & their own interests will at length prevail, will gather them into the fold of their country, and will compleat that entire union of opinion, which gives to a nation the blessing of harmony, and the benefit of all it's strength.

15   I shall now enter on the duties to which my fellow-citizens have again called me. & shall proceed in the spirit of those principles which they have approved. I fear not that any motives of interest may lead me astray: I am sensible of no passion which could seduce me knowingly from the path of justice: but the weaknesses of human nature, & the limits of my own understanding will produce errors of judgment sometime injurious to your interests. I shall need therefore all the indulgence I have heretofore experienced; the want of it will certainly not lessen with increasing years. I shall need too the favor of that being in whose hands we are, who led our fathers, as Israel of old, from their native land, & planted them in a country flowing with all the necessaries and comforts of life: who has covered our infancy with his providence & our riper years with his wisdom & power: and to whose goodness I ask you to join with me in supplications, that he will so enlighten the minds of your servants, guide their councils, & prosper their measures, that whatsoever they do, shall result in your good, & shall secure to you the peace, friendship, & approbation of all nations.

Th. Jefferson.

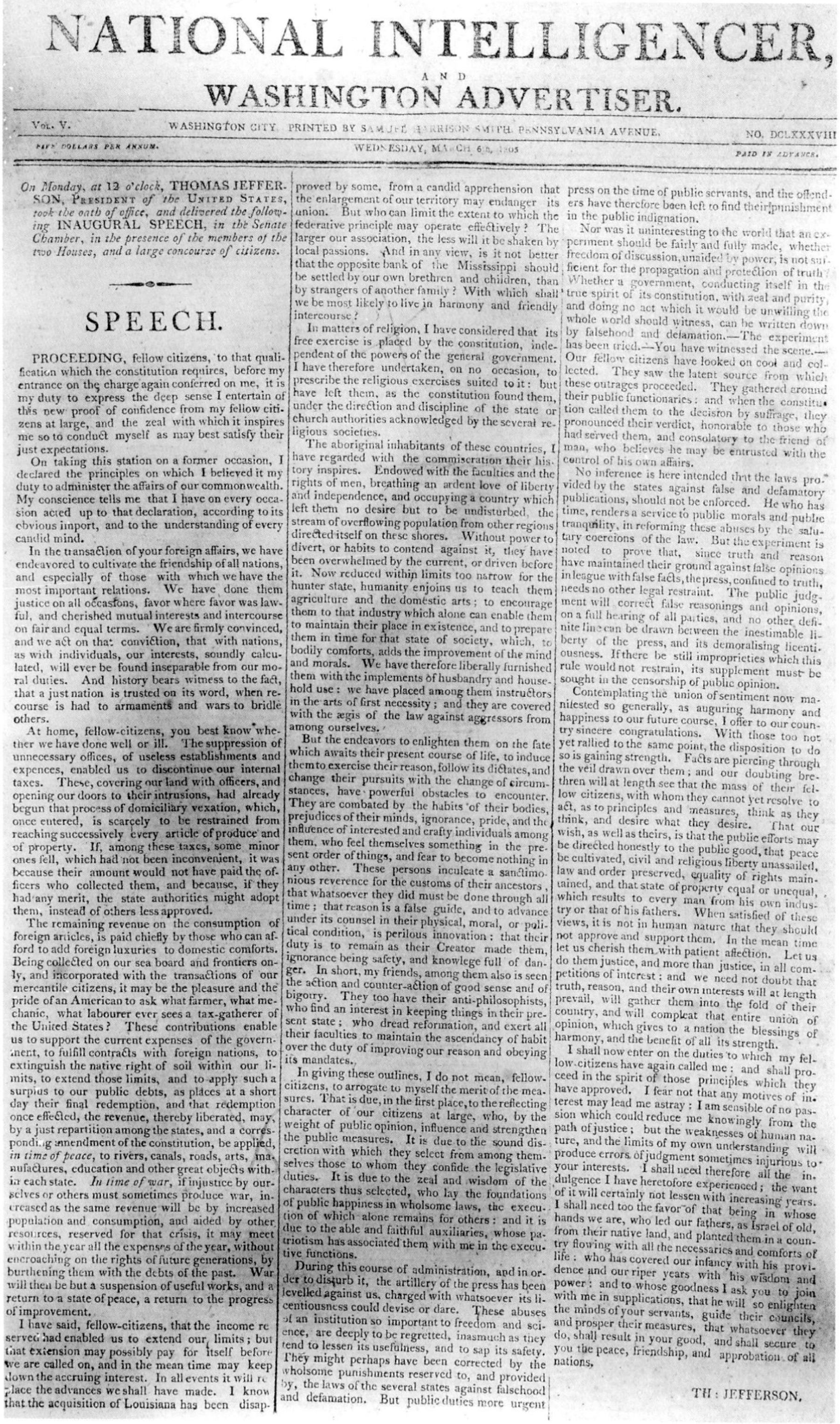

NATIONAL INTELLIGENCER,

AND

WASHINGTON ADVERTISER.

VOL. V. WASHINGTON CITY. PRINTED BY SAMUEL HARRISON SMITH, PENNSYLVANIA AVENUE. NO. DCLXXXVIII

FIVE DOLLARS PER ANNUM. WEDNESDAY, MARCH 6th, 1805 PAID IN ADVANCE.

On Monday, at 12 *o'clock,* THOMAS JEFFERSON, PRESIDENT *of the* UNITED STATES, *took the oath of office, and delivered the following* INAUGURAL SPEECH, *in the Senate Chamber, in the presence of the members of the two Houses, and a large concourse of citizens.*

SPEECH.

PROCEEDING, fellow citizens, to that qualification which the constitution requires, before my entrance on the charge again conferred on me, it is my duty to express the deep sense I entertain of this new proof of confidence from my fellow citizens at large, and the zeal with which it inspires me so to conduct myself as may best satisfy their just expectations.

On taking this station on a former occasion, I declared the principles on which I believed it my duty to administer the affairs of our commonwealth. My conscience tells me that I have on every occasion acted up to that declaration, according to its obvious import, and to the understanding of every candid mind.

In the transaction of your foreign affairs, we have endeavored to cultivate the friendship of all nations, and especially of those with which we have the most important relations. We have done them justice on all occasions, favor where favor was lawful, and cherished mutual interests and intercourse on fair and equal terms. We are firmly convinced, and we act on that conviction, that with nations, as with individuals, our interests, soundly calculated, will ever be found inseparable from our moral duties. And history bears witness to the fact, that a just nation is trusted on its word, when recourse is had to armaments and wars to bridle others.

At home, fellow-citizens, you best know whether we have done well or ill. The suppression of unnecessary offices, of useless establishments and expences, enabled us to discontinue our internal taxes. These, covering our land with officers, and opening our doors to their intrusions, had already begun that process of domiciliary vexation, which, once entered, is scarcely to be restrained from reaching successively every article of produce and of property. If, among these taxes, some minor ones fell, which had not been inconvenient, it was because their amount would not have paid the officers who collected them, and because, if they had any merit, the state authorities might adopt them, instead of others less approved.

The remaining revenue on the consumption of foreign articles, is paid chiefly by those who can afford to add foreign luxuries to domestic comforts. Being collected on our sea board and frontiers only, and incorporated with the transactions of our mercantile citizens, it may be the pleasure and the pride of an American to ask what farmer, what mechanic, what labourer ever sees a tax-gatherer of the United States? These contributions enable us to support the current expenses of the government, to fulfill contracts with foreign nations, to extinguish the native right of soil within our limits, to extend those limits, and to apply such a surplus to our public debts, as places at a short day their final redemption, and that redemption once effected, the revenue, thereby liberated, may, by a just repartition among the states, and a corresponding amendment of the constitution, be applied, *in time of peace*, to rivers, canals, roads, arts, manufactures, education and other great objects within each state. *In time of war*, if injustice by ourselves or others must sometimes produce war, increased as the same revenue will be by increased population and consumption, and aided by other resources, reserved for that crisis, it may meet within the year all the expenses of the year, without encroaching on the rights of future generations, by burthening them with the debts of the past. War will then be but a suspension of useful works, and a return to a state of peace, a return to the progress of improvement.

I have said, fellow-citizens, that the income reserved had enabled us to extend our limits; but that extension may possibly pay for itself before we are called on, and in the mean time may keep down the accruing interest. In all events it will replace the advances we shall have made. I know that the acquisition of Louisiana has been disapproved by some, from a candid apprehension that the enlargement of our territory may endanger its union. But who can limit the extent to which the federative principle may operate effectively? The larger our association, the less will it be shaken by local passions. And in any view, is it not better that the opposite bank of the Mississippi should be settled by our own brethren and children, than by strangers of another family? With which shall we be most likely to live in harmony and friendly intercourse?

In matters of religion, I have considered that its free exercise is placed by the constitution, independent of the powers of the general government. I have therefore undertaken, on no occasion, to prescribe the religious exercises suited to it: but have left them, as the constitution found them, under the direction and discipline of the state or church authorities acknowledged by the several religious societies.

The aboriginal inhabitants of these countries, I have regarded with the commiseration their history inspires. Endowed with the faculties and the rights of men, breathing an ardent love of liberty and independence, and occupying a country which left them no desire but to be undisturbed, the stream of overflowing population from other regions directed itself on these shores. Without power to divert, or habits to contend against it, they have been overwhelmed by the current, or driven before it. Now reduced within limits too narrow for the hunter state, humanity enjoins us to teach them agriculture and the domestic arts; to encourage them to that industry which alone can enable them to maintain their place in existence, and to prepare them in time for that state of society, which, to bodily comforts, adds the improvement of the mind and morals. We have therefore liberally furnished them with the implements of husbandry and household use: we have placed among them instructors in the arts of first necessity; and they are covered with the ægis of the law against aggressors from among ourselves.

But the endeavors to enlighten them on the fate which awaits their present course of life, to induce them to exercise their reason, follow its dictates, and change their pursuits with the change of circumstances, have powerful obstacles to encounter. They are combated by the habits of their bodies, prejudices of their minds, ignorance, pride, and the influence of interested and crafty individuals among them, who feel themselves something in the present order of things, and fear to become nothing in any other. These persons inculcate a sanctimonious reverence for the customs of their ancestors, that whatsoever they did must be done through all time; that reason is a false guide, and to advance under its counsel in their physical, moral, or political condition, is perilous innovation: that their duty is to remain as their Creator made them, ignorance being safety, and knowlege full of danger. In short, my friends, among them also is seen the action and counter-action of good sense and of bigotry. They too have their anti-philosophists, who find an interest in keeping things in their present state; who dread reformation, and exert all their faculties to maintain the ascendancy of habit over the duty of improving our reason and obeying its mandates.

In giving these outlines, I do not mean, fellow-citizens, to arrogate to myself the merit of the measures. That is due, in the first place, to the reflecting character of our citizens at large, who, by the weight of public opinion, influence and strengthen the public measures. It is due to the sound discretion with which they select from among themselves those to whom they confide the legislative duties. It is due to the zeal and wisdom of the characters thus selected, who lay the foundations of public happiness in wholsome laws, the execution of which alone remains for others: and it is due to the able and faithful auxiliaries, whose patriotism has associated them with me in the executive functions.

During this course of administration, and in order to disturb it, the artillery of the press has been levelled against us, charged with whatsoever its licentiousness could devise or dare. These abuses of an institution so important to freedom and science, are deeply to be regretted, inasmuch as they tend to lessen its usefulness, and to sap its safety. They might perhaps have been corrected by the wholsome punishments reserved to, and provided by, the laws of the several states against falsehood and defamation. But public duties more urgent press on the time of public servants, and the offenders have therefore been left to find their punishment in the public indignation.

Nor was it uninteresting to the world that an experiment should be fairly and fully made, whether freedom of discussion, unaided by power, is not sufficient for the propagation and protection of truth? Whether a government, conducting itself in the true spirit of its constitution, with zeal and purity, and doing no act which it would be unwilling the whole world should witness, can be written down by falsehood and defamation.—The experiment has been tried.—You have witnessed the scene.—Our fellow citizens have looked on cool and collected. They saw the latent source from which these outrages proceeded. They gathered around their public functionaries: and when the constitution called them to the decision by suffrage, they pronounced their verdict, honorable to those who had served them, and consolatory to the friend of man, who believes he may be entrusted with the control of his own affairs.

No inference is here intended that the laws provided by the states against false and defamatory publications, should not be enforced. He who has time, renders a service to public morals and public tranquility, in reforming these abuses by the salutary coercions of the law. But the experiment is noted to prove that, since truth and reason have maintained their ground against false opinions in league with false facts, the press, confined to truth, needs no other legal restraint. The public judgment will correct false reasonings and opinions, on a full hearing of all parties, and no other definite line can be drawn between the inestimable liberty of the press, and its demoralising licentiousness. If there be still improprieties which this rule would not restrain, its supplement must be sought in the censorship of public opinion.

Contemplating the union of sentiment now manifested so generally, as auguring harmony and happiness to our future course, I offer to our country sincere congratulations. With those too not yet rallied to the same point, the disposition to do so is gaining strength. Facts are piercing through the veil drawn over them; and our doubting brethren will at length see that the mass of their fellow citizens, with whom they cannot yet resolve to act, as to principles and measures, think as they think, and desire what they desire. That our wish, as well as theirs, is that the public efforts may be directed honestly to the public good, that peace be cultivated, civil and religious liberty unassailed, law and order preserved, equality of rights maintained, and that state of property equal or unequal, which results to every man from his own industry or that of his fathers. When satisfied of these views, it is not in human nature that they should not approve and support them. In the mean time let us cherish them with patient affection. Let us do them justice, and more than justice, in all competitions of interest: and we need not doubt that truth, reason, and their own interests will at length prevail, will gather them into the fold of their country, and will compleat that entire union of opinion, which gives to a nation the blessings of harmony, and the benefit of all its strength.

I shall now enter on the duties to which my fellow-citizens have again called me: and shall proceed in the spirit of those principles which they have approved. I fear not that any motives of interest may lead me astray: I am sensible of no passion which could reduce me knowingly from the path of justice; but the weaknesses of human nature, and the limits of my own understanding will produce errors of judgment sometimes injurious to your interests. I shall need therefore all the indulgence I have heretofore experienced; the want of it will certainly not lessen with increasing years. I shall need too the favor of that being in whose hands we are, who led our fathers, as Israel of old, from their native land, and planted them in a country flowing with all the necessaries and comforts of life: who has covered our infancy with his providence and our riper years with his wisdom and power: and to whose goodness I ask you to join with me in supplications, that he will so enlighten the minds of your servants, guide their councils, and prosper their measures, that whatsoever they do, shall result in your good, and shall secure to you the peace, friendship, and approbation of all nations.

TH: JEFFERSON.

Fig. 5-4. Washington *National Intelligencer,* March 6, 1805. Reprinting of Thomas Jefferson's second inaugural address, earlier published as a supplement to the March 4 issue. American Antiquarian Society.

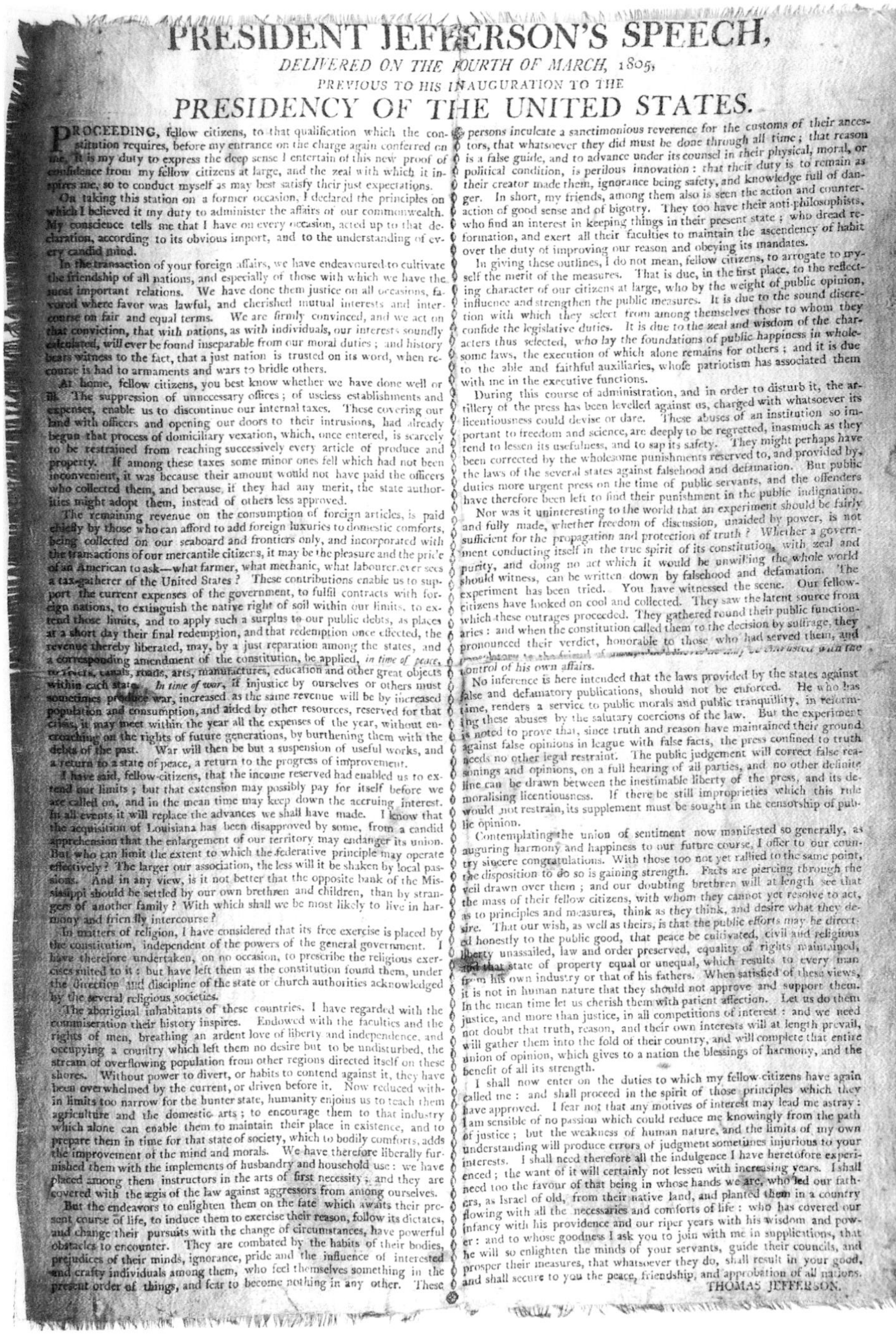

PRESIDENT JEFFERSON'S SPEECH,

DELIVERED ON THE FOURTH OF MARCH, 1805,

PREVIOUS TO HIS INAUGURATION TO THE

PRESIDENCY OF THE UNITED STATES.

PROCEEDING, fellow citizens, to that qualification which the constitution requires, before my entrance on the charge again conferred on me, it is my duty to express the deep sense I entertain of this new proof of confidence from my fellow citizens at large, and the zeal with which it inspires me, so to conduct myself as may best satisfy their just expectations.

On taking this station on a former occasion, I declared the principles on which I believed it my duty to administer the affairs of our commonwealth. My conscience tells me that I have on every occasion, acted up to that declaration, according to its obvious import, and to the understanding of every candid mind.

In the transaction of your foreign affairs, we have endeavoured to cultivate the friendship of all nations, and especially of those with which we have the most important relations. We have done them justice on all occasions, favored where favor was lawful, and cherished mutual interests and intercourse on fair and equal terms. We are firmly convinced, and we act on that conviction, that with nations, as with individuals, our interests soundly calculated, will ever be found inseparable from our moral duties; and history bears witness to the fact, that a just nation is trusted on its word, when recourse is had to armaments and wars to bridle others.

At home, fellow citizens, you best know whether we have done well or ill. The suppression of unnecessary offices; of useless establishments and expenses, enable us to discontinue our internal taxes. These covering our land with officers and opening our doors to their intrusions, had already begun that process of domiciliary vexation, which, once entered, is scarcely to be restrained from reaching successively every article of produce and property. If among these taxes some minor ones fell which had not been inconvenient, it was because their amount would not have paid the officers who collected them, and because, if they had any merit, the state authorities might adopt them, instead of others less approved.

The remaining revenue on the consumption of foreign articles, is paid chiefly by those who can afford to add foreign luxuries to domestic comforts, being collected on our seaboard and frontiers only, and incorporated with the transactions of our mercantile citizens, it may be the pleasure and the pride of an American to ask—what farmer, what mechanic, what labourer ever sees a tax-gatherer of the United States? These contributions enable us to support the current expenses of the government, to fulfil contracts with foreign nations, to extinguish the native right of soil within our limits, to extend those limits, and to apply such a surplus to our public debts, as places at a short day their final redemption, and that redemption once effected, the revenue thereby liberated, may, by a just reparation among the states, and a corresponding amendment of the constitution, be applied, *in time of peace*, to rivers, canals, roads, arts, manufactures, education and other great objects within each state. *In time of war*, if injustice by ourselves or others must sometimes produce war, increased as the same revenue will be by increased population and consumption, and aided by other resources, reserved for that crisis, it may meet within the year all the expenses of the year, without encroaching on the rights of future generations, by burthening them with the debts of the past. War will then be but a suspension of useful works, and a return to a state of peace, a return to the progress of improvement.

I have said, fellow-citizens, that the income reserved had enabled us to extend our limits; but that extension may possibly pay for itself before we are called on, and in the mean time may keep down the accruing interest. In all events it will replace the advances we shall have made. I know that the acquisition of Louisiana has been disapproved by some, from a candid apprehension that the enlargement of our territory may endanger its union. But who can limit the extent to which the federative principle may operate effectively? The larger our association, the less will it be shaken by local passions. And in any view, is it not better that the opposite bank of the Missisippi should be settled by our own brethren and children, than by strangers of another family? With which shall we be most likely to live in harmony and friendly intercourse?

In matters of religion, I have considered that its free exercise is placed by the constitution, independent of the powers of the general government. I have therefore undertaken, on no occasion, to prescribe the religious exercises suited to it: but have left them as the constitution found them, under the direction and discipline of the state or church authorities acknowledged by the several religious societies.

The aboriginal inhabitants of these countries, I have regarded with the commiseration their history inspires. Endowed with the faculties and the rights of men, breathing an ardent love of liberty and independence, and occupying a country which left them no desire but to be undisturbed, the stream of overflowing population from other regions directed itself on these shores. Without power to divert, or habits to contend against it, they have been overwhelmed by the current, or driven before it. Now reduced within limits too narrow for the hunter state, humanity enjoins us to teach them agriculture and the domestic arts; to encourage them to that industry which alone can enable them to maintain their place in existence, and to prepare them in time for that state of society, which to bodily comforts, adds the improvement of the mind and morals. We have therefore liberally furnished them with the implements of husbandry and household use: we have placed among them instructors in the arts of first necessity; and they are covered with the ægis of the law against aggressors from among ourselves.

But the endeavors to enlighten them on the fate which awaits their present course of life, to induce them to exercise their reason, follow its dictates, and change their pursuits with the change of circumstances, have powerful obstacles to encounter. They are combated by the habits of their bodies, prejudices of their minds, ignorance, pride and the influence of interested and crafty individuals among them, who feel themselves something in the present order of things, and fear to become nothing in any other. These persons inculcate a sanctimonious reverence for the customs of their ancestors, that whatsoever they did must be done through all time; that reason is a false guide, and to advance under its counsel in their physical, moral, or political condition, is perilous innovation: that their duty is to remain as their creator made them, ignorance being safety, and knowledge full of danger. In short, my friends, among them also is seen the action and counteraction of good sense and of bigotry. They too have their anti-philosophists, who find an interest in keeping things in their present state; who dread reformation, and exert all their faculties to maintain the ascendency of habit over the duty of improving our reason and obeying its mandates.

In giving these outlines, I do not mean, fellow citizens, to arrogate to myself the merit of the measures. That is due, in the first place, to the reflecting character of our citizens at large, who by the weight of public opinion, influence and strengthen the public measures. It is due to the sound discretion with which they select from among themselves those to whom they confide the legislative duties. It is due to the zeal and wisdom of the characters thus selected, who lay the foundations of public happiness in wholesome laws, the execution of which alone remains for others; and it is due to the able and faithful auxiliaries, whose patriotism has associated them with me in the executive functions.

During this course of administration, and in order to disturb it, the artillery of the press has been levelled against us, charged with whatsoever its licentiousness could devise or dare. These abuses of an institution so important to freedom and science, are deeply to be regretted, inasmuch as they tend to lessen its usefulness, and to sap its safety. They might perhaps have been corrected by the wholesome punishments reserved to, and provided by, the laws of the several states against falsehood and defamation. But public duties more urgent press on the time of public servants, and the offenders have therefore been left to find their punishment in the public indignation.

Nor was it uninteresting to the world that an experiment should be fairly and fully made, whether freedom of discussion, unaided by power, is not sufficient for the propagation and protection of truth? Whether a government conducting itself in the true spirit of its constitution, with zeal and purity, and doing no act which it would be unwilling the whole world should witness, can be written down by falsehood and defamation. The experiment has been tried. You have witnessed the scene. Our fellow-citizens have looked on cool and collected. They saw the latent source from which these outrages proceeded. They gathered round their public functionaries: and when the constitution called them to the decision by suffrage, they pronounced their verdict, honorable to those who had served them, and [illegible] with the control of his own affairs.

No inference is here intended that the laws provided by the states against false and defamatory publications, should not be enforced. He who has time, renders a service to public morals and public tranquillity, in reforming these abuses by the salutary coercions of the law. But the experiment is noted to prove that, since truth and reason have maintained their ground against false opinions in league with false facts, the press confined to truth needs no other legal restraint. The public judgement will correct false reasonings and opinions, on a full hearing of all parties, and no other definite line can be drawn between the inestimable liberty of the press, and its demoralising licentiousness. If there be still improprieties which this rule would not restrain, its supplement must be sought in the censorship of public opinion.

Contemplating the union of sentiment now manifested so generally, as auguring harmony and happiness to our future course, I offer to our country sincere congratulations. With those too not yet rallied to the same point, the disposition to do so is gaining strength. Facts are piercing through the veil drawn over them; and our doubting brethren will at length see that the mass of their fellow citizens, with whom they cannot yet resolve to act, as to principles and measures, think as they think, and desire what they desire. That our wish, as well as theirs, is that the public efforts may be directed honestly to the public good, that peace be cultivated, civil and religious liberty unassailed, law and order preserved, equality of rights maintained, and that state of property equal or unequal, which results to every man from his own industry or that of his fathers. When satisfied of these views, it is not in human nature that they should not approve and support them. In the mean time let us cherish them with patient affection. Let us do them justice, and more than justice, in all competitions of interest: and we need not doubt that truth, reason, and their own interests will at length prevail, will gather them into the fold of their country, and will complete that entire union of opinion, which gives to a nation the blessings of harmony, and the benefit of all its strength.

I shall now enter on the duties to which my fellow-citizens have again called me: and shall proceed in the spirit of those principles which they have approved. I fear not that any motives of interest may lead me astray: I am sensible of no passion which could reduce me knowingly from the path of justice; but the weakness of human nature, and the limits of my own understanding will produce errors of judgment sometimes injurious to your interests. I shall need therefore all the indulgence I have heretofore experienced; the want of it will certainly not lessen with increasing years. I shall need too the favour of that being in whose hands we are, who led our fathers, as Israel of old, from their native land, and planted them in a country flowing with all the necessaries and comforts of life: who has covered our infancy with his providence and our riper years with his wisdom and power: and to whose goodness I ask you to join with me in supplications, that he will so enlighten the minds of your servants, guide their councils, and prosper their measures, that whatsoever they do, shall result in your good, and shall secure to you the peace, friendship, and approbation of all nations.

THOMAS JEFFERSON.

Fig. 6-1. *President Jefferson's Speech, Delivered on the Fourth of March, 1805, Previous to His Inauguration to the Presidency of the United States.* Printed on silk, [1805]. American Antiquarian Society.

Chapter VI

Responses at Home

Thomas Jefferson's second inaugural speech would not gain the lasting renown of his first, but the text would be widely circulated, criticized by some, and admired by many. In an editorial in the *National Intelligencer*, Samuel Harrison Smith lauded the address:

> It announces the continuance of those pure principles of republicanism, which four years ago recommended Thomas Jefferson to the suffrages of a free people, and whose practical application has since justified the confidence then bestowed. It is his rare felicity, to be able to say that power has not corrupted his heart, or disturbed the even tenor of a life devoted to the good of his country. Rich in the confidence of his fellow citizens, he has abused none of the powers which this confidence conferred. The sentiments of such a man are at all times interesting; but peculiarly so at the period, when he is entering on a new term of office. . . . They are, fortunately for the cause of human rights, and for the dignity of human nature, convictions of the superiority of republican over all other institutions—convictions that man is able to maintain his freedom and advance his happiness far better than any agent can do it for him.[1]

The text of Jefferson's speech spread as rapidly through the country as had that of his first inaugural address four years earlier. Among readers anxiously awaiting its publication was Levi Lincoln of Massachusetts, who, before resigning at the end of December 1804, had been attorney general in Jefferson's cabinet. Writing to Jefferson a few days after the inauguration, Lincoln ended his letter by revealing: "On the 4th of March, my feelings in spite of myself, carried me to Washington, and reassociated me on the joyous occasion, with the political objects of my esteem, confidence and affection; But not hearing your communication, am waiting with impatience, great impatience, to see it."[2]

To repeat the record of swift publication achieved with Jefferson's first inaugural address, the Baltimore *American* made special arrangements for the early publication of his second inaugural address. Printing the complete text of the speech in the *American* on March 5, 1805, the editors proudly announced: "The President's Speech reached the office of the American (per express) last night, between 11 and 12 o'clock; and the Editors experience a peculiar satisfac-

---

1. *National Intelligencer* (Washington), March 6, 1805.

2. Lincoln to Jefferson, March 9, 1805, Thomas Jefferson Papers, Library of Congress.

tion, in being enabled, by anticipating the mail, thus early to present it to their numerous patrons." The editors added their opinion that the president's speech "will afford a rich treat to all who can peruse it, under the happy influence of reason, truth, and candor."

Federalist Senator William Plumer, who read Jefferson's speech in the Baltimore *American* on his way home to New Hampshire, recorded his reaction in his *Memorandum* book:

> The President says, *his Conscience tells him he has on every occasion acted up to the declaration contained in his former inaugural speech.* In that address he explicitly condemned political intolerance—declared all were federalists, all were republicans—Yet in a few days after that, he removed many deserving men from office, because they were federalists. . . .
>
> He is equally imprudent, but more mean, in explicitly censuring and condemning former Administrations and lavishing encomiums on himself for effecting a discontinuance of the Internal Revenues. . . .
>
> But after all it must be confessed that this man has talents—and those of the popular kind. It seems to be a great and primary object with him never to pursue a measure if it becomes unpopular.[3]

By March 7, the text of Jefferson's second inaugural address had reached Philadelphia, where it was published in both the Republican *Aurora* and the Federalist *United States Gazette* on that date. The Federalist editor announced the publication in a curiously partisan notice:

JUST RECEIVED,
AND NOW TO BE SEEN IN THIS CITY GRATIS
INAUGURAL SPEECH,
No. 2.

as great a curiosity as any one No. of the gun boats, and well deserving of the attention of all students and practitioners in the art and mystery of gull-catching.[4]

Two days after its publication in Philadelphia, the president's speech could be read in the New York *American Citizen* on March 9. Among other printings throughout the nation, Jefferson's address appeared in the Richmond *Enquirer* on March 8, in the Newark *Centinel of Freedom* on March 12, and in the Hartford *American Mercury* and Boston *Independent Chronicle* on March 14. On the following day it was published in the Charleston, South Carolina, *City Gazette* and in *Kline's Carlisle Weekly Gazette* in Pennsylvania. The *Eastern Argus* in Portland, District of Maine, printed the text on March 22 (fig. 6-2).

In publishing the text of Jefferson's address in the Boston *Democrat* on March 16, 1805, the publisher filled the entire front page with a handsomely printed text, which he also made available for sale in a broadside (fig. 6-3). He wrote:

> This document cannot be raised in the estimation of our readers, by any comments within our power to advance. To pay our small tribute of respect for its author, we have directed our attention for its display in the Democrat, in some degree correspondent with its invaluable merit. Those who wish it preserved as an ornament, to adorn the parlor, while it will afford a rich treasure of instruction for their budding offspring; are respectfully informed that we have printed a number on elegant WHITE SATIN, to answer so desirable a purpose.

Like his speech at his first inauguration, Jefferson's second address would be translated into German and published in the Harrisburg, Pennsylvania, *Härrisburger Morgenröthe Zeitung*, appearing in the issue of March 23. Readers of the Peacham, Vermont, *Green Mountain Patriot*

---

3. Everett S. Brown, ed., *William Plumer's Memorandum of Proceedings in the United States Senate, 1803–1807*, 315–16.

4. Such a notice was not included when Jefferson's speech was printed in the *United States Gazette for the Country* on March 12.

had to wait until April 9 to read the full text published in that weekly paper.

In the Louisiana Territory—acquired during Jefferson's first term as president—the New Orleans *Louisiana Gazette* published Jefferson's second inaugural address on April 12. Reprinted from the Philadelphia *Aurora,* the text appeared in New Orleans only five days earlier than it would be published in London.[5]

In an editorial accompanying the publication of Jefferson's address in the Worcester, Massachusetts, *National Aegis* on March 20, editor Sewall Goodridge wrote:

> With pride and pleasure, we present to our readers the Inaugural Speech of Thomas Jefferson, upon his second election, as president of the United States. It breathes the honest confidence of conscious merit, yet in no instance does it betray the arrogant pride of 'vain boasting.' . . . It refutes the confined and narrow axiom, that the pursuits of science and the labors of state are incompatible. It combines the most profound moral philosophy with the most acute political differences.
>
> . . . The Speech of Mr. Jefferson is addressed to the great body of the people; in the emphatic language of a Republican, to his *'fellow-citizens at large.'* . . . The citizens of the Union are requested to review his official conduct, and to compare it with the engagements, which he made, on entering on his office. He makes no appeal to their feelings. To their sober judgment, to their unbiased reason, does he address himself. . . .
>
> We earnestly hope, that the elegant and excellent speech of Mr. Jefferson, may receive a general perusal. We recommend it to the attention of all, who would have a fair criterion, by which to decide on the *principles* of our Republican President.

On the same date that this glowing praise of Jefferson appeared in this Massachusetts paper, the Federalist *New York Evening Post,* founded in 1801 by Alexander Hamilton, criticized Jefferson for even delivering a second inaugural address. Under the heading "Inaugural Speech No. 2," the editor wrote:

> Mr. Jefferson has made this address without any precedent for it, and without any apparent reason but that of ingratiating himself with the people, and exhibiting a sort of defence against those severe but just animadversions which have been made upon his conduct during the greater part of his administration.—And we congratulate the community that the Chief Magistrate has not yet arrived at that state when merited public censure ceases to touch his sensibility.

The editor followed with a detailed critique of Jefferson's address, continued in subsequent issues of his paper.[6]

The Federalist *United States Gazette* earlier had employed the title "Inaugural Address No. 2" to call attention to Jefferson's not having followed the precedent of President Washington, who had not delivered an address at his second inauguration. Subsequent presidents winning reelection have followed Jefferson's example, rather than Washington's.

Publishing Jefferson's address in the Newark, New Jersey, *Centinel of Freedom* on March 12, the editor called attention to the celebrations of March 4 throughout the nation, writing:

> *The fourth of March,* we observe by our papers received from different parts of the union, has been celebrated by the republican citizens with the éclat and public spirit worthy so great and

5. On April 16, 1805, the *Louisiana Gazette* published "His Majesty's Speech" of January 15, 1805, to the British House of Lords, and "The Emperor's Speech," Paris, of December 17, 1804.

6. *New York Evening Post,* March 21, 22, 1805.

EASTERN ARGUS.

No. 29, of Vol. II. *PORTLAND*, FRIDAY, *March* 22, 1805. *Whole No.* 80.

Inaugural Speech!

Columbia. Washington, *March* 4.

THIS day, at twelve o'clock, THOMAS JEFFERSON, President of the United States, took the Oath of Office, and delivered the following *Inaugural Speech*, in the Senate-Chamber, in the preſence of the Members of the two Houſes of Congreſs, and a large concourſe of Citizens :—

PROCEEDING, *Fellow-Citizens*, to that qualification which the Conſtitution requires, before my entrance on the charge again conferred on me, it is my duty to expreſs the deep ſenſe I entertain of this new proof of confidence from my fellow-citizens at large, and the zeal with which it inſpires me ſo to conduct myſelf as may beſt ſatisfy their juſt expectations.

On taking this ſtation on a former occaſion, I declared the principles on which I believed it my duty to adminiſter the affairs of our Commonwealth. My conſcience tells me that I have on every occaſion acted up to that declaration according to its obvious import, and to the underſtanding of every candid mind.

In the tranſaction of your foreign affairs, we have endeavored to cultivate the friendſhip of all nations, and eſpecially of thoſe with which we have the moſt important relations. We have done them juſtice on all occaſions, favor where favor was lawful, and cheriſhed mutual intereſts and intercourſe on fair and equal terms ; we are firmly convinced, and we act on that conviction, that with nations, as with individuals, our intereſts, ſoundly calculated, will ever be found inſeparable from our moral duties. And hiſtory bears witneſs to the fact, that a juſt nation is truſted on its word, when recourſe is had to armaments & wars to bridle others.

At home, fellow-citizens, you beſt know whether we have done well or ill. The ſuppreſſion of unneceſſary offices, of uſeleſs eſtabliſhments and expences, enabled us to diſcontinue our internal taxes. Theſe, covering our land with officers, and opening our doors to their intruſions, had already begun that proceſs of domiciliary vexation, which, once entered, is ſcarcely to be reſtrained from reaching ſucceſſively every article of produce and of property. If, among theſe taxes, ſome minor ones fell, which had not been inconvenient, it was becauſe their amount would not have paid the officers who collected them, and becauſe, if they had any merit, the ſtate authorities might adopt them, inſtead of others leſs approved.

The remaining revenue on the conſumption of foreign articles, is paid chiefly by thoſe who can afford to add foreign luxuries to domeſtic comforts. Being collected on our ſea board and frontiers only, and incorporated with the tranſactions of our mercantile citizens, it may be the pleaſure and the pride of an American to aſk what farmer, what mechanic, what labourer, ever ſees a tax-gatherer of the United States ? Theſe contributions enable us to ſupport the current expences of the government, to fulfill contracts with foreign nations, to extinguiſh the native right of ſoil within our limits, to extend thoſe limits, and to apply ſuch a ſurplus to our public debts, as places at a ſhort day their final redemption, and that redemption once effected, the revenue thereby liberated, may, by a juſt repartition among the ſtates, and a correſponding amendment of the conſtitution, be applied, *in time of peace*, to rivers, canals, roads, arts, manufactures, education and other great objects within each ſtate. *In time of war*, if injuſtice by ourſelves or others muſt ſometimes produce war, increaſed, as the ſame revenue will be by increaſed population and conſumption, & aided by other reſources, reſerved for that criſis, it may meet within the year all the expenſes of the year, without encroaching on the rights of future generations, by burthening them with the debts of the paſt. War will then be but a ſuſpenſion of uſeful works, and a return to a ſtate of peace, a return to the progreſs of improvement.

I have ſaid, fellow-citizens, that the income reſerved had enabled us to extend our limits ; but that extenſion may poſſibly pay for itſelf before we are called on, and in the mean time may keep down the accruing intereſt. In all events it will replace the advances we ſhall have made. I know that the acquiſition of Louiſiana has been diſapproved by ſome, from a candid apprehenſion that the enlargement of our territory may endanger its union ; but who can limit the extent to which the federative principle may operate effectively ? The larger our aſſociation, the leſs will it be ſhaken by local paſſions, and in any view, is it not better that the oppoſite bank of the Miſſiſippi ſhould be ſettled by our own brethren and children, than by ſtrangers of another family ? With which ſhall we be moſt likely to live in harmony & friendly intercourſe ?

In matters of Religion I have conſidered that its free exerciſe is placed by the conſtitution independent of the powers of the general government. I have therefore undertaken, on no occaſion, to preſcribe the religious exerciſes ſuited to it ; but have left them, as the conſtitution found them, under the direction and diſcipline of the ſtate or church authorities acknowledged by the ſeveral religious ſocieties.

The aboriginal inhabitants of theſe countries, I have regarded with the commiſeration their hiſtory inſpires. Endowed with the faculties and the rights of men, breathing an ardent love of liberty and independence, and occupying a country which left them no deſire but to be undiſturbed, the ſtream of overflowing population from other regions directed itſelf on theſe ſhores. Without power to divert, or habits to contend againſt it, they have been overwhelmed by the current or driven before it. Now reduced within limits too narrow for the hunter ſtate, humanity enjoins us to teach them agriculture and the domeſtic arts ; to encourage them to that induſtry which alone can enable them to maintain their place in exiſtence. and to prepare them in time for that ſtate of ſociety, which, to bodily comforts, adds the improvement of the mind and morals. We have therefore liberally furniſhed them with the implements of huſbandry and houſehold uſe : we have placed among them inſtructors in the arts of firſt neceſſity ; and they are covered with the ægis of the law againſt aggreſſors from among ourſelves.

But the endeavors to enlighten them on the fate which awaits their preſent courſe of life, to induce them to exerciſe their reaſon, follow its dictates, and change their purſuits with the change of circumſtances, have powerful obſtacles to encounter. They are combated by the habits of their bodies, prejudices of their minds, ignorance, pride, and the influence of intereſted and crafty individuals among them, who feel themſelves ſomething in the preſent order of things, & fear to become nothing in any other. Theſe perſons inculcate a ſanctimonious reverence for the cuſtoms of their anceſtors ; that whatſoever they did muſt be done through all time ; that reaſon is a falſe guide, and to advance under its counſel in their phyſical, moral, or political condition, is perilous innovation : that their duty is to remain as their Creator made them, ignorance being ſafety, and knowledge full of danger. In ſhort, my friends, among them alſo is ſeen the action and counter-action of good ſenſe and of bigotry. They too have their anti-philoſophiſts, who find an intereſt in keeping things in their preſent ſtate ; who dread reformation, and exert all their faculties to maintain the aſcendancy of habit over the duty of improving our reaſon and obeying its mandates.

In giving theſe outlines, I do not mean, fellow-citizens, to arrogate to myſelf the merit of the meaſures. That is due, in the firſt place, to the reflecting character of our citizens at large, who, by the weight of public opinion, influence and ſtrengthen the public meaſures. It is due to the ſound diſcretion with which they ſelect from among themſelves thoſe to whom they confide the legiſlative duties. It is due to the zeal and wiſdom of the characters thus ſelected, who lay the foundations of public happineſs in wholeſome laws, the execution of which alone remains for others : and it is due to the able and faithful auxiliaries, whoſe patriotiſm has aſſociated them with me in the executive functions.

During this courſe of adminiſtration, & in order to diſturb it, the artillery of the preſs has been levelled againſt us, charged with whatſoever its licentiouſneſs could deviſe or dare. Theſe abuſes of an inſtitution ſo important to freedom and ſcience, are deeply to be regretted, inaſmuch as they tend to leſſen its uſefulneſs, and to ſap its ſafety. They might perhaps have been corrected by the wholſome puniſhments reſerved to, and provided by, the laws of the ſeveral ſtates againſt falſehood and defamation. But public duties more urgent preſs on the time of public ſervants, and the offenders have therefore been left to find their puniſhment in the public indignation.

Nor was it unintereſting to the world that an experiment ſhould be fairly & fully made, whether freedom of diſcuſſion, unaided by power, is not ſufficient for the propagation and protection of truth ? whether a government, conducting itſelf in the true ſpirit of its conſtitution, with zeal and purity, and doing no act which it would be unwilling the whole world ſhould witneſs, can be written down by falſehood and defamation.—The experiment has been tried.—You have witneſſed the ſcene.—Our fellow-citizens have looked on cool and collected. They ſaw the latent ſource from which theſe outrages proceeded. They gathered around their public functionaries : & when the conſtitution called them to the deciſion by ſuffrage, they pronounced their verdict, honorable to thoſe who had ſerved them, and conſolatory to the friend of man, who believes he may be entruſted with the control of his own affairs.

No inference is here intended that the laws provided by the ſtates againſt falſe & defamatory publications ſhould not be enforced. He who has time, renders a ſervice to public morals and public tranquility, in reforming theſe abuſes by the ſalutary coerſions of the law. But the experiment is noted to prove that, ſince truth and reaſon have maintained their ground againſt falſe opinions in league with falſe facts, the preſs, confined to truth, needs no other legal reſtraint. The public judgment will correct falſe reaſonings and opinions, on a full hearing of all parties, and no other definite line can be drawn between the ineſtimable liberty of the preſs, & its demoralizing licentiouſneſs. If there be ſtill improprieties which this rule would not reſtrain, its ſupplement muſt be ſought in the cenſorſhip of public opinion.

Contemplating the union of ſentiment now manifeſted ſo generally, as auguring harmony and happineſs to our future courſe I offer to our country ſincere congratulations. With thoſe too not yet rallied to the ſame point, the diſpoſition to do ſo is gaining ſtrength. Facts are piercing through the veil drawn over them ; and our doubting brethren will at length ſee that the maſs of their fellow-citizens, with whom they cannot yet reſolve to act, as to principles and meaſures, think as they think, and deſire what they deſire. That our wiſh, as well as theirs, is that the public efforts may be directed honeſtly to the public good, that peace be cultivated, civil and religious liberty unaſſailed, law and order preſerved, equality of rights maintained, and that ſtate of property equal or unequal, which reſults to every man from his own induſtry or that of his fathers. When ſatisfied of theſe views, it is not in human nature that they ſhould not approve and ſupport them. In the mean time let us cheriſh them with patient affection. Let us do them juſtice, and more than juſtice, in all competitions of intereſt : and we need not doubt that truth, reaſon, and their own intereſts will at length prevail, will gather them into the fold of their country, and will compleat that entire union of opinion, which gives to a nation the bleſſings of harmony, & the benefit of all its ſtrength.

I shall now enter on the duties to which my fellow-citizens have again called me : and ſhall proceed in the ſpirit of thoſe principles which they have approved. I fear not that any moties of intereſt may lead me aſtray : I am ſenſible of no paſſion which could reduce me knowingly from the path of juſtice ; but the weakneſſes of human nature, and the limits of my own underſtanding, will produce errors of judgment ſometimes injurious to your intereſts. I ſhall need therefore all the indulgence I have heretofore experienced ; the want of it will certainly not leſſen with increaſing years. I ſhall need too the favor of that Being in whoſe hands we are, who led our fathers, as Iſrael of old, from their native land, and planted them in a country flowing with all the neceſſaries and comforts of life : who has covered our infancy with his providence, and our riper years with his wiſdom and power : and to whoſe goodneſs I aſk you to join with me in ſupplications, that he will ſo enlighten the minds of your ſervants, guide their councils, and proſper their meaſures, that whatſoever they do, ſhall reſult in your good, & ſhall ſecure to you the peace, friendſhip, and approbation of all nations.

TH : JEFFERSON.

TRIPOLINE WAR.

Copy of a Letter from Commodore Preble, *to the Secretary of the Navy.—[Continued.]*

Auguſt 5th. We were at anchor with the ſquadron about two leagues north from the city of Tripoli, the Argus in chaſe of a ſmall veſſel to the weſtward, which ſhe ſoon came up with, and brought within hail. She proved to be a French privateer of 4 guns, which put into Tripoli a few days ſince for water, and left it this morning. I prevailed on the Capt. for a conſideration, to return to Tripoli, for the purpoſe of landing 14 very badly wounded Tripolitans which I put on board his veſſel with a letter to the prime miniſter, leaving it at the option of the Baſhaw to reciprocate this generous mode of conducting the war. The ſending theſe unfortunate men on ſhore to be taken care of by their friends, was an act of humanity on our part, which I hope will make a proper impreſſion on the minds of the barbarians—but I doubt it. All hands were buſily employed altering the rig of the three prizes from latten veſſels to ſloops, and preparing for a ſecond attack. Obſerved one of the enemy's ſchooners and the brig (two corſairs) in the harbor to be diſmaſted, was informed by the French captain, that the damage theſe veſſels received in the action of the 3d, had occationed their maſts being taken out. The 7th, the French privateer came out, and brought me a letter from the French Conſul, in which he obſerves, that our attack of the 3d inſtant had diſpoſed the Baſhaw to accept of reaſonable terms ; and invited me to ſend a boat to the rocks with a flag of truce, which was declined, as the white flag was not hoiſted at the baſhaw's caſtle. At 9, A. M. with a very light breeze from the Eaſtward, and a ſtrong current, which obliged the Conſtitution to remain at anchor, I made the ſignal for the light veſſels to weigh, and the gun and bomb boats to caſt off and ſtand in ſhore towards the Weſtern batteries, the prize boats having been completely fitted for ſervice, and the command of them given to lieutenants Crane, of the Vexen, Thorn, of the Enterprize, and Caldwell, of the Syren ;—the whole advanced with ſails and oars. The orders were for the bombs to take a poſition in a ſmall bay to the weſtward of the city, where but few of the enemy's guns could be brought to bear on them, but from whence they could annoy the town with ſhells. The gun-boats, to ſilence a battery of ſeven heavy guns, which guarded the approach to that poſition, and the brigs and ſchooners to ſupport them, in caſe the enemy's flotilla ſhould venture out. At half paſt 1, P. M. a breeze from N. N. E. I weighed with the Conſtitution, and ſtood in for the town, but the wind being on ſhore made it imprudent to engage the batteries with the ſhip, as in caſe of a maſt being ſhot away, the loſs of the veſſel would probably enſue, unleſs a change of wind ſhould favour our getting off. At half paſt 2, P. M. the bomb and gun-boats having gained their ſtations, the ſignal was made for them to attack the town and batteries. Our bombs immediately commenced throwing ſhells, and the gun-boats opened a ſharp and well directed fire on the town and batteries within point blank ſhot, which was warmly returned by the enemy. The ſeven gun battery in leſs then two hours was ſilenced, except one gun—I preſume the others were diſmounted by our ſhot, as the walls were almoſt totally deſtroyed. At a quarter paſt 3, P. M. a ſhip hove in ſight to the northward, ſtanding for the town ; made the Argus' ſignal to chaſe.—At half paſt 3 one of our prize gun-boats was blown up by a hot ſhot from the enemy, which paſſed through her magazine. She had on board 28 officers, ſeamen and marines ; 10 of whom were killed, and 6 wounded. Among the killed were James R. Caldwell, firſt lieut. of the Syren, & midſhipman John S. Dorſey, both excellent officers ; midſhipman Spence and 11 men were taken up unhurt.—Captain Decatur, whoſe diviſion this boat belonged to, and who was near her at the time ſhe blew up, reports to me that Mr. Spence was ſuperintending the loading of the gun at that moment, and notwithſtanding the boat was ſinking, he and the brave fellows ſurviving, finiſhed charging, gave three cheers as the boat went from under them, and ſwam to the neareſt boats, where they aſſiſted during the remainder of the action. The enemy's gun-boats and gallies (15 in number) were all in motion cloſe under the batteries, and appeared to meditate an attack on our boats ; the Conſtitution, Nautilus and Enterprize were to windward, ready at every hazard to cut them off, from the harbor, if they ſhould venture down ; while the Syren and Vixen were near our boats to ſupport and cover any of them that might be diſabled. The enemy thought it moſt prudent, however, to retire to their ſnug retreat behind the rocks, after firing a few ſhot. Our boats, in two diviſions, under captains Somers & Decatur, were all conducted, as were our bomb-veſſels, by lieuts. Dent and Robinſon. The town muſt have ſuffered much from this attack, and the batteries, particularly the ſeven gun-battery, muſt have loſt many men. At half paſt 5 P. M. the wind began to freſhen from the N. N. E. I made the ſignal for the gun and bomb boats to retire from action, and for the veſſels to which they were attached, to take them in tow. The Argus made ſignal that the ſtrange ſail was a friend. In this day's action No. 4 had a 24 pound ſhot through her hull ; No. 6 had her latteen yard ſhot away ; No. 8 a 24 pound ſhot through her hull, which killed two men. Some of the other boats had their rigging and ſails conſiderably cut. We threw 48 ſhells, and about 500 24 pound ſhot into the town and batteries. All the officers & men engaged in the action behaved with the utmoſt intrepidity. At half paſt 6 all the boats were in tow, and the ſquadron ſtanding to the N. W. At 8 the John Adams, Capt. Chauncey, from the U. States, joined company. At 9 the ſquadron anchored, Tripoli bearing S. E. 5 miles diſtant. Gun boat No. 3 was this day commanded by Mr. Brooks, maſter of the Argus, and No. 6 by lieut. Wadſworth, of the Conſtitution.

Killed—Gun-boat No. 9, 1 lieut. 1 midſhipman, 1 boatſwain's-mate, 1 quarter gunner, 1 ſergeant of marines, & 5 ſeamen—Ditto gun-boat No. 8. 2 ſeamen—Total 12.—Wounded—gun-boat No. 9, 6 ſeamen, two of which mortally.

[*To be continued.*]

Fig. 6-2. *Eastern Argus,* Portland, Maine, March 22, 1805. American Antiquarian Society.

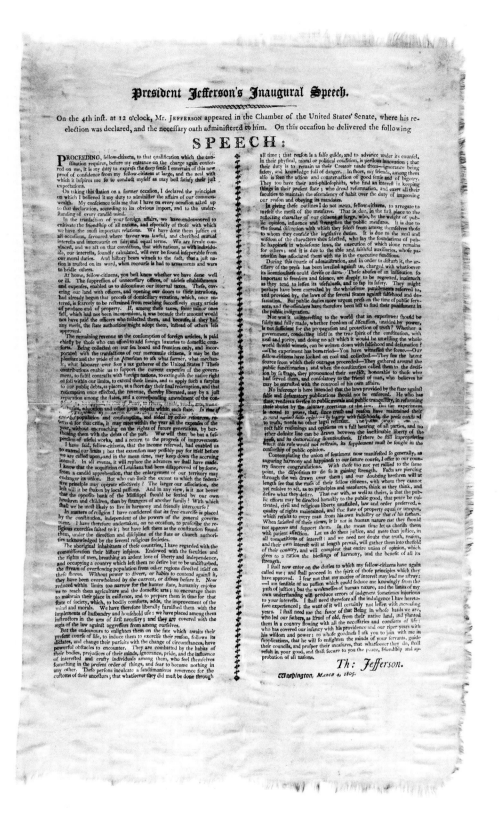

Fig. 6-3. *President Jefferson's Inaugural Speech.* Washington, March 4, 1805. Printed on silk, [1805]. Rare Book Division, Library of Congress.

momentous occasion. Nor is it the least aston-ishing that an event so propitious to them, and so salutary to the freedom of the nation, should call forth the feeling expressions of an enlight-ened and discerning people. . . . With pride and exultation, they welcome the *fourth of March, 1801* which inducted THOMAS JCEFFERSON to the office of President of the nation—and which introduced a new order of things. It was on this memorable day the fetters of aristocracy, forged by our opponents, were wrent in twain.

Although Jefferson's 1805 inaugural address appears to have been as widely published in the newspapers as his 1801 speech, his second address attracted less attention than his first. Periodicals reprinting the address included the Hudson, New York, *Monthly Register, and Review of the United States* for March 1805 and the Hudson *Balance and Columbian Repository* of March 19, 1805. The Federalist editor of the *Balance* prefaced the publication with a note say-ing: "We had almost forgotten to mention that Mr. Jefferson is again elected President, and Mr. Clinton, Vice-President; indeed we might not have thought of it now, had we not discovered in the papers, the subjoined inaugural speech said to have been delivered."[7]

Jefferson's second inaugural address was reprinted in pamphlets and broadsides, but it appears to have been reproduced less often than his first address. The text appeared in one eight-page pamphlet titled simply *President's Speech.*[8] A broadside published in Newport, Rhode Island, on March 14 also was titled *President's Speech* (fig. 6-4). Handsome editions of Jefferson's address were printed on silk, and examples can be found today in the special col-lections of several major libraries (figs. 6-1 and 6-3).[9]

Demand for mementos of Jefferson's second inaugural may have been less than for those of his first inauguration. Nonetheless, the daybook of John Doggett, a Roxbury, Massachusetts, glass and mirror importer and picture framer, contains a number of entries recording the sale of frames for prints of Jefferson's second inaugural address.[10]

7. *Balance and Columbian Repository* 4 (March 19, 1805): 90–91.

8. Rare Book Division, Library of Congress.

9. Prints at the American Antiquarian Society, the Library of Congress, and the University of Virginia.

10. Entries for June 6, 26, July 6, 13, 1805, Daybook of John Doggett, Roxbury, Mass., 1802–1809, Henry Francis du Pont Winterthur Museum, Winterthur, Del.

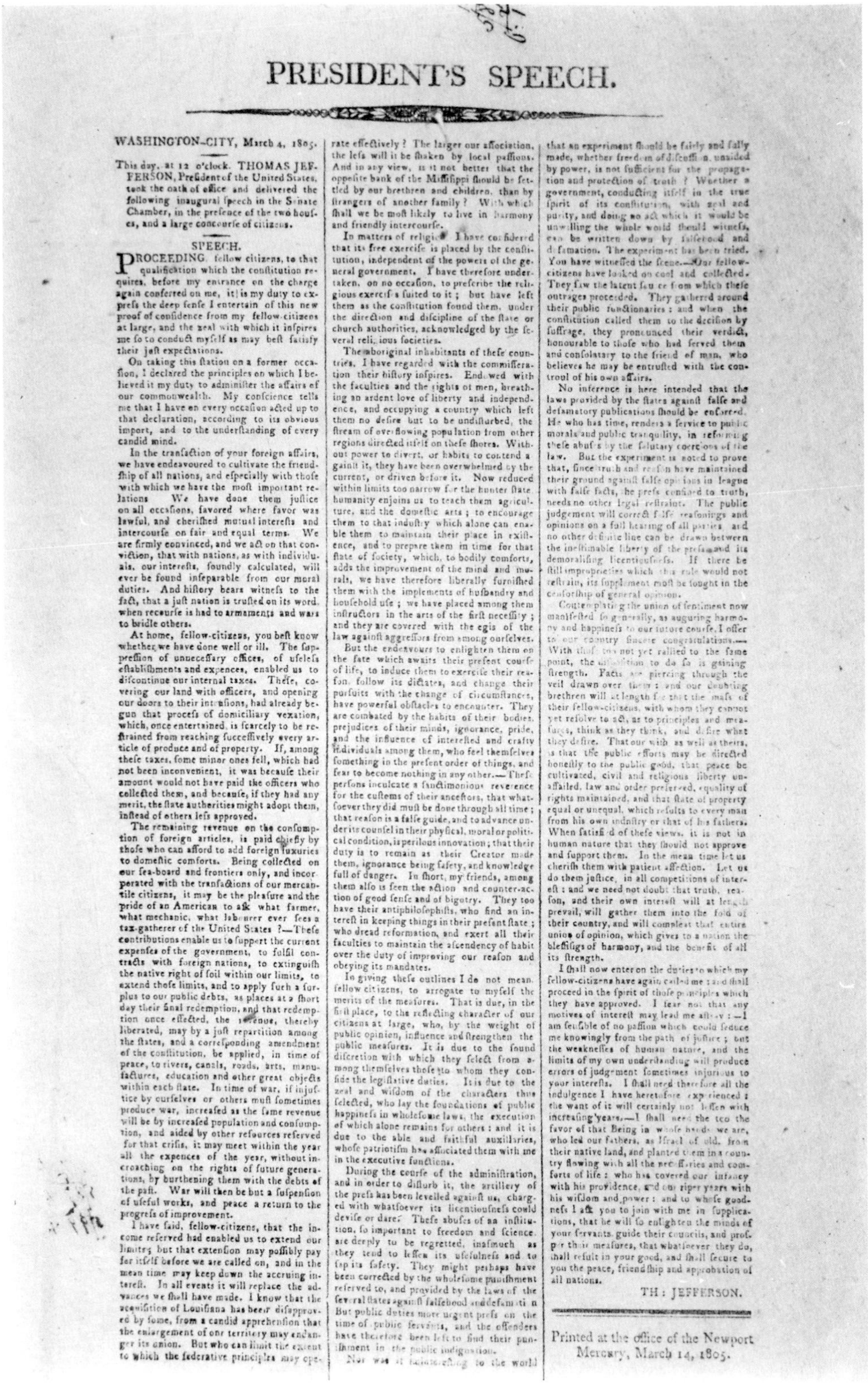

PRESIDENT'S SPEECH.

WASHINGTON-CITY, March 4, 1805.

This day, at 12 o'clock, THOMAS JEFFERSON, President of the United States, took the oath of office and delivered the following inaugural speech in the Senate Chamber, in the presence of the two houses, and a large concourse of citizens.

SPEECH.

PROCEEDING, fellow citizens, to that qualification which the constitution requires, before my entrance on the charge again conferred on me, it is my duty to express the deep sense I entertain of this new proof of confidence from my fellow-citizens at large, and the zeal with which it inspires me so to conduct myself as may best satisfy their just expectations.

On taking this station on a former occasion, I declared the principles on which I believed it my duty to administer the affairs of our commonwealth. My conscience tells me that I have on every occasion acted up to that declaration, according to its obvious import, and to the understanding of every candid mind.

In the transaction of your foreign affairs, we have endeavoured to cultivate the friendship of all nations, and especially with those with which we have the most important relations. We have done them justice on all occasions, favored where favor was lawful, and cherished mutual interests and intercourse on fair and equal terms. We are firmly convinced, and we act on that conviction, that with nations, as with individuals, our interests, soundly calculated, will ever be found inseparable from our moral duties. And history bears witness to the fact, that a just nation is trusted on its word, when recourse is had to armaments and wars to bridle others.

At home, fellow-citizens, you best know whether we have done well or ill. The suppression of unnecessary offices, of useless establishments and expences, enabled us to discontinue our internal taxes. These, covering our land with officers, and opening our doors to their intrusions, had already begun that process of domiciliary vexation, which, once entertained, is scarcely to be restrained from reaching successively every article of produce and of property. If, among these taxes, some minor ones fell, which had not been inconvenient, it was because their amount would not have paid the officers who collected them, and because, if they had any merit, the state authorities might adopt them, instead of others less approved.

The remaining revenue on the consumption of foreign articles, is paid chiefly by those who can afford to add foreign luxuries to domestic comforts. Being collected on our sea-board and frontiers only, and incorporated with the transactions of our mercantile citizens, it may be the pleasure and the pride of an American to ask what farmer, what mechanic, what labourer ever sees a tax-gatherer of the United States?—These contributions enable us to support the current expenses of the government, to fulfil contracts with foreign nations, to extinguish the native right of soil within our limits, to extend those limits, and to apply such a surplus to our public debts, as places at a short day their final redemption, and that redemption once effected, the revenue, thereby liberated, may by a just repartition among the states, and a corresponding amendment of the constitution, be applied, in time of peace, to rivers, canals, roads, arts, manufactures, education and other great objects within each state. In time of war, if injustice by ourselves or others must sometimes produce war, increased as the same revenue will be by increased population and consumption, and aided by other resources reserved for that crisis, it may meet within the year all the expences of the year, without incroaching on the rights of future generations, by burthening them with the debts of the past. War will then be but a suspension of useful works, and peace a return to the progress of improvement.

I have said, fellow-citizens, that the income reserved had enabled us to extend our limits; but that extension may possibly pay for itself before we are called on, and in the mean time may keep down the accruing interest. In all events it will replace the advances we shall have made. I know that the acquisition of Louisiana has been disapproved by some, from a candid apprehension that the enlargement of our territory may endanger its union. But who can limit the extent to which the federative principles may operate effectively? The larger our association, the less will it be shaken by local passions. And in any view, is it not better that the opposite bank of the Mississippi should be settled by our brethren and children, than by strangers of another family? With which shall we be most likely to live in harmony and friendly intercourse.

In matters of religion I have considered that its free exercise is placed by the constitution, independent of the powers of the general government. I have therefore undertaken, on no occasion, to prescribe the religious exercises suited to it; but have left them as the constitution found them, under the direction and discipline of the state or church authorities, acknowledged by the several religious societies.

The aboriginal inhabitants of these countries, I have regarded with the commisseration their history inspires. Endowed with the faculties and the rights of men, breathing an ardent love of liberty and independence, and occupying a country which left them no desire but to be undisturbed, the stream of overflowing population from other regions directed itself on these shores. Without power to divert, or habits to contend against it, they have been overwhelmed by the current, or driven before it. Now reduced within limits too narrow for the hunter state, humanity enjoins us to teach them agriculture, and the domestic arts; to encourage them to that industry which alone can enable them to maintain their place in existence, and to prepare them in time for that state of society, which, to bodily comforts, adds the improvement of the mind and morals, we have therefore liberally furnished them with the implements of husbandry and household use; we have placed among them instructors in the arts of the first necessity; and they are covered with the egis of the law against aggressors from among ourselves.

But the endeavours to enlighten them on the fate which awaits their present course of life, to induce them to exercise their reason, follow its dictates, and change their pursuits with the change of circumstances, have powerful obstacles to encounter. They are combated by the habits of their bodies, prejudices of their minds, ignorance, pride, and the influence of interested and crafty individuals among them, who feel themselves something in the present order of things, and fear to become nothing in any other.—These persons inculcate a sanctimonious reverence for the customs of their ancestors, that whatsoever they did must be done through all time; that reason is a false guide, and to advance under its counsel in their physical, moral or political condition, is perilous innovation; that their duty is to remain as their Creator made them, ignorance being safety, and knowledge full of danger. In short, my friends, among them also is seen the action and counter-action of good sense and of bigotry. They too have their antiphilosophists, who find an interest in keeping things in their present state; who dread reformation, and exert all their faculties to maintain the ascendency of habit over the duty of improving our reason and obeying its mandates.

In giving these outlines I do not mean, fellow citizens, to arrogate to myself the merits of the measures. That is due, in the first place, to the reflecting character of our citizens at large, who, by the weight of public opinion, influence and strengthen the public measures. It is due to the sound discretion with which they select from among themselves those to whom they confide the legislative duties. It is due to the zeal and wisdom of the characters thus selected, who lay the foundations of public happiness in wholesome laws, the execution of which alone remains for others: and it is due to the able and faithful auxiliaries, whose patriotism has associated them with me in the executive functions.

During the course of the administration, and in order to disturb it, the artillery of the press has been levelled against us, charged with whatsoever its licentiousness could devise or dare. These abuses of an institution, so important to freedom and science, are deeply to be regretted, inasmuch as they tend to lessen its usefulness and to sap its safety. They might perhaps have been corrected by the wholesome punishment reserved to, and provided by the laws of the several states against falsehood and defamation. But public duties more urgent press on the time of public servants, and the offenders have therefore been left to find their punishment in the public indignation.

Nor was it uninteresting to the world that an experiment should be fairly and fully made, whether freedom of discussion, unaided by power, is not sufficient for the propagation and protection of truth? Whether a government, conducting itself in the true spirit of its constitution, with zeal and purity, and doing no act which it would be unwilling the whole world should witness, can be written down by falsehood and defamation. The experiment has been tried. You have witnessed the scene.—Our fellow-citizens have looked on cool and collected. They saw the latent source from which these outrages proceeded. They gathered around their public functionaries: and when the constitution called them to the decision by suffrage, they pronounced their verdict, honourable to those who had served them and consolatory to the friend of man, who believes he may be entrusted with the controul of his own affairs.

No inference is here intended that the laws provided by the states against false and defamatory publications should be enforced. He who has time, renders a service to public morals and public tranquility, in reforming these abuses by the salutary coercions of the law. But the experiment is noted to prove that, since truth and reason have maintained their ground against false opinions in league with false facts, the press confined to truth, needs no other legal restraint. The public judgement will correct false reasonings and opinions on a full hearing of all parties, and no other definite line can be drawn between the inestimable liberty of the press and its demoralising licentiousness. If there be still improprieties which this rule would not restrain, its supplement must be sought in the censorship of general opinion.

Contemplating the union of sentiment now manifested so generally, as auguring harmony and happiness to our future course, I offer to our country sincere congratulations.—With those too not yet rallied to the same point, the disposition to do so is gaining strength. Facts are piercing through the veil drawn over them: and our doubting brethren will at length see that the mass of their fellow-citizens, with whom they cannot yet resolve to act, as to principles and measures, think as they think, and desire what they desire. That our wish as well as theirs, is that the public efforts may be directed honestly to the public good, that peace be cultivated, civil and religious liberty unassailed, law and order preserved, equality of rights maintained, and that state of property equal or unequal, which results to every man from his own industry or that of his fathers. When satisfied of these views, it is not in human nature that they should not approve and support them. In the mean time let us cherish them with patient affection. Let us do them justice, in all competitions of interest: and we need not doubt that truth, reason, and their own interest will at length prevail, will gather them into the fold of their country, and will compleat that entire union of opinion, which gives to a nation the blessings of harmony, and the benefit of all its strength.

I shall now enter on the duties to which my fellow-citizens have again called me: and shall proceed in the spirit of those principles which they have approved. I fear not that any motives of interest may lead me astray:—I am sensible of no passion which could seduce me knowingly from the path of justice; but the weaknesses of human nature, and the limits of my own understanding will produce errors of judgement sometimes injurious to your interests. I shall need therefore all the indulgence I have heretofore experienced: the want of it will certainly not lessen with increasing years.—I shall need too the favor of that Being in whose hands we are, who led our fathers, as Israel of old, from their native land, and planted them in a country flowing with all the necessaries and comforts of life: who has covered our infancy with his providence, and our riper years with his wisdom and power: and to whose goodness I ask you to join with me in supplications, that he will so enlighten the minds of your servants, guide their councils, and prosper their measures, that whatsoever they do, shall result in your good, and shall secure to you the peace, friendship and approbation of all nations.

TH: JEFFERSON.

Printed at the office of the Newport Mercury, March 14, 1805.

Fig. 6-4. *President's Speech.* Broadside, printed at the office of the *Newport Mercury,* March 14, 1805. Newport Historical Society, Newport, Rhode Island.

GAZETTE NATIONALE ou LE MONITEUR UNIVERSEL.

A dater du 7 nivôse an 8, les Actes du Gouvernement et des Autorités constituées, contenus dans le Moniteur, sont officiels.

N° 213. Mardi, 3 floréal an 13 de la République (23 avril 1805.)

EXTÉRIEUR.

ETATS-UNIS D'AMERIQUE.

Washington, 5 mars (14 ventose.)

M. Burr a pris congé du sénat, dans la séance du 2 mars, et a quitté la ville le même jour.

Dans la séance du 4 mars, Thomas Jefferson a été installé dans ses fonctions de président du congrès pour quatre ans, à commencer de ce jour, ainsi que Georges Clinton, nouveau vice-président.

Après qu'ils eurent prêté le serment constitutionnel, M. Jefferson a remis aux deux chambres une adresse, dans laquelle il témoigne à ses concitoyens la reconnaissance que ce nouveau gage d'estime lui inspire, et la ferme résolution où il est de s'en rendre digne. Il déclare qu'il continuera à se conduire d'après les principes qu'il a montrés dans sa premiere administration.

« Dans la conduite des affaires étrangeres, dit-il, nous nous sommes efforcés de cultiver l'amitié de toutes les nations, spécialement de celles avec qui nous avons les plus importantes relations; nous leur avons rendu justice en toute occasion; nous les avons favorisées là où la faveur était permise, et entretenu nos intérêts, notre commerce réciproques dans les termes les plus équitables. Nous sommes fermement convaincus, et nous agissons d'après cette conviction, qu'entre nations comme entre individus, nos intérêts, bien entendus ne sont jamais séparés de nos devoirs et de notre morale; et l'histoire nous prouve qu'on en croit une nation juste sur sa parole, tandis qu'on n'emploie que la voie des armes pour discuter avec les autres. »

Quant à la gestion des affaires intérieures, le président expose que les impôts publics ont été aussi modérés qu'on a pu le faire; que la plus grande partie porte sur des objets de luxe et d'importation; qu'ils ont été employés à payer les dépenses courantes du gouvernement, à remplir les engagemens contractés avec les nations étrangeres, à étendre le territoire des Etats, à payer la dette publique, de maniere que l'extinction totale en soit prompte, et qu'alors on puisse employer les revenus de l'Etat, en tems de paix, à des travaux publics, tels que des canaux et des routes, ou à l'encouragement des manufactures, au perfectionnement de l'éducation, etc.; en tems de guerre, à obtenir l'indépendance et la dignité des Etats.

Le président témoigne qu'il n'ignore pas que l'acquisition de la Louisiane a été désapprouvée par quelques personnes, dans la crainte que l'agrandissement du territoire des Etats ne compromît leur union; mais il pense qu'on ne peut limiter l'étendue d'un Etat gouverné dans le système fédératif, et que, dans tous les cas, il vaut mieux avoir des freres sur les rives du Mississipi que des étrangers d'une autre famille.

En matiere de religion, le libre exercice des cultes est garanti par la constitution, indépendant du pouvoir du gouvernement. Le président les laissera, comme il les a trouvés, sous la direction particuliere et la discipline des autorités ecclésiastiques reconnues par les différentes sociétés religieuses.

M. Jefferson examinant ensuite la condition actuelle des habitans originaires du territoire des Etats, les considere avec la commisération que leur sort inspire; il les voit ardens pour leur indépendance, réduits à reculer toujours devant une population civilisée qui s'accroît sans cesse, resserrés dans des pays où la chasse suffit à peine à leur existence. L'humanité nous fait un devoir, dit-il, de leur enseigner l'agriculture et les arts domestiques. Nous leur avons envoyé des instrumens aratoires, et nous les avons placés sous l'égide de nos lois contre ceux d'entre nous qui voudraient les opprimer; mais les efforts que nous avons tentés pour les éclairer ont été combattus jusqu'ici par les habitudes, l'ignorance, les préjugés et l'orgueil de ceux qui sont intéressés à les tenir dans cet état sauvage, de peur de perdre leur crédit s'ils en sortaient. Ces gens leur donnent un respect religieux pour les coutumes de leurs ancêtres, leur persuadent que la raison est un guide trompeur, une innovation dangereuse; que leur devoir est de rester tels que le créateur les a formés, l'ignorance étant une voie de salut et la science une source de dangers. Enfin, ces peuples ont aussi leurs anti-philosophes qui sont intéressés à les tenir dans cet état sauvage, qui craignent une réforme, et qui usent de tous leurs moyens pour déconcerter les efforts que nous faisons pour les civiliser.

Passant ensuite à des objets intérieurs, le président rappele avec quelle indécence on a abusé dans ces derniers tems, contre lui-même, de la liberté de la presse: il expose que, par ces abus, elle perd toute utilité; que les auteurs auraient pu être punis suivant la rigueur des lois contre la calomnie et la diffamation; mais que les affaires publiques occupant plus l'attention des magistrats, les auteurs de ces libelles n'ont encore été punis que par l'indignation générale. Maintenant le président demande s'il ne serait pas utile d'examiner, d'après l'épreuve qu'on en a faite, si un gouvernement qui se conduit dans l'esprit de sa constitution avec zele et pureté, qui ne fait rien dont il ne puisse prendre l'Univers entier pour témoin, peut être attaqué si violemment par des déclamations calomnieuses? D'ailleurs, il estime que, d'après l'effet de ces calomnies, d'après l'issue de tant d'intrigues, l'opinion publique a tiré elle-même une ligne entre la licence immorale de la presse et son inestimable liberté: c'est à elle de suppléer à l'impuissance de la loi.

Le président termine son adresse par conjurer ses concitoyens de se réunir avec lui d'intentions et de moyens pour faire le bonheur de la patrie et et conserver l'amitié, l'estime et l'approbation de toutes les nations.

REPUBLIQUE HELVETIQUE.

Bâle, le 16 avril (26 germinal.)

On assure que M. de Crumpipen a été chargé par la cour, d'inviter S. Exc. le landamman à envoyer, dans le cours de l'été prochain, un député à Vienne, chargé de pleins pouvoirs pour conclure un traité définitif sur les points de contestations qui subsistent entre la Suisse et l'Autriche.

Berne, le 11 avril (21 germinal.)

On écrit de Schaffhouse, que le cercueil renfermant les restes de feu M. l'avoyer Steigner, y arriva le 8 du courant, escorté par plusieurs parens du défunt: il fut déposé à l'auberge de la Couronne, devant laquelle les autorités firent placer une garde d'honneur.

Du 12. L'inhumation des restes de feu M. l'avoyer Steigner aura lieu, à ce qu'on assure, mercredi 17 du courant.

REPUBLIQUE BATAVE.

La Haye, le 16 avril (26 germinal.)

Les régistres des votes ont été fermés aujourd'hui ici, et dans toute l'étendue de la république; la majorité a voté pour l'acceptation de la nouvelle constitution.

Le corps-législatif a tenu aujourd'hui la premiere séance de la session de printems, dans laquelle elle a nommé les douze orateurs de la session.

ANGLETERRE.

Londres, le 8 avril (18 germinal.)

Lord Melleville vient d'adresser la lettre suivante aux commissaires de la comptabilité maritime:

Messieurs, en lisant votre dixieme rapport, j'y ai remarqué le paragraphe dont la teneur suit:

« Si la crainte de divulguer des transactions délicates et secretes du gouvernement, semble exiger, de la part de lord Melville, quelques restrictions sur les informations qu'on lui demande relativement aux avances faites aux autres départemens, nous ne voyons pas que cette appréhension puisse l'autoriser à refuser de répondre, lorsqu'on l'interpelle de dire s'il a tiré aucun profit ou avantage de l'usage ou de l'emploi des fonds destinés au service de la marine? Si sa seigneurie a reçu des sommes égales à celles qu'elle a avancées aux autres départemens, et si elle les a employées à mesure qu'elles lui sont rentrées, il est clair qu'il n'a pu résulter pour elle aucun profit ou avantage de semblables transactions; c'est un fait qui paraît constant quelque contraire qu'il puisse être, aux yeux du parlement, à la sauve-garde des fonds publics. »

Je crois devoir établir les observations suivantes, afin de placer sous leur véritable point de vue les motifs qui m'ont déterminé à ne point répondre à votre question, et que vous paraissez n'avoir pas pesés attentivement.

« Lorsque vous vous êtes adressés à moi pour obtenir les informations dont il s'agit, je vous ai démontré que je n'avais aucunes pieces matérielles sur lesquelles je pusse appuyer le compte que vous me demandiez; et dans une conférence avec M. Trotter (caissier de la marine) avant mon examen du 15 novembre dernier, j'ai appris que dans les comptes qu'il a tenus relativement à mes intérêts particuliers, il a tellement mêlé l'emploi de ses propres fonds avec celui des fonds publics qu'il avait en mains, qu'il m'était impossible de déterminer, d'une maniere précise, si les avances qu'il a eu occasion de faire pour moi, dans le cours de son compte particulier avec moi, ont été prises sur les sommes qui constituent sa balance avec MM. Coutts. Cette circonstance, dont je sais que M. Trotter vous a fait part, me met dans l'impossibilité de donner aucune autre réponse que celle que j'ai déjà faite à la question générale: *Si M. Trotter a employé aucuns des fonds destinés au service courant de la marine, pour mon intérêt particulier?* C'est cette circonstance qui a déterminé ma réponse à l'autre question relative à la maniere dont M. Trotter a employé les fonds qu'il avait en maniement.

Lorsque vous me fites la question: « Si j'avais ordonné à M. Trotter, ou si je l'avais autorisé à employer à mon profit les fonds destinés au service courant de la marine? » Ma réponse fut que je ne me rappellais pas l'avoir jamais fait. Cette réponse, je la fais encore. Quand vous m'eussiez demandé si je m'étais entendu avec M. Trotter pour tirer avantage en commun de la garde des fonds publics, ou si, en aucun tems, j'en avais tiré moi-même, je vous aurais déclaré, sans hésiter, comme je le déclare en ce moment, que jamais il n'exista aucun arrangement, aucun accord de cette espece entre M. Trotter et moi; que je n'ai jamais su me prévaloir de tels avantages, et quels que soient les émolumens que puisse avoir M. Trotter, en raison de ses fonctions, ils lui sont propres, et je les ignore.

Quant aux avances que M. Trotter a pu faire pour mon compte particulier, je me considere comme son propre débiteur, et il n'y a, dans cette circonstance, d'autre relation entre lui et moi que celle que je pourrais avoir avec tout autre homme d'affaires qui aurait pu faire des avances pour moi, en gérant mes affaires que je lui aurais confiées. Il m'est impossible de déterminer, d'après les documens ou pieces qui se trouvent en mes mains, à combien ont pu se monter ces avances à une époque quelconque. Les comptes que vous avez insérés dans votre rapport, ne m'ont jamais passé sous les yeux, et c'est dans ce rapport seulement que je les ai vus pour la premiere fois. Il n'en est aucun qui me regarde, et je n'y suis pour rien. Ils contiennent une variété de sommes qui sont censées m'avoir été délivrées, et qui n'ont jamais passé dans mes mains. On n'y donne aucun crédit aux diverses sommes reçues par M. Trotter pour mon compte, en raison de mon traitement de trésorier de la marine, et d'autres émolumens qu'il avait coutume de recevoir. On n'y fait aucune mention de la caution qu'il avait pour le remboursement de tout ce qui pouvait lui être du des fonds particuliers.

A l'égard des fonds de la marine qui m'ont été avancés et que j'ai, dit-on, employés à d'autres objets, je ne crois pas nécessaire de faire de nouvelles observations, sinon de déclarer que toutes ces sommes sont rentrées dans les coffres dont elles étaient sorties, n'ayant jamais été employées pour mon avantage particulier. Avant de conclure, je crois devoir relever une inexactitude que j'ai remarquée dans l'appendix, n° 7, page 162. On m'y fait cette question: « Avez-vous tiré profit ou » avantage du fonds destiné au service courant » de la marine, dans l'intervalle des 19 août » 1802 au 31 avril 1803; ou du 1er février 1784 » au 31 décembre 1785, période pendant laquelle » vous avez rempli les fonctions de trésorier de » la marine? » J'ai répondu à cette question, en me référant à la réponse que j'avais déja faite à une question semblable. Cette réponse est inexacte dans ce qu'elle se rapporte au mélange qu'a fait M. Trotter, de ses fonds, dans son compte particulier avec MM. Coutts. M. Trotter n'était pas payeur avant l'année 1786. En conséquence, les circonstances relatives au compte de M. Trotter, qui m'empêcherent de répondre à votre premiere question, ne s'appliquent pas aux époques spécifiées dans la réponse dont est mention. C'est pourquoi je puis sans difficulté déclarer que, durant ces intervalles, je ne tirai jamais aucun avantage de l'usage ou de l'emploi des fonds destinés au service de la marine. Ces faits une fois établis, il est presqu'inutile de dire que je suis prêt à les vérifier en personne. *Signé*, MELLEVILLE.

Fig. 7-1. *Gazette Nationale ou Le Moniteur Universel,* Paris, April 23, 1805. Ellis Library, University of Missouri–Columbia.

Chapter VII

Noticed Abroad

European publishers in 1805 gave widespread notice to Thomas Jefferson's speech upon taking the presidential oath of office for the second time. The *Times* of London printed the full text of the address in the issue of April 17. *Cobbett's Weekly Political Register* (London) published it on April 27. Among other magazines reprinting the inaugural address were the *European Magazine and London Review* for April and the London *Monthly Magazine* for May 1.

Napoleon Bonaparte was the first consul of France when the text of Jefferson's first inaugural address was translated into French and published in full in the Paris *Gazette Nationale ou Le Moniteur Universel* on April 20, 1801 (fig. 4-3). Four years later, when Jefferson delivered his second inaugural address, Napoleon was emperor of France. Although the American president's 1805 address was promptly reported at length on the first page of *Le Moniteur* on April 23, 1805 (fig. 7-1), only one paragraph was printed in full. The remainder of the address was reported in summary form. Among passages omitted were Jefferson's words: "It may be the pleasure and the pride of an American to ask what farmer, what mechanic, what labourer ever sees a tax-gatherer of the United States?"

The *Journal de Paris* reported on Jefferson's second inaugural address in the leading news item for the issue of April 23, but the single-paragraph report was limited to a summation of the major policies enunciated. Among those reported were Jefferson's promises to cultivate the friendship of all nations, pay the public debt, encourage commerce and industry, and guarantee religious freedom.

Jefferson's friends in France—the Marquis de Lafayette among them—thought the president's speech had been "speedily enough" received in Paris, and they were much pleased with it.[1] But they were dissatisfied with the treatment of the address in the French press. On April 22—the day before *Le Moniteur* reported Jefferson's address—the Paris English-language paper *Argus: or London Reviewed in Paris* published the complete English text.[2] On the same day, Lafayette wrote to Jefferson, commending his "admirable speech," and adding: "I was the more pleased

1. Lafayette to Madison, April 22, 1805, microfilm of Lafayette Papers in Chateau La Grange, Manuscript Division, Library of Congress.
2. I am indebted to Carol Armbruster, European Division, Library of Congress, for obtaining a photographic copy of this issue from the Bibliothèque Nationale, Paris.

211

(Num. 52.)

GIORNALE ITALIANO

Milano : Maggio 1805.

Res italas armis tuteris ; moribus ornes ;
Legibus emendes . . . .

Hor. Ep. II. 1.

NUOVE POLITICHE

WASHINGTON 5 Marzo.

Per chi leggendo riflette ed applica , merita d'essere riportato il discorso del nuovo Presidente degli Stati-Uniti , Tommaso Jefferson.

Jeri è stato installato nelle sue funzioni di Presidente del Congresso per 4 anni, come Giorgio Clinton in quelle di vice-presidente. Dopo il giuramento da essi prestato, Jefferson ha presentato alle due camere un indirizzo , del quale giova l' estrarre i seguenti tratti.

Proseguirà a regolarsi secondo i principj della prima sua amministrazione. . . . Nella condotta degli affari esteri avrà gran cura di conservare sul più amichevole piede i rapporti colle altre nazioni . . . . . . « Serbiamoci sempre, dic' egli , giusti e probi riguardo ad esse in ogni affar di commercio e di politica . . . . e sia convinto ognun di noi, che tra le nazioni , come tra gl' individui , il vero e solido interesse non va mai disgiunto dall' adempimento dei doveri e dalla sana morale . . . La storia ci prova, che una nazione proba si crede sulla parola , mentre per discutere e terminar gli affari coll'altre, per lo più non si adopran che l' armi . . . »

Quanto agli affari interni , il presidente assicura che le imposizioni sono le minori possibili , e che la più gran parte pesa sopra oggetti di lusso e di importazione . . . Non hanno servito mai , che alle spese correnti del Governo ; all' osservanza degli obblighi coi Governi esteri ; a stendere il territorio ; a pagare il debito pubblico, onde resti estinto al più presto , e possano in seguito impiegarsi le rendite in tempo di pace in oggetti di pubblica utilità , cioè canali , strade , manifatture , educazione ec. : in tempo di guerra a sostenere l' indipendenza e la dignità dello Stato . . . .

Sa il Presidente , che l' acquisto della Luigiana è riprovato da taluni che temono che l' ingrandimento del territorio non comprometta l' unione . . . . egli crede però che non possano mettersi limiti all' estensione di uno Stato che per sistema è federativo : e che è sempre molto meglio aver dei fratelli sulle rive del confinante Mississipi , che dei popoli lontani di tutt' altra famiglia e discendenza . . . .

In materia di religione , il libero esercizio dei culti è garantito dalla costituzione , e indipendente dal potere governativo. Il Presidente li lascerà , come li ha trovati , sotto la direzione e disciplina delle autorità ecclesiastiche d'ogni particolare società religiosa.

Esamina poscia il sig. Jefferson la condizione attuale degli abitanti del territorio che ora gli Stati-Uniti posseggono , e li considera con quella commiserazione che ispirano . . . . Ravvisa in essi un desiderio costante d'indipendenza . . . . li vede ridotti a retrocedere dinanzi a una popolazione incivilita che sempre cresce e li domina , rinchiusi ormai entro paesi di boschi e foreste, ove a stento vivon di caccia. « E' un dovere d' umanità , dic' egli , l' insegnar loro

l' agricoltura e l' arti domestiche. . . . abbiam dato ad essi gl' istrumenti arativi. . . . li difendiam colle leggi dall' oppressione di alcuni fra noi : ma questi pensieri e sforzi nostri per istruirli son tuttavia combattuti dalle abitudini , dall' ignoranza , dai pregiudizj loro, dall' avidità e dall'orgoglio di quelli che sono interessati a mantenerli nel loro stato selvaggio , per timore che si sottraggano. Costoro accrescono a tale oggetto il rispetto religioso che hanno que' popoli per i costumi dei loro antenati , li persuadono che *la ragione è una guida fallace , una pericolosa novità* , che il dover loro è di rimaner tai quali formolli il creatore , perchè *l' ignoranza è la via della salute , e la scienza una sorgente d' errori e pericoli* . . . Que' popoli hanno anch' essi i loro pseudofilosofi, che temono la riforma , e fan di tutto per tener lontano l'incivilimento a cui vuol ridurli il Governo. «

Passa di poi il Presidente ad oggetti interni , e declama contro l' abuso della libertà della stampa . . . riflettendo che i sommi affari dello Stato hanno obbligato il Governo a lasciare il castigo de' rei alla sola generale indignazione . . . Egli ne prende occasione a risentirsi delle calunniose diffamazioni delle quali è stato oggetto egli stesso , quando può chiamare a testimonio e giudice delle sue azioni il mondo intero... Egli confida nel sentimento di quella generale giustizia ed opinione pubblica che sa separare l' immorale licenziosità della stampa dalla inestimabile sua libertà . e finisce coll' esortare i suoi concittadini ad unirsi a lui colle intenzioni e coi mezzi i più proprj a conservare colla interna prosperità , la stima e l'amicizia di tutte l' altre nazioni.

LONDRA 8 Aprile.

L' attual situazione delle Antille continua ad occupar la pubblica attenzione. Il *Mercurio della Barbada* (de' 27 febbrajo), dà i seguenti ulteriori dettagli sulla spedizione fatta colà dal nemico. — » Se imponenti forze non giungono prontamente a soccorrere le isole del Vento , esse saranno minacciate da ulteriori pericoli. Un bastimento inglese partito dalla Martinica è stato incontrato in alto mare dalla fregata l' *Unicorno* , già arrivata qui nella Barbada , e dal rapporto da quella fatto non solo si conferma la notizia sparsa , che il nemico avea grandi forze nelle isole del Vento , ma ha soggiunto pure che sette vascelli di linea francesi , accompagnati da proporzionato numero di bastimenti da trasporto e di fregate, dovean seguire la prima spedizione , e con quella combinare un' attacco generale contro tutte le possessioni inglesi. E secondo lo stesso rapporto il nemico ha diretto un'altra forte spedizione per prendere d'assalto S. Lucia. — Si teme, e con ragione, che alcuni vascelli ravvisati jeri dalla nostra costa , faccian parte de' nuovi rinforzi aspettati di Francia dal nemico. Questo timore è stato accresciuto da un bastimento americano, il quale gl' incontrò jeri mattina , e dalla loro maniera di manovrare , li credette francesi. Esso li vide molto da vicino per distinguere che due di quelli erano vascelli di linea , ed aveano seco cinque bastimenti inferiori. «

Fig. 7-2. *Giornale Italiano,* Milan, May 1, 1805. Biblioteca Universitaria, Bologna, under concession of the Ministero per i Beni Culturali e Ambientali.

with it as it was perfectly suited not to the situation, but to the wants of this part of the world, and of course to the feelings of those who can not give up the hope of its final enfranchisement." Not long afterward, in another letter to Jefferson, Lafayette commented further on the publication of Jefferson's address in France, writing: "We had your speech printed in the *Argus*. But in the other papers they imprudently curtailed and altered it. Two translations are making, one here, the other by our friend Dupont—and if the Gazettes dare not give it out, it shall be printed and distributed by us." At about the same time, Samuel DuPont de Nemours was writing to Jefferson: "I have translated your speech that our gazettes have wilfully mutilated. We will have it printed in two columns, English on one side, French on the other."[3]

On May 1, the *Giornale Italiano* in Milan published a detailed summary of Jefferson's second inaugural address on its front page (fig. 7-2). On the following day *Il Corrière Milanese* published a similar but somewhat longer summary (fig. 7-3). In Pisa, Jefferson's longtime friend Philip Mazzei in June held in his hand a borrowed copy of an American newspaper containing Jefferson's complete address. Instructed to return the newspaper after one day, Mazzei copied Jefferson's address for later translation—a task he completed before the end of June. Mazzei planned to send a copy of his translation to a close friend in Florence, Giovanni Fabbroni, who was also a friend of Jefferson's. Commenting on the speech in a letter to Fabbroni, Mazzei noted: "In the inaugural address Jefferson delivered on reas-

suming the presidency there are two most interesting passages: one with reference to the aborigines and the other to the freedom of the press."[4]

By July 1, Mazzei had received a copy of the address from Jefferson himself. Writing again to Fabbroni, whom he called Nanni, Mazzei explained:

> I have so many things to do, so much to write, and my memorary is so enfeebled that I don't remember if in my previous letter I mentioned my transcription of Jefferson's address which I would send tonight to Nardo[5] to give to you as soon as he had read it, etc. Here is what I am writing him today:
>
> `I was thinking of the annoying difficulty you would have in deciphering my scribbled transcription of Jefferson's address from the English original, when the other night the United States consul brought me a letter from its author containing the printed copy enclosed herewith. Now, mind you, a week from today I want to send it to Prince Czartoryski in St. Petersburg. My conditions are that you read it at once; that as soon as you have read it, give it to Nanni and that either you or Nanni let me have it here by Sunday morning.'[6]

This letter is particularly revealing because Polish Prince Adam Czartoryski—who had been brought to Russia by Catherine II and was an early and strong influence on the adolescent Alexander—was now the effective foreign minister of Russia under Czar Alexander I.

---

3. Lafayette to Jefferson, April 22, 1805, in Gilbert Chinard, ed., *The Letters of Lafayette and Jefferson*, 240; Lafayette to Jefferson, May 1, 1805, microfilm of Lafayette Papers in Chateau La Grange, Manuscript Division, Library of Congress; DuPont to Jefferson, April 29, 1805, in Gilbert Chinard, ed., *The Correspondence of Jefferson and DuPont de Nemours*, 94, translated from the French text published by Chinard.

4. Mazzei to Giovanni Fabbroni, June 28, 1805, in Marchione, ed., *Mazzei Writings*, 3:384. While minister to France, Jefferson in May 1785 sent Fabbroni a copy of his *Notes on the State of Virginia*; Julian Boyd et al., eds., *The Papers of Thomas Jefferson* (Princeton, N.J., 1950–), 8:161.

5. Nardo was Bernardo Lessi, an auditor during the regime of the Grand Duke Leopold of Tuscany. See Marchione, ed., *Mazzei Writings*, 3:394n.

6. Mazzei to Giovanni Fabbroni, July 1, 1805, in ibid., 3:384–85.

IL CORRIERE MILANESE

N.º 35.   Milano Giovedì 2 Maggio 1805.

STATI UNITI D'AMERICA.

Washington 5 marzo.

Nella seduta di jeri il sig. Jefferson è stato installato nelle sue funzioni di presidente del congresso per 4 anni, cominciando da oggi, come pure il sig. Clinton nuovo vice-presidente. Dopo ch'ebbero prestato il giuramento costituzionale, il sig. Jefferson ha consegnato alle due camere un indirizzo, nel quale esprime ai suoi concittadini la gratitudine, che questo nuovo pegno di stima gli ispira e la ferma risoluzione, in cui è di rendersene degno. Egli dichiara che proseguirà a condursi, giusta gli stessi principj, che ha moderati nella sua prima amministrazione. Nella condotta degli affari esteri, dic'egli, ci siamo sforzati di coltivare l'amicizia di tutte le nazioni e specialmente di quelle, colle quali abbiamo i più importanti rapporti; abbiamo resa loro giustizia in ogni occasione; le abbiamo favorite laddove il favore era permesso ed abbiamo mantenuto il nostro commercio ed i nostri reciproci interessi entro i termini i più equi. Siamo fermamente convinti ed operiamo coerentemente a questa convinzione che fra nazioni così come fra individui, i nostri interessi ben intesi, non vadano giammai divisi dai nostri doveri e dalla nostra morale e la storia ci dimostra che una nazione è creduta giusta sulla sua parola, mentre con altre non altrimenti si discute che colla via dell'armi. Quanto alla gestione degli affari interni, il presidente espone che le pubbliche imposte sono state moderate il più possibile; che la maggior parte percuote oggetti di lusso e di importazione; che sono state adoperate nel pagare le spese correnti del governo; nell'adempire gli impegni contratti colle nazioni estere, nell'estendere il territorio degli Stati e nel pagare il debito pubblico; di modocchè sollecita ne sia l'estinzione totale e che allora si possano impiegare i redditi dello stato, in tempo di pace a dei pubblici lavori, come canali e strade od all'incoraggimento delle manifatture, al perfezionamento dell'educazione ec., in tempo di guerra a sostenere l'indipendenza e la dignità degli Stati. Il presidente aggiugne non ignorare egli che l'acquisizione della Luigiana è stata riprovata da alcuni individui per tema che l'ingrandimento del territorio degli Stati non ne comprometta la loro unione; ma egli è d'avviso non potersi limitare l'estensione di uno Stato governato nel sistema federativo ed in tutti i casi essere miglior cosa avere dei fratelli sulle sponde del Mississipi che degli esteri di un'altra famiglia. In punto di religione, l'esercizio libero dei culti è garantito dalla costituzione indipendente dal potere del governo. Il presidente li lascerà come li ha trovati, sotto la direzione particolare e la disciplina delle autorità ecclesiastiche riconosciute dalle diverse società religiose. Il sig. Jefferson esaminando poscia la condizione attuale degli abitanti originarj

del territorio degli Stati, li risguarda colla commiserazione, che ispira la loro sorte; egli li mira ardenti per la loro indipendenza, ridotti a ritrocedere mai sempre avanti ad una popolazione civilizzata, che si accresce continuamente, circoscritti in paesi, ove la caccia basta appena alla loro esistenza. L'umanità ci prescrive, dic'egli, d'insegnar loro l'agricoltura e le arti domestiche. Abbiamo spediti loro degli stromenti aratorj e li abbiamo posti sotto l'egida delle nostre leggi, contro quelli fra noi, che volessero opprimerli; ma gli sforzi da noi tentati per illuminarli, sono stati combattuti fin qua dall'abitudine, dall'ignoranza, dai pregiudizj e dall'orgoglio di quelli, che sono interessati a tenerli in questo stato selvaggio per tema di perdere il loro credito, se ne uscissero. Queste persone ispirano loro un religioso rispetto pei costumi dei loro antenati; li persuadono che la ragione è una guida ingannevole, una pericolosa innovazione; che il loro dovere è di rimanere tali, quali il creatore li ha formati, essendo l'ignoranza strada di salute e la dottrina una sorgente di pericoli. Così anche quei popoli hanno i loro anti filosofi, i quali sono interessati a mantenerli in questo stato selvaggio; che temono una riforma e che usano di tutti i loro mezzi per isconcertare gli sforzi, che noi facciamo ad oggetto di incivilirli. Quindi passando a degli oggetti interni, il presidente rammenta con quale indecenza si è abusato in questi ultimi tempi, contro lui medesimo, della libertà della stampa: egli espone che per tali abusi, essa perde tutto il vantaggio; che gli autori avrebbero potuto essere puniti giusta il rigore delle leggi contro la calunnia e la diffamazione; ma che gli affari pubblici occupando assai più l'attenzione dei magistrati, gli autori di questi libelli non sono stati ancor puniti che dalla generale indignazione. Il presidente domanda ora, se opportuno non sarebbe l'esaminare conformemente alla prova, che ne è stata fatta, se un governo, che si conduce, giusta lo spirito della sua costituzione con izelo e purezza, che non fa nulla, di cui non possa prendere il mondo intero per testimonio, possa essere attaccato così violentemente con delle declamazioni calunniose? D'altronde egli è d'avviso che conseguentemente all'effetto di queste calunnie, conseguentemente all'esito di tanti intrighi, l'opinione pubblica abbia fissata essa stessa una linea di demarcazione fra la licenza immorale della stampa e la sua inestimabile libertà. Tocca ad essa a supplire all'impotenza delle leggi. Il presidente conchiude il suo indirizzo collo scongiurare i suoi concittadini a riunirsi seco lui d'intenzioni e di mezzi per fare la felicità della patria e conservare l'amicizia, la stima e l'approvazione di tutte le nazioni.

Semelino 11 aprile

Le disposizioni militari dei serviani insorti, prendono tuttodì un carattere più imponente. Da

Fig. 7-3. *Il Corrière Milanese,* Milan, May 2, 1805. Biblioteca di Storia Moderna e Contemporanea, Rome.

Czartoryski was also a good friend of Mazzei's, and he had met Jefferson while Jefferson was minister to France. In the spring of 1802, Mazzei had made a trip to St. Petersburg to see Czartoryski. Writing to Jefferson before leaving Pisa, Mazzei confided: "Young Prince Cz[artoryski], a true friend of mine, whom you met in Paris, is an intimate friend of Alexander. That is why I am undertaking such a long and perilous trip while going on my 72nd year."[7] Mazzei would return to Pisa in October 1802.

In July 1805, in a letter to Scipione Piattoli—an Italian priest who had once been Czartoryski's tutor—Mazzei wrote in reference to Jefferson's second inaugural address:

> You may also have read in gazettes his inaugural address delivered on reassuming the presidency on March 4 ult. After I had translated it from an American gazette, I received it from him, and tonight I am sending it on to our Guardian Angel [Czartoryski] together with this letter. . . .
>
> You will find what he says on the freedom of the press entirely to your liking; you will admire his stated opinion that even the most unbridled license should not be legally punishable, after he himself had been its target.[8]

Mazzei had a very high opinion of Czartoryski, calling him not only "our Guardian Angel" but also "that great and worthy man." He recalled in regard to Jefferson's first inaugural address that Czartoryski had read it to his friends—along with later proposals by Jefferson adopted by Congress. He also remembered that Czartoryski had remarked: "this shows how much good a single man of talent and heart can do."[9] Mazzei's references to Jefferson's first and second inaugural addresses being sent to, and commented upon by, Czartoryski suggest that Czar Alexander I also would have been acquainted with Jefferson's inaugural addresses.

In sending Mazzei a copy of his 1805 inaugural speech, Jefferson had compared it with his first inaugural address: "As that of 1801 was a declaration of principles, this of 1805 is an account of practice on those principles, a compte rendu, which the nature of the occasion obliged me to be summary. The head of Indians was a little extended with an ironical eye to the modern declaimers against philosophy." In reply, Mazzei assured Jefferson that his second address was "not at all inferior to your first."[10]

Jefferson's second inaugural address was extensively reported in the German-speaking states of Europe. The Altona-Hamburg *Altonaischer Mercurius* printed the text on April 29 (fig. 7-4). On the same date, it also appeared in the *Kolnische Zeitung,* published in Cologne, then under French control. The *Hamburgische Neue Zeitung,* in which Jefferson's first inaugural address had been published four years earlier, printed the second address on April 30 (fig. 7-6). Modestly edited to reduce its length, it appeared also in the *Staats- und Gelehrte Zeitung des Hamburgischen unparthenischen Correspondenten.* The *Frankfurter Kaiserlich-Reichs-Ober-Post-Amts-Zeitung,* on May 4, offered only a brief report focusing on matters that would most interest Europeans (fig. 7-5). On the same date, the *Berlinische Nachrichten* published a longer summary of the speech (fig. 7-7). The nearly complete text appeared in the *Leipziger Zeitungen* on May 7

---

7. Janet M. Hartley, *Alexander I,* 15–16; Mazzei to Jefferson, April 10, 1802, in Marchione, ed., *Mazzei Writings,* 3:258–60.

8. Mazzei to Scipione Piattoli, July 3, 1805, in Marchione, ed., *Mazzei Writings,* 3:386–87.

9. Ibid., 3:387.

10. Jefferson to Mazzei, March 10, 1805, and Mazzei to Jefferson, July 20, 1805, in ibid., 3:376, 391. See also Jefferson's "Notes of a draft for second inaugural address," in Ford, ed., *Works of Thomas Jefferson,* 10:127–28, quoted above in Chapter 5.

Altonaischer

Anno 1805   **No. 68**

MERCVRIVS

Montag, den 29 April.

— 1171 —

daß ihm aufs neue geschenkte Vertrauen und äussert sich darauf über die Staatsangelegenheiten mit folgenden Worten:

„In Betreibung Ihrer ausländischen Angelegenheiten, Mitbürger, haben wir uns bemühet, die Freundschaft aller Nationen, und besonders derer zu unterhalten, mit welchen wir die wichtigsten Beziehungen haben. Wir haben ihnen bey jeder Gelegenheit Gerechtigkeit wiederfahren lassen, Gefälligkeiten, wo Gefälligkeiten gesetzmäßig waren, und haben gegenseitiges Interesse und Verkehr nach Billigkeit befördert; wir sind fest überzeugt, daß unser richtig verstandenes Interesse, sowohl in Hinsicht der Nationen, als der Individuen, von unsern moralischen Pflichten unzertrennlich ist, und bewähret es die Geschichte, daß man einer gerechten Nation auf ihr Wort traut, während Krieg und Rüstungen nothwendig sind, um andere im Zaum zu halten. Im Innern, Mitbürger, wissen Sie am besten, ob wir gut oder schlecht gehandelt haben. Die Aufhebung unnöthiger Aemter und unnützer Einrichtungen und Kosten setzte uns in den Stand, unsere innere Zollabgaben abzuschaffen. Sie bedeckten das Land mit einer Menge Beamten, öfneten deren Zudringlichkeiten unsere Thüren und hatten schon zu Hausdurchsuchungen Anlaß gegeben. Wenn unter den abgeschaften Abgaben sich einige geringere befanden, welche füglich hätten beybehalten werden können, so geschahe es, weil deren Betrag zur Besoldung der Einnehmer nicht zugereicht haben würde. Die noch bestehenden Abgaben von dem Verbrauch ausländischer Waaren, werden hauptsächlich von denen bezahlt, welche sich fremde Luxusartikel anschaffen können; und da diese nur an den Seeküsten und Gränzorten von den Kaufleuten erhoben werden, so kann es die Freude und der Stolz eines Amerikaners seyn, zu fragen: welcher Ackersmann, welcher Handwerker, welcher Arbeiter bekommt je einen Steuereinnehmer der vereinigten Staaten zu sehn? Mit diesen noch bestehenden Abgaben bestreiten wir die laufenden Kosten der Regierung, die Verbindlichkeiten mit fremden Nationen, erweitern unsere Gränzen und verwenden einen solchen Ueberschuß auf die Abtragung der öffentlichen Schuld daß solche in kurzem ganz getilgt seyn wird, und wir nachher in Friedenszeiten diese Gelder auf Flüsse, Kanäle, Landstraßen, Manufacturen, öffentliche Erziehung u. s. w. werden verwenden können. In Kriegszeiten, wenn unsere eigene oder fremde Ungerechtigkeit zuweilen einen Krieg erregen sollte, werden unsere durch vermehrte Bevölkerung vermehrten Einkünfte und die zu einer solchen Crisis aufbewahrten Hülfsquellen hinreichen, jährlich die Kosten jedes Jahres zu bestreiten, ohne die künftige Generation mit Schulden zu belasten. Dann wird der Krieg nur ein Aufschub nützlicher Unternehmungen seyn, und die Rückkehr zum Frieden wird die Rückkehr zur Vervollkommnung werden. Ich habe gesagt, Bürger, daß die Einkünfte uns in den Stand gesetzt haben, unsere Gränzen zu erweitern. Diese Erweiterung wird auf alle Fälle die Vorschüsse, die wir darauf verwendet haben, vergüten. Ich weiß, daß die Erwerbung von Louisiana von denen getadelt worden, welche befürchten, daß eine Vergrößerung unsers Gebiets dessen Einigkeit gefährden möge; wer kann aber

— 1172 —

dem Umfange Gränzen setzen, zu welchem der föderative Grundsatz in der That führen kann? — Je grösser unser Länderverein wird, je weniger wird er durch lokale Leidenschaften erschüttert werden, und ist es denn in jeder Hinsicht nicht besser, daß das entgegengesetzte Ufer des Mißißippi von unsern eigenen Brüdern und Kindern, als von Ausländern eines andern Stammes bebaut werde? Mit welchen von beyden ist Eintracht und freundschaftliches Verkehr wahrscheinlicher?"

„Die ursprünglichen Bewohner dieses Landes habe ich mit jenem Mitleiden angesehn, welches ihre Geschichte einflößt. Der Strom einer überflüssigen Bevölkerung hat sich aus andern Gegenden der Welt nach diesen Ufern gezogen. Ohne Kraft, ihn zurück zu weisen, und ausser Stande, gegen ihn zu streiten, sind die ursprünglichen Einwohner von dem Strom überwältigt, oder verjagt worden. Jetzt, da ihr Gränzen für das Jagdleben zu beschränkt sind, gebietet uns die Menschheit, sie im Ackerbau und häuslichen Künsten zu unterrichten und sie zu der Industrie aufzumuntern, die sie allein in den Stand setzen kann, ihre Existenz zu behaupten und sich zu dem gesellschaftlichen Stande vorzubereiten, der die körperlichen Bequemlichkeiten mit der Bildung der Seele und Moral vereinigt. Ich habe sie demnach reichlich mit Ackerbau- und Hausgeräthschaften versehn, habe Lehrer in den Künsten der ersten Nothwendigkeit unter sie geschickt und sie mit dem Schilde des Gesetzes gegen Angreifer aus unsern Mitteln versehn. Meine Bemühungen aber, sie über die bevorstehende Veränderung ihrer Lebensart aufzuklären, sie zur Anwendung ihrer Vernunft und zur Veränderung ihrer Beschäftigungen bey veränderten Umständen zu bewegen, haben mit mächtigen Hindernissen zu kämpfen. Ihre körperlichen Gewohnheiten, Vorurtheile, Unwissenheit, Stolz und der Einfluß eigennütziger, starker Personen unter ihnen, die bey der gegenwärtigen Ordnung der Dinge etwas unter ihnen gelten, und bey einer Veränderung in Nichts zu versinken fürchten, kämpfen dagegen. Diese Menschen dringen auf eine heilige Ehrfurcht für die alten Gebräuche der Vorfahren und daß das, was jene thaten, immer geschehen müsse. Sie behaupten, die Vernunft sey ein falscher Führer und rathe bloß gefährliche Neuerungen; es sey Pflicht, so zu bleiben, wie der Schöpfer uns geschaffen habe; Unwissenheit sey Sicherheit, Kenntnisse brächten Gefahr. Kurz, meine Freunde, man sieht auch unter diesen Wilden den gesunden Menschenverstand mit der Scheinheiligkeit kämpfen; auch da haben ihre Antiphilosophien, welche ein Interesse dabey finden, daß alles beym alten bleibe, welche eine Reformation fürchten und alle Kräfte aufbieten, um die Macht der Gewohnheit über die Pflicht, die Vernunft zu bilden und deren Gebote zu befolgen, zu behaupten." (Hierauf klagt der Präsident, daß das Geschrey der Presse während seiner Verwaltung gegen ihn gerichtet worden, und zwar mit aller der Bitterkeit, welche die Licenz nur hervorbringen kann. Er spricht weitläuftig über diesen Punkt und sagt am Schluß:)

„Ich werde nun die Amtspflichten antreten, zu welchen meine Mitbürger mich aufs neue berufen haben. Ich werde den Geist

— 1173 —

der von Ihnen schon genehmigten Grundsätze dabey befolgen. Ich fürchte nicht, daß eigennützige Absichten mich irre führen oder irgend eine Leidenschaft mich irgend von dem Pfade der Gerechtigkeit ableiten werde; die Schwäche der menschlichen Natur aber und die Beschränktheit meiner Einsichten kann mich zu irrigen Maaßregeln führen, die Ihrem Interesse zuweilen nachtheilig seyn können. Ich werde also aller Nachsicht bedürfen, die ich vorher erhalten habe. Ich beuge mich gegen jenes Wesen, in dessen Händen wir sind, und welches unsere Väter, wie ehemals die Kinder Israel, aus ihrem Vaterlande geführt und in ein Land verpflanzt hat, in welchem alle Bedürfnisse und Annehmlichkeiten des Lebens vorhanden sind. Ich bitte Sie, ihr Flehen mit dem meinigen zu vereinigen, daß er das Gemüth Ihrer Beamten erleuchte, deren Rathschläge leite und deren Maaßregeln segne, damit alles zu Ihrem Guten ausschlage und Ihnen Friede, Freundschaft und Beyfall aller Völker sichere.

Thomas Jefferson."

Fig. 7-4. *Altonaischer Mercurius*, Altona-Hamburg, April 29, 1805. Staats- und Universitäts Bibliothek Carl von Ossietzky, Hamburg.

Nro. 71.

Samſtägige
Frankfurter
Kaiſerl. Reichs-Ober-Poſt-Amts-Zeitung
vom 4. Mai 1805.

Wien, vom 27. April.

Se. Maj. der Kaiſer haben geruhet den Feldmarſchalllieutenant und kommandirenden General im Banat, Grafen Johann v. Soro, mit dem Feldzeugmeiſterskarakter in den Ruheſtand zu ſetzen, den Feldmarſchalllieutenant und Generalquartiermeiſter, Peter v. Duka, zum kommandirenden General im Banat zu ernennen, und die Stelle eines Generalquartiermeiſters dem Feldmarſchalllieutenant und Inhaber eines Küraſſierregiments, Frhrn. Karl v. Mack, zu übertragen.

Se. k. H. der Erzh. Karl ſind im Begriffe das Hoftriegsrathsgebäude zu verlaſſen, und in die Metternichſchen Gärten am Rennwege zu ziehen.

Der Erzherzoge k. k. H. H. haben bereits ihren Aufenthalt in Schönbronn genommen.

Vor einigen Tagen iſt der neue Vicepräſident der Oberſten Juſtizſtelle, Frhr v. Karg feierlich vorgeſtellt worden, nachdem Se. Exzell. in die Hände des Präſidenten den gewöhnlichen Eid abgelegt hatten.

Waſhington, vom 8. März.

Am 2 d nahm Hr. Burr, der hauptſächlich wegen ſeines Duells mit General Hamilton nicht wieder zum Vicepräſidenten gewählt worden iſt, vom Senat Abſchied, und verließ Waſhington am gleichen Tage Geſtern wurde Hr. Thomas Jefferſon in die Funktionen eines Präſidenten neuerdings auf 4 Jahre, ſo wie Hr. Georges Clinton in die eines Vicepräſidenten, inſtalirt Nach Ableiſtung des verfaſſungsmäßigen Eides übergab Hr Jefferſon beiden Kammern eine Adreſſe, worinn er die

Erkenntlichkeit, die ihm dieſer neue Beweis der Achtung ſeiner Mitbürger einflöße, ſo wie ſeinen feſten Vorſatz, ſich deren ferner würdig zu machen, ausdrückt. Er erklärt, er werde fortfahren, ſein Betragen nach ſeinen bisherigen Grundſätzen einzurichten; im Auslande die Freundſchaft aller Nationen beizubehalten, im Innern weiſe zu regieren, die Abgaben zu vermindern, die Staatsſchuld abzuführen, den Gewerbsfleiß und den Handel zu ermuntern trachten, im Bezug auf die Religion alle von der Konſtitution erlaubte Gottesverehrungen beſchützen u. ſ. w. Er vertheidigte die Erwerbung von Louiſiana gegen diejenigen, welche von dieſer Vergröſerung des Staatsgebiets einen Nachtheil für die Union beſorgen; die Gröſe eines nach dem Föderativſyſtem regierten Staates ſey nicht zu beſchränken, und auf jeden Fall ſey es beſſer, Brüder als Fremde an den Ufern des Miſſiſſipi zu wiſſen. Zulezt beſchwerte er ſich über die ungezähmten Angriffe, die ſich einige Winkelſchriftſteller durch Mißbrauch der Preßfreiheit gegen ihn erlaubt hätten, und beruft ſich auf die öffentl. Meinung, welche bereits eine Gränzlinie zwiſchen der Preßfrechheit und der unſchätzbaren Preßfreiheit gezogen habe. An ihr ſey es, für die Ohnmacht des Geſetzes zu entſchädigen ꝛc.

Konſtantinopel, vom 26. März.

Zu Zujukdere iſt ein ruſſiſches Linienſchiff und eine Fregatte mit 500 Mann Truppen an Bord angekommen; eine Brik, die einige Tage früher angelangt war, ſoll zum Transport der Truppen nach Korfu beſtimmt ſeyn, die den Winter hier zugebracht haben, denn das

Fig. 7-5. *Frankfurter Kaiserlich-Reichs-Ober-Post-Amts-Zeitung,* Frankfurt, May 4, 1805. Staats- und Universitats Bibliothek, Bremen.

69 Stück. Dienstag, den 30 April 1805.

Schreiben aus Washington, vom 4 März.
Heute legte Hr. Jefferson als neu erwählter Präsident der vereinigten Staaten den Eid ab und hielt im Senat eine Rede, folgenden wesentlichen Inhalts:

Mitbürger!

Ehe ich mein mit abermals aufgetragenes Amt antrete, halte ich es für meine Pflicht, die Empfindungen und den Eifer auszudrücken, mit welchem mich dieser neue Beweis Ihres Vertrauens beseelt. Ich habe schon vormals die Grundsätze aus einander gesetzt, nach welchen ich die Angelegenheiten dieser Republik zu verwalten entschlossen war. Mein Gewissen sagt mir, daß ich mich denselben gemäß verhalten habe.

In der Besorgung der auswärtigen Angelegenheiten haben wir uns bemüht, die Freundschaft aller Nationen zu cultiviren, und besonders derer, mit welchen wir in wichtigen Verhältnissen stehen. Wir haben ihnen jederzeit Gerechtigkeit wiederfahren lassen, sie begünstiget, wo Begünstigung erlaubt war und das gegenseitige Interesse und Einverständniß unter billigen Bedingungen gesucht; denn wir sind überzeugt, daß, wie bey Individuen, so auch bey Nationen, das wahre Interesse derselben von moralischen Pflichten unzertrennbar ist, und die Geschichte beweiset, daß eine gerechte Nation bey ihrem Wort Vertrauen fand, wenn man Kriege und Bewaffnungen nöthig hatte, um andere im Zaum zu halten.

Sie wissen, Mitbürger, ob wir uns zu Hause wohl oder übel befunden haben. Die Unterdrückung überflüssiger Aemter, Etablissements und Ausgaben sehte uns in Stand, unsre innern Taxen aufzuheben. Die Taxen von ausländischen Artikeln werden vorzüglich von denen bezahlt, welche ihre häuslichen Bequemlichkeiten durch fremden Luxus vermehren können. Da sie bloß in Seehäfen und an den Gränzen gesammlet werden, so kann der Americaner mit Freude und Stolz fragen, wo der Pächter, Handwerksmann und Arbeiter sey, der einen Zoll-Einnehmer jemals sähe? Diese Contributionen sehen uns in Stand, die öffentlichen Ausgaben zu bestreiten. Die gänzliche Tilgung der National-Schuld steht nahe bevor. Ist diese erfolgt, so kann der jährliche Ueberschuß der Einnahme zu Candlen, Künsten, Manufacturen, zur Erziehung und zu andern großen öffentlichen Zwecken allein angewandt werden. In Kriegszeiten — wenn Ungerechtigkeiten von unserer oder von anderer Seite einmal Krieg veranlassen sollten — werden von dem Ueberschuß der Einnahme die Ausgaben des Kriegs bestritten werden können, ohne den Rechten der künftigen Generationen zu nahe zu treten, indem man sich mit den Schulden der vorhergegangenen Generation belastet. Der Krieg wird dann bloß eine Suspension nützlicher Werke und die Rückkehr zum Friedensstande die Rückkehr zu den Fortschritten inländischer Verbesserungen seyn.

Ich habe es bemerkt, Mitbürger, daß das reservirte Einkommen des Staats uns in Stand gesetzt hat, unsre Gränzen zu erweitern. Aber diese Erweiterung wird das dafür Aufgewandte bald selbst wieder bezahlen. Ich weiß, die Acquisition Louisiana's ist von einigen gemißbilligt worden, aus Besorgniß, daß die Erweiterung des Territoriums unsere Union schwächen möchte. Aber wer vermag die Erweiterung zu beschränken, welche das föderative Princip in der That bewirken kann? Je weiter unsre Association sich erstreckt, um so weniger kann sie durch Local-Leidenschaften erschüttert werden, und ist es nicht in jeder Rücksicht besser, daß das gegenseitige Ufer des Mißisipi von unsern eignen Brüdern und Kindern bevölkert werde, als von fremden? Mit welchen werden wir am leichtesten harmoniren?

Die benachbarten Indianer, die ursprünglichen Einwohner dieses Landes, habe ich mit dem Mitleiden betrachtet, welches ihre Geschichte einflößt. Die Menschlichkeit verpflichtet uns, da sie jetzt für ein Jäger-Leben auf zu enge Gränzen beschränkt sind, sie den Ackerbau und die häuslichen Künste zu lehren, sie zur Industrie zu ermuntern und sie für einen gesellschaftlichen Zustand vorzubereiten. Wir haben ihnen deswegen Ackerwerkzeuge und nützlichen Hausrath mitgetheilt, Lehrer in den nothwendigsten ersten Künsten unter sie gesandt und wir bedecken sie mit

Fig. 7-6. *Hamburgische Neue Zeitung*, Hamburg, April 30, 1805. Staats- und Universitats Bibilothek Carl von Ossietzky, Hamburg.

dem Schuß unsrer Rechte gegen alle Aggreſſion aus unſrer Mitte. Indeſſen haben die Bemühungen, ſie zu erleuchten und ihren Zuſtand zu beſſern, noch mächtige Hinderniſſe. Körperliche Gewohnheit, Vorurtheile, Unwiſſenheit, Stolz und der Einfluß eigennüßiger, liſtiger Individuen unter ihnen ſtehen denſelben entgegen. Dieſe Menſchen, die ſich in der jetzigen Ordnung der Dinge als ein Etwas fühlen und in einer andern Ordnung Nichts zu ſeyn befürchten, lehren eine heilige Ehrfurcht gegen die Gebräuche ihrer Vorfahren; ſie lehren, daß die Vernunft ein ſchlimmer Führer ſey; daß es ihre Pflicht wäre, ſo zu bleiben, wie ihr Schöpfer ſie geſchaffen habe; daß die Unwiſſenheit Sicherheit und Kenntniß ſehr gefährlich ſey. Kurz, meine Freunde, auch unter ihnen kämpfen Vernunft und Bigotterie wider einander. Sie haben ihre Antiphiloſophen, welche ihren Vortheil dabey finden, die Sachen in ihrer alten Verfaſſung zu laſſen, die eine Reformation fürchten und alle ihre Kraft anwenden, um den Einfluß der Gewohnheit gegen die Pflicht zu behaupten, die Vernunft zu vervollkommnen und deren Geſetzen zu gehorchen.

Während meiner Adminiſtration iſt zur Störung derſelben das Geſchütz der Preſſe gegen uns gerichtet und alles uns zur Laſt gelegt worden, was die Frechheit nur erſinnen konnte. Dieſe Mißbräuche einer Einrichtung, die ſo wichtig für Freyheit und Wiſſenſchaft iſt, ſind ſehr zu beklagen, indem ſie deren Nutzen ſchwächen. Sie hätten vielleicht durch einige nützliche Beſtrafungen gebeſſert werden können, wie ſie das Geſetz gegen Verläumdung und Unwahrheiten vorſchreibt. Aber Pflichten von höherm Gewicht liegen den öffentlichen Beamten ob und die Uebelthäter ſind deswegen bloß der Strafe des öffentlichen Unwillens überlaſſen worden. Auch war es nicht unintereſſant, einmal zu verſuchen, ob nicht die Freyheit der Discuſionen, ohne der Macht zu bedürfen, hinlänglich ſey, Wahrheiten zu verbreiten und zu erhalten, und um zu ſehen, ob ein redliches Gouvernement durch Unwahrheiten und Verläumdung niedergeſchrieben werden kann. Die Probe iſt gemacht worden und glücklich ausgefallen. Unſre Mitbürger ſahen dem Getümmel der Schreyer ruhig zu, bemerkten die verborgene Quelle der Schmähungen, ſammleten ſich um ihre öffentlichen Beamten und erklärten ſich überall für dieſe.

Ich will daraus nicht den Schluß ziehen, daß die Geſetze gegen Diffamation nicht in Kraft erhalten werden ſollten; allein die Erfahrung hat bewieſen, daß, da Wahrheit und Vernunft ſich gegen falſche Meynungen, verbunden mit falſchen Factis, behauptet haben, die Preſſe, die auf Wahrheit beſchränkt wird, keiner andern geſetzmäßigen Einſchränkung bedarf. Das öffentliche Urtheil wird, nach Anhören aller Partheyen, falſche Meynungen und Raiſonnements corrigiren und es kann keine andere beſtimmte Gränzlinie zwiſchen der unſchätzbaren Freyheit der Preſſe und ihrer unmoraliſchen Frechheit gezogen werden.

Wenn ich die Einigkeit der Geſinnungen betrachte, welche ſich jetzt im Allgemeinen ſo deutlich offenbart und Eintracht und Glück für die Zukunft verſpricht, ſo muß ich unſerm Lande aufrichtig Glück wünſchen.

Unſre noch zweifelnden Brüder werden es endlich einſehen, daß die Maſſe ihrer Mitbürger, mit deren Maaßregeln und Grundſätzen ſie ſich noch nicht verſöhnen können, doch weiter deſſen und wünſchen, was ſie wünſchen.

Ich werde nun die Amtspflichten antreten, zu welchen meine Mitbürger mich aufs neue berufen haben. Ich werde den Geiſt der von Ihnen ſchon genehmigten Grundſätze dabey befolgen. Ich fürchte nicht, daß eigennützige Abſichten mich irre führen oder irgend eine Leidenſchaft mich von dem Pfade der Gerechtigkeit ableiten werde; die Schwäche der menſchlichen Natur aber und die Beſchränktheit meiner Einſichten kann mich zu irrigen Maaßregeln führen, die Ihrem Intereſſe zuweilen nachtheilig ſeyn können. Ich werde alſo aller Nachſicht bedürfen, die ich vorher erhalten habe. Ich beuge mich gegen jenes Weſen, in deſſen Händen wir ſind, und welches unſre Väter, wie ehemals die Kinder Iſraels, aus ihrem Vaterlande geführt und in ein Land verpflanzt hat, in welchem alle Bedürfniſſe und Annehmlichkeiten des Lebens vorhanden ſind. Ich bitte Sie, Ihr Flehen mit dem meinigen zu vereinigen, daß es die Gemüther Ihrer Beamten erleuchte, deren Rathſchläge leite und deren Maaßregeln ſegne, damit alles zu Ihrem Beſten ausſchlage und Ihnen Frieden, Freundſchaft und den Beyfall aller Völker ſichere.

Thomas Jefferſon.

Schreiben aus Hanau, vom 23 April.

Die Pferdeſeuche hat ſich aus Ober- und Niederſachſen auch bis hieher erſtreckt.

Für die verwittwete Churfürſtin von Bayern und den Grafen Arco iſt zu Maynz eine Yacht gemiethet, um auf dem Rhein nach Düſſeldorf zu fahren.

Der Königl. Preußiſche Reſident von Harnier in München iſt zugleich als Landgräfl. Heßiſcher Miniſter-Reſident daſelbſt angeſtellt.

Schreiben aus Stockholm, vom 19 April.

Das große Luſtlager, welches zu Bonnarpshed in Schonen gehalten werden ſoll, fängt am 1ſten Junii an und wird 17 Tage dauern. Es wird nicht nur aus den Regimentern in Schonen, ſondern auch aus den Bataillons derjenigen Regimenter beſtehen, von denen ſich jetzt ein Theil in Pommern befindet. Das Hauptquartier ſoll zu Herrevards Kloſter ſeyn.

Ein Unbekannter hat zur Bezeugung ſeiner Freude über die glückliche Rückkunft Ihrer Majeſtäten und über die Geburt der Prinzeßin Amalie Marie Charlotte dem Grafen von Mörner, Chef en Second der Schwediſchen Garden eine Summe von 4000 Rthlrn. Banco zugeſtellt, um zur Errichtung eines Hospitals für alte verwundete und verabſchiedete Soldaten gebraucht zu werden. Der Graf von Mörner und die Schwediſchen Garde-Officiers haben zugleich beſchloſſen, zur Vermehrung dieſes Fonds jährlich zu 6 Procent die Intereſſen eines Capitals von 4166 Reichsthalern zu bezahlen. Ihre Königl. Majeſtäten haben dieſen edlen Entſchluß ſehr wohlgefällig aufgenommen und werden auch jährlich einen Beytrag zum Beſten des Inſtituts geben, welches nach unſrer verehrten Königin Friederike Dorotheen-Hospital genannt werden ſoll.

No. 54.   Sonnabend, den 4ten Mai 1805.

Spanien.

Die Infanterie erhält eine neue Organisation. Die blaue Uniform, die abgeschafft worden war, wird wieder eingeführt, und alle Korps sollen in Brigaden, jede zu 4 Regimentern, vertheilt werden. — Die Armee in Gallizien ist 28,000 Mann stark. Man versichert, daß sie bestimmt sey, die Seehäfen und festen Plätze Portugals zu besetzen. Das Ausrüsten der Flotte zu Ferrol ist am 28 März vollendet worden, und die Schiffe sind bereit, auf das erste Zeichen in See zu gehen. Diese Flotte besteht, ohne die französischen Schiffe und außer den Fregatten und Korvetten, aus 12 Linienschiffen. Die bisher zu Kadix ausgerüstete Flotte enthält ebenfals 12 Linienschiffe, worunter eines von 100, ein zweites von 114, und ein drittes von 134 Kanonen sich befindet. Hierzu kommen 4 franz. Linienschiffe, jedes von 76 Kanonen, zwei Fregatten von 38; 12 Kanonenböte zu Kadix und 18 zu Algesiras.

Grosbritanien.

Hr. Melville hat an die Kommissär der Seekomptabilität einen weitläuftigen Brief zu seiner Rechtfertigung ergehen lassen. Er erörtert vorzüglich darin die Frage, ob Hr. Trotter einige für den laufenden Dienst der Marine bestimmte Gelder zu seinem Privat-Interesse verwendet hätte, und sagt: In dem Falle, wo man mich gefragt hätte, ob ich mich mit Hrn. Trotter, (Kassirer bei der Marine) verstanden hätte, um gemeinsamen Vortheil von der Bewahrung der öffentlichen Gelder zu ziehen, oder ob ich jemal selbst daraus Vortheil gezogen hätte, würde ich ohne Bedenklichkeit erkläret haben, wie ich es diesen Augenblick erkläre, daß niemal einige Uebereinkunft, niemal ein Einverständniß von dieser Art zwischen Herrn Trotter und mir bestand; daß ich mir nie dergleichen Vortheile zu verschaffen gemußt habe, und wie auch immer die Vortheile, seyn, die Hr. Trotter zufolge seiner Verrichtungen, haben mag, sie sind ihm eigen, und ich kenne sie nicht. In Rüksicht der Fonds der Marine, die ich, wie man sagt, zu andern Gegenständen angewendet haben soll, will ich nur erklären, daß alle diese Summen in die Kassen zurückgeflossen sind, woher sie kamen,

Nordamerikanische Staaten.

Der bekannte Burr hat in der Sitzung am 2ten März vom Senat in Waßington Abschied genommen und am nämlichen Tage die Stadt verlassen. Hr. Jefferson wurde am 4ten März auf vier Jahre als Präsident eingesetzt, so wie Georges Clinton als neuer Vizepräsident. Die Adresse, welche er nach geleistetem Eide an die beiden Häuser übergab, ist besonders merkwürdig: Jefferson erklärt unter andern darin, er werde fortfahren sich nach den Grundsätzen zu betragen, die er in seiner ersten Verwaltung gezeigt hat. In der Leitung der auswärtigen Angelegenheiten, sagt er, haben wir uns bestrebt, die Freundschaft aller Nationen beizubehalten... Wir sind fest überzeugt, und wir handeln nach dieser Ueberzeugung, daß unter Nationen, wie unter Individuen, unser wohlverstandenes Interesse, niemal von unsern Pflichten und unserer Moral getrennt ist. In Betreff der Betreibung der innern Angelegenheiten bemerkt der Präsident, daß die öffentlichen Auflagen so gemäßigt gewesen sind, als man sie machen konnte; daß die meisten Auflagen nur auf Gegenständen des Luxus und der Ausfuhr haften; daß sie zur Bezahlung der laufenden Ausgaben der Regierung, zur Erfüllung der mit den fremden Nationen eingegangenen Verbindlichkeiten, zur Ausdehnung des Gebietes der Staaten, zur Abtragung der Nationalschuld so verwendet worden sind, daß die gänzliche Austilgung derselben bald da seyn werde, und daß man alsdann die Einkünfte des Staates, in Friedenszeiten, zu öffentlichen Arbeiten, Kanälen und Heerstraßen, oder zur Ermunterung der Manufakturen, zur Vervollkommnung der Erziehung ꝛc. in Kriegszeiten, zur Erhaltung der Unabhängigkeit und der Würde des Staates anwenden könne... Der Präsident bezeugt, er wisse wohl, daß die Erwerbung von Luisiana von einigen Personen gemisbilligt worden sey, in der Furcht, daß die Vergrößerung des Gebietes des Staates seine Eintracht aufs Spiel setze; allein er denkt, daß man die Ausbreitung eines im föderativen Sistem verwalteten Staates nicht beschränken kann, und daß es in allen Fällen besser ist, Brüder an den Ufern des Mississipi, als Ausländer einer andern Familie zu haben. In Betreff der Religion, ist die freie Ausübung des Gottesdienstes durch die Staatsverfassung verbürget, unabhängig von der Macht der Regierung. Der Präsident wird ihn lassen, wie er ihn gefunden hat, unter der besonderen Leitung und der Disziplin der geistlichen Authoritäten, die von verschiedenen religiösen Gesellschaften anerkannt sind. Hr. Jefferson untersucht endlich den dermaligen Zustand der Landeseingebornen, und bemitleidet ihre Robheit. Die Menschheit macht es uns zur Pflicht, sagt er, ihnen den Ackerbau und

Fig. 7-7. *Berlinische Nachrichten*, Berlin, May 4, 1805. Institut fur Zeitungsforschung, Dortmund.

die häuslichen Künste zu lehren. Wir haben ihnen Werkzeuge zum Pflügen geschikt, und sie unter den Schild unserer Gesetze wider diejenigen gestellt, welche sie gerne unterdrücken wollten; allein die Anstrengungen, welche wir versucht haben, um sie aufzuklären, sind bisher von den Gewohnheiten der Unwissenheit, den Vorurtheilen, und dem Stolze derjenigen bekämpfet worden, die dabei betheiligt sind, um sie in jenem wilden Zustande zu halten, und aus Furcht ihr Zutrauen zu verlieren, wenn sie daraus hervorgingen. Diese Leute bringen ihnen eine heilige Ehrfurcht gegen die Gewohnheiten ihrer Vorfahren bei; überreden sie, daß die Vernunft ein trügerischer Wegweiser, eine gefährliche Neuerung ist, daß ihre Pflicht ist, so zu bleiben, wie der Schöpfer sie gebildet hat, indem die Unwissenheit ein Weg zum Heile, und die Wissenschaft eine Quelle von Gefahren sey. Endlich haben diese Völker auch ihre Afterphilosophen, die eine Reformation fürchten, und die alle Mittel brauchen, unsere Bemühungen zu ihrer Ausbildung zu vereiteln. ... Hierauf kömmt der Präsident auf innere Gegenstände, und eifert sonderlich wider die Preßfreiheit, und behauptet, daß sie durch ihre Misbräuche jeden Vortheil verliert. Sollte es nicht nützlich seyn, fragt er, zu untersuchen, ob eine Regierung, die sich nach dem Geiste der Konstitution mit reinem Eifer beträgt; die nichts thut, worüber sie nicht die ganze Welt zum Zeugen nehmen könne, gewaltsam durch verläumderische Deklamationen angegriffen werden könne? Die öffentliche Meinung, sagt er, hat selbst eine Linie zwischen der unsittlichen Zügellosigkeit der Presse und ihrer unschätzbaren Freiheit gezogen. Sie muß ins Mittel treten, wenn das Gesetz ohnmächtig ist. Der Präsident schließt seine Adresse mit der Beschwörung seiner Mitbrüder, ihre Gesinnungen und Mittel mit ihm zu vereinigen, um das Glük des Vaterlandes zu befördern, und die Freundschaft, die Hochachtung und den Beifall aller Nationen zu erhalten.

Rußland.

Die Schöpfung von Haydn ward am 17ten März zum Bessten der Witwen der Musiker in Petersburg, in einem dazu eingerichteten schönen Saale aufgeführt. Ueber 600 Billets, zu 5 Rubeln, waren verkauft. Der Kaiser, der wegen Kabinetsgeschäften nicht zugegen seyn konnte, hatte, nebst der Kaiserinn Mutter, sehr ansehnliche Summen zu dieser milden Stiftung beigetragen. Den 4ten April wurde das Requiem von Mozart zu dem nämlichen Zwek aufgeführt.

Handelssache. — Der Zucker war, wie gewöhnlich, einer der wichtigsten Artikel der Einfuhr im vergangenen Jahre. Der Werth davon beläuft auf 4 Millionen 400,000 Rubel. Von dieser Einfuhr fallen 13 Millionen auf Rechnung der russischen und 7 Mill. 336,000 Rubel auf Rechnung der englischen Kaufleute. — Die Sage von einer Beschädigung des Hafens von Odessa war ungegründet. Der schöpferische Geist Alexanders hat aus diesem öden Flecken in wenigen Jahren einen ansehnlichen Ort emporsteigen lassen. Inzwischen haben die Fortschritte dieser Stadt den Blik des Monarchen auf einen andern Punkt des schwarzen Meeres gerichtet. Rußlands Handel auf dem schwarzen Meere brauchte nämlich außer Odessa einen andern Ausgang für seine mannigfaltigen Produkte. Kein Platz schien dazu geeigneter zu seyn, als Caffa in der Krimm, diese ehemals so glänzende Handelsstadt der Genueser, jetzt unter dem Namen Theodosia bekannt. Die Wiedererschaffung dieses Ortes, der noch mehrere bedeutende Ueberbleibsel seiner ehemaligen Größe besitzt, war lange der Gegenstand der Sorgfalt des Monar-

chen. Mehrere ausländische Handelshäuser sind bereits mit ansehnlichen Kapitalien dahin gezogen. Der Kaiser schont keine Kosten für die Wohlfahrt dieser Stadt, und hat ihr zum Befehlshaber einen Mann gegeben, dessen große Eigenschaften den wohlthätigsten Einfluß auf den russischen Handel haben, und die eheste Blüthe desselben glüklich verbürgen.

— Von Petersburg aus wird unterm 1ten April der Nachricht widersprochen, als wenn der russische Hof freien Durchmarsch von Truppen durch das preussische Gebiet begehrt und eine abschlägige Antwort erhalten hätte. Man müßte, so sagt die Petersburger Hofzeitung, die Denkart des russischen Kabinettes wenig kennen, wenn man annehmen wollte, daß es eine solche abschlägige Antwort nicht voraus gesehen, oder sich sehr derselben hätte aussetzen wollen.

Italien.

Neapel. — Der Reichsmarschall Kellermann wird, wie es heißt, den Divisionsgeneral St. Cyr im Oberbefehl der franz. Armee im Neapolitanischen ablösen. — In der Kirche der Benediktinerabtei Campajo, unfern Aquino, der Vaterstadt Juvenals, dieses strengen Richters der zügellosen Sprache und Lebensart im Gewühle des alten Roms, hat man den 13ten April ein Denkmahl gefunden, daß er der Ceres geweiht hatte. Es erhellt nebsthin daraus, daß er Tribun der ersten Kohorte der Dalmaten und zweimal Flamen unter Vespasian gewesen sey, dessen unwürdiger Sohn den 90jährigen Greis, den er nicht zu strafen wagte, und doch als seiner Verdorbenheit strenge Geißel um sich dulden wollte, als Präfekten nach Aegypten schikte.

Piemont. — Die Minister der auswärtigen Angelegenheiten und des Innern, sind den 13ten April in Turin angekommen. Den 14ten nahmen sie Besitz von den Zimmern, die für sie im kaiserl. Pallaste bestimmt sind. Hierauf speiseten sie im Schlosse Stupinis. Auch viele andere Personen aus dem Gefolge Ihrer Kaiserl. Maj. sind gegen den 14ten April in Turin eingetroffen.

Ein kaiserl. Dekret, das in Turin bekannt gemacht wurde, betrifft die Domängüter und enthält folgende Verfügungen: Die Privatpersonen oder öffentliche Anstalten, welchen von den in der 27ten Militärdivision angestellten Regierungen, Domängüter freiwillig bewilligt worden sind, sollen vom 4ten Germinal an, bis zum 1ten nächsten Messidor dem Minister des Innern und der Finanzen, ihre Gesuche und schriftliche Vorstellungen vorlegen, um die Bestätigung dieser Bewilligungen zu erhalten. Wenn diese Vorstellungen nicht vor dem 1ten Vendemiär beigebracht sind, so hören die Bewilligungen geradezu auf. Der Sequester wird unverzüglich wieder auf die Nationalgüter gelegt werden, die in den besagten Konzessionen oder Bewilligungen begriffen sind, und diejenigen, denen die Güter bewilligt werden, empfangen aus der Hand des Sequesters die Früchte besagter Güter bis zum 1ten nächsten Vendem. Der Sequester soll gleichfals wieder auf alle Güter gelegt werden, die zur Bezahlung der Lieferanten verkauft wurden, deren Rechnungen nicht ganz schließlich berichtigt sind; indessen sollen die Früchte davon durch den Sequester den wirklichen Besitzern besagter Güter entrichtet werden, bis darüber anders verordnet sey.

Deutschland.

Oestreich. — Fürst von Schwarzenberg, Vizepräsident des Hofkriegsrathes, ist zum geheimen Rathe er-

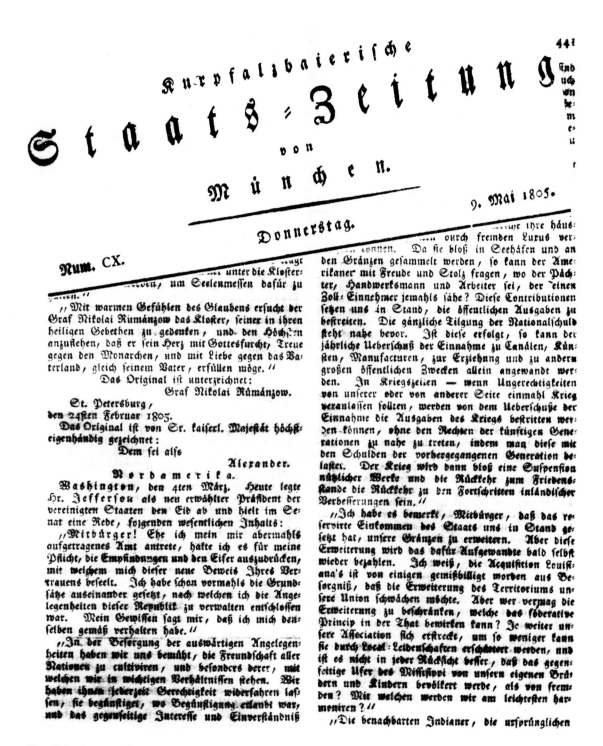

Fig. 7-8. *Staats-Zeitung von Munchen,* Munich, May 9, 10, 1805. Staats- und Universitats Bibliothek, Bremen.

442

Einwohner dieses Landes, habe ich mit dem Mitleiden betrachtet, welches ihre Geschichte einflößt. Die Menschlichkeit verpflichtet uns, da sie jetzt für ein Jäger-Leben auf zu enge Gränzen beschränkt sind, sie den Ackerbau und die häuslichen Künste zu lehren, sie zur Industrie zu ermuntern, und sie für einen gesellschaftlichen Zustand vorzubereiten. Wir haben ihnen deßwegen Ackerwerkzeuge und nützlichen Hausrath mitgetheilt, Lehrer in den nothwendigsten ersten Künsten unter sie gesandt und wir bedecken sie mit dem Schutze unserer Rechte gegen alle Aggression aus unserer Mitte. Indessen haben die Bemühungen, sie zu erleuchten und ihren Zustand zu bessern, noch mächtige Hindernisse. Körperliche Gewohnheit, Vorurtheile, Unwissenheit, Stolz und der Einfluß eigennütziger, listiger Individuen unter ihnen stehen denselben entgegen. Diese Menschen, die sich in der jetzigen Ordnung der Dinge als ein Etwas fühlen und in einer andern Ordnung Nichts zu sein befürchten, lehren eine heilige Ehrfurcht gegen die Gebräuche ihrer Vorfahrer; sie lehren, daß die Vernunft ein schlimmer Führer sei; daß es ihre Pflicht wäre, so zu bleiben, wie ihr Schöpfer sie geschaffen habe; daß die Unwissenheit, Sicherheit, und Unkenntniß sehr gefährlich sei. Kurz, meine Freunde, auch unter ihnen kämpfen Vernunft und Bigotterie wider einander. Sie haben ihre Antiphilosophen, welche ihren Vortheil dabei finden, die Sachen in ihrer alten Verfassung zu lassen, die eine Reformation fürchten und alle ihre Kraft anwenden, um den Einfluß der Gewohnheit gegen die Pflicht zu behaupten, die Vernunft zu vervollkommnen und deren Gesetzen zu gehorchen.''

,,Während meiner Administration ist zur Störung derselben das Geschütz der Presse gegen uns gerichtet und alles uns zur Last gelegt worden, was die Frechheit nur ersinnen konnte. Diese Mißbräuche einer Einrichtung, die so wichtig für Freiheit und Wissenschaft ist, sind sehr zu beklagen, indem sie deren Nutzen schwächen. Sie hätten vielleicht durch einige nützliche Bestrafungen gebessert werden können, wie sie das Gesetz gegen Verläumbung und Unwahrheiten vorschreibt. Aber Pflichten von höherem Gewicht liegen den öffentlichen Beamten ob, und die Uebelthäter sind deßwegen bloß der Strafe des öffentlichen Unwillens überlassen worden. Auch war es nicht uninteressant, einmahl zu versuchen, ob nicht die Freiheit der Discussionen, ohne der Macht zu bedürfen, hinlänglich sei, Wahrheiten zu verbreiten und zu erhalten, und um zu sehen, ob ein redliches Gouvernement durch Unwahrheiten und Verläumbung niedergeschrieben werden kann. Die Probe ist gemacht worden und glücklich ausgefallen. Unsre Mitbürger sahen dem Getümmel der Schreier

ruhig zu, bemerkten die verborgene Quelle der Schmähungen, sammelten sich um ihre öffentlichen Beamten und erklärten sich überall für diese.''

(Der Beschluß folgt).

446

tag wiederhohlt

10. Mai 1805.

Freitag.

die Rückkehr in ...ntern.

Nord-Amerika.

Washington, den 4ten März. Beschluß der Rede des Präsidenten Jefferson bei seiner Eidesleistung im Senat.

,,Ich will daraus nicht den Schluß ziehen, daß die Gesetze gegen Diffamation nicht in Kraft erhalten werden sollten; allein die Erfahrung hat bewiesen, daß, da Wahrheit und Vernunft sich gegen falsche Meinungen, verbunden mit falschen Factis, behauptet haben, die Presse, die auf Wahrheit beschränkt wird, keiner anderen gesetzmäßigen Einschränkung bedarf. Das öffentliche Urtheil wird, nach Anhören aller Parteien, falsche Meinungen und Raisonnements corrigiren, und es kann keine andere bestimmte Gränzlinie zwischen der unschätzbaren Freiheit der Presse und ihrer unmoralischen Frechheit gezogen werden.''

,,Wenn ich die Einigkeit der Gesinnungen betrachte, welche sich itzt im Allgemeinen so deutlich offenbart, und Eintracht und Glück für die Zukunft verspricht, so muß ich unserm Lande aufrichtig Glück wünschen. Unsere noch zweifelnden Brüder werden es endlich einsehen, daß die Masse ihrer Mitbürger, mit deren Maßregeln und Grundsätzen sie sich noch nicht versöhnen können, doch weiser denkt und wünscht, was auch sie wünschen.''

,,Ich werde nun die Amtspflichten antreten, zu welchen meine Mitbürger mich aufs Neue berufen haben. Ich werde den Geist der von Ihnen schon genehmigten Grundsätze dabei befolgen. Ich fürchte nicht, daß eigennützige Absichten mich irre führen oder irgend eine Leidenschaft mich von dem Pfade der Gerechtigkeit ableiten werde; die Schwäche der menschlichen Natur aber und die Beschränktheit meiner Einsichten kann mich zu irrigen Maßregeln führen, die Ihrem Interesse zuweilen nachtheilig sein können. Ich werde also aller Nachsicht bedürfen, die ich vorher erhalten habe. Ich beuge mich gegen jenes Wesen, in dessen Händen wir sind, und welches unsere Väter, wie ehemahls die Kinder Israels, aus ihrem Vaterlande geführt und in ein Land verpflanzt hat, in welchem alle Bedürfnisse und Annehmlichkeiten des Lebens vorhanden sind. Ich bitte Sie, Ihr Flehen mit dem meinigen zu vereinigen, daß es die Gemüther Ihrer Beamten erleuchte, deren Rathschläge leite und deren Maßregeln segne, damit alles zu Ihrem Besten ausschlage und Ihnen Frieden, Freundschaft und den Beifall aller Völker sichere. Thomas Jefferson.''

and 8; and the text was printed in the Munich *Staats-Zeitung von München* in the issues of May 9 and 10 (fig. 7-8). The entire text appeared in the *Baireuther Zeitung* published in Bayreuth, Bavaria, on May 10. The Austrian *Gratzer Zeitung* published the complete address on May 20. In the issues of May 25 and 29 the *Wiener Zeitung* presented Jefferson's words to Vienna readers.

The widespread republication of Jefferson's second inaugural address in a monarchically dominated continent threatened by the expansionist Emperor Napoleon of France is revealing of the political crosscurrents sweeping Europe and of the emerging—though still meager—influence of the United States.

Fig. 8-1. Silhouette of Thomas Jefferson by Raphaelle Peale, [Washington, D.C., 1804]. Embossed with the name PEALE immediately under the bust. Thomas Jefferson Memorial Foundation, Monticello.

Epilogue

From Washington, D.C., to Philadelphia and New York; from Baltimore, Maryland, to Lexington, Kentucky, and the Northwest territory; from Richmond, Virginia, to Charleston, South Carolina, and the Georgia frontier; from Boston, Massachusetts, to Peacham, Vermont, and Montreal; from Quebec to London and Paris; from The Hague to Hamburg and Berlin; from Milan to Vienna and Leipzig; and from other cities, large and small, in America and in Europe, the texts of Thomas Jefferson's presidential inaugural addresses of 1801 and 1805 spread with varying speed and completeness in English, French, German, Dutch, Italian—and no doubt other languages—to a wider and more interested audience than has previously been recognized.

Jefferson's widely circulated first inaugural address displayed an elected leader whose words to his own countrymen had meaning and application to peoples beyond the boundaries of his nation. Readers could sense Jefferson's devotion to the rule of law, political freedom, and the will of the majority. They could grasp his commitment to self-government, to religious freedom, and to the rights of minorities. Many of the rights and freedoms that Americans had won were still beyond the reach of numerous peoples elsewhere, and Jefferson's words provided a beacon of hope.

In his second inaugural address Jefferson directed attention to the Indian population in America, but nowhere in either inaugural address did he address the issue of slavery in the United States. While recognizing the condition of Indians as a national concern, he regarded slavery as subject to the authority of the states, which had the power to prohibit or to protect slavery. Himself a slaveholder who opposed slavery but continued to own slaves, Jefferson as president offered no national leadership toward dealing with the future of slavery in the United States.

That Jefferson's inaugural addresses were commonly reprinted in newspapers in the United States may be expected, but that these addresses were widely republished outside the United States has not been adequately recognized. Jefferson's words were not welcomed in every European state, but both his first and second inaugural addresses were reprinted extensively in Europe.

Some of Jefferson's contemporaries clearly recognized that his inaugural addresses could have influence beyond the borders of the United States. That was strikingly demonstrated when the Marquis de Lafayette and other friends of Jefferson's in France arranged to have his second inaugural address translated and printed after the Paris *Gazette Nationale ou Le Moniteur Universel* published only a summary of the text. Indications that Czar Alexander I of Russia read both of Jefferson's inaugural addresses suggest how widely the American president's speeches circulated abroad privately, if not always publicly.

Jefferson's care in preserving the manuscript texts of both of his addresses was in accord with his common practice of saving copies of his letters and other papers. The high attention that he gave to the content of both addresses demonstrated the importance he placed on their composition. That after two hundred years these addresses are worthy of reading and contemplation provides added evidence of how truly remarkable was this American president.

Bibliography

MANUSCRIPTS

Carey, Mathew. Papers, Account Books. American Antiquarian Society.

Doggett, John. Daybook. Henry Francis DuPont Winterthur Museum.

Gallatin, Albert. Papers. New-York Historical Society.

Jefferson, Thomas. Papers. Manuscripts Division, Library of Congress.

———. Papers. Coolidge Collection, Massachusetts Historical Society.

———. Papers. University of Virginia.

Lafayette family. Papers. Chateau La Grange, microfilm, Manuscripts Division, Library of Congress.

Monroe, James. Papers. Manuscripts Division, Library of Congress.

Morris, Gouverneur. Papers. Manuscripts Division, Library of Congress.

Nicholas, Wilson Cary. Papers. Manuscripts Division, Library of Congress.

Rodney, Thomas. Papers. Manuscripts Division, Library of Congress.

Rutledge, John. Papers. University of North Carolina, Chapel Hill.

Smith, Margaret Bayard (Mrs. Samuel H.). Papers. Manuscripts Division, Library of Congress.

Smith, William Loughton. Papers. Manuscripts Division, Library of Congress.

NEWSPAPERS

United States

American (Baltimore, Md.)
American Citizen (New York, N.Y.)
American Mercury (Hartford, Conn.)
Aurora (Philadelphia, Pa.)
Centinel of Freedom (Newark, N.J.)
City Gazette (Charleston, S.C.)
Columbian Centinel (Boston, Mass.)
Connecticut Courant (Hartford)
Democrat (Boston, Mass.)
Eastern Argus (Portland, Me.)
Enquirer (Richmond, Va.)
Examiner (Richmond, Va.)
Farmers' Museum, or Literary Gazette (Walpole, N.H.)
Gazette of the United States (Philadelphia, Pa.)
General Advertiser (Philadelphia, Pa.)
Green Mountain Patriot (Peacham, Vt.)
Härrisburger Morgenröthe Zeitung (Harrisburg, Pa.)
Independent Chronicle (Boston, Mass.)
Kline's Weekly Carlisle Gazette (Carlisle, Pa.)
Louisiana Gazette (New Orleans)
Maryland Gazette (Annapolis)
Massachusetts Spy, or Worcester Gazette (Worcester)
Mercury and New England Palladium (Boston, Mass.)
National Aegis (Worcester, Mass.)
National Intelligencer (Washington, D.C.)
New-York Evening Post (New York, N.Y.)
Providence Gazette (Providence, R.I.)
Scioto Gazette (Chillicothe, Ohio)

Stewart's Kentucky Herald (Lexington)
Times (Alexandria, Va.)
United States Gazette (Philadelphia)
Universal Gazette (Washington, D.C.)
Virginia Argus (Richmond)
Washington Federalist (Georgetown, Md.)

Canada

Gazette de Montreal
Montreal Gazette
Royal Gazette and New-Brunswick Advertiser

Great Britain

Courier de Londres (London)
The Times (London)

Europe

Allgemeine Zeitung (Augsburg)
Altonaischer Mercurius (Altona-Hamburg)
Argus: or London Reviewed in Paris (Paris)
Baireuther Zeitung (Bayreuth, Bavaria)
Berlinische Nachrichten (Berlin)
Berlinische Zeitung (Berlin)
Binnenlandsche Bataafsche Courant (The Hague)
Corrière Milanese (Milan)
Frankfurter Kaiserlich-Reichs-Ober-Post-Amts-Zeitung (Frankfurt)
Gazette Nationale ou Le Moniteur Universel (Paris)
Giornale Italiano (Milan)
Gratzer Zeitung (Graz, Austria)
Hamburgische Neue Zeitung (Hamburg)
Journal de Paris (Paris)
Kolnische Zeitung (Cologne)
Leipziger Zeitung (Leipzig)
Redattore Cisalpino (Milan)
Staats- und Gelehrte Zeitung des Hamburgischen unparthenischen Correspondenten (Hamburg)
Staats-Zeitung von München (Munich)
Wiener Zeitung (Vienna)

South America

Aurora de Chile (Santiago)

JOURNALS AND MAGAZINES

Anti-Jacobin Review and Magazine (London)
Balance and Columbian Repository (Hudson, N.Y.)
Baltimore Weekly Magazine (Baltimore, Md.)
Cobbett's Weekly Political Magazine (Dublin)
Connecticut Magazine, and Gentleman's and Lady's Monthly Museum (Bridgeport)
Edinburgh Weekly Journal (Edinburgh)
European Magazine and London Review (London)
Monthly Magazine (London)
Monthly Register, and Review of the United States (Hudson, N.Y.)
Port Folio (Philadelphia)
Universal Magazine (London)
Walker's Hibernian Magazine (Dublin)

BOOKS

Abbot, W. W., Dorothy Twohig, et al., eds. *The Papers of George Washington.* Presidential Series. 9 vols. to date. Charlottesville, Va., 1987–.

Adams, Charles Francis, ed. *The Memoirs of John Quincy Adams, Comprising Portions of His Diary from 1797 to 1848.* 12 vols. Philadelphia, 1874–1877.

Adams, Henry, ed. *The Writings of Albert Gallatin.* 3 vols. 1879. Rpt. New York, 1960.

Alberts, Robert C. *The Golden Voyage: The Life and Times of William Bingham, 1752–1804.* Boston, 1969.

Betts, Edwin M., and James A Bear, Jr., eds. *Family Letters of Thomas Jefferson.* Columbia, Mo., 1966.

Boyd, Julian P., et al. *The Papers of Thomas Jefferson.* 28 vols. to date. Princeton, N.J., 1950–.

Brown, Everett S., ed. *William Plumer's Memorandum of Proceedings in the United States Senate, 1803–1807.* 1923. Rpt. New York, 1969.

Butterfield, L. H., ed. *Letters of Benjamin Rush.* 2 vols. Princeton, N.J., 1951.

Chinard, Gilbert, ed. *The Correspondence of Jefferson and DuPont de Nemours.* Baltimore, 1931.

———. *The Letters of Lafayette and Jefferson.*

Baltimore, 1929.

Cunningham, Noble E., Jr. *The Image of Thomas Jefferson in the Public Eye: Portraits for the People.* Charlottesville, Va., 1981.

———. *In Pursuit of Reason: The Life of Thomas Jefferson.* Baton Rouge, La., 1987.

———. *The Jeffersonian Republicans in Power: Party Operations, 1801–1809.* Chapel Hill, N.C., 1963.

———. *Popular Images of the Presidency: From Washington to Lincoln.* Columbia, Mo., 1991.

———. *The Process of Government under Jefferson.* Princeton, N.J., 1978.

Cunningham, Noble E., Jr., ed. *Circular Letters of Congressmen to Their Constituents, 1789–1829.* 3 vols. Chapel Hill, N.C., 1978.

Ford, Paul L., ed. *The Works of Thomas Jefferson.* 12 vols. Federal edition, New York, 1904.

Hamilton, Stanislaus M., ed. *The Writings of James Monroe.* 7 vols. 1898–1903; rpt. New York, 1969.

Harris, C. M., ed. *Papers of William Thornton.* Charlottesville, Va., 1995.

Hartley, Janet M. *Alexander I.* London and New York, 1994.

Humphreys, Frank L. *Life and Times of David Humphreys.* New York, 1917.

Hunt, Gaillard, ed. *The First Forty Years of Washington Society in the Family Letters of Margaret Bayard Smith.* 1906. Rpt. New York, 1965.

Johnson, Herbert A., Charles T. Cullen, and Charles F. Hobson, eds. *The Papers of John Marshall.* 10 vols. to date. Chapel Hill, N.C., 1974–.

Kerber, Linda K. *Federalists in Dissent: Imagery and Ideology in Jeffersonian America.* Ithaca and London, 1970.

King, Charles R., ed. *The Life and Correspondence of Rufus King.* 6 vols. New York, 1894–1900.

Kline, Mary-Jo, and Joanne Wood Ryan, eds. *Political Correspondence and Public Papers of Aaron Burr.* 2 vols. Princeton, N.J., 1993.

Malone, Dumas. *Jefferson the President: First Term, 1801–1805.* Boston, 1970.

———. *Jefferson the President: Second Term, 1805–1809.* Boston, 1974.

Marchione, Margherita, ed. *Philip Mazzei: Selected Writings and Correspondence.* 3 vols. Prato, Italy, 1983.

Peterson, Merrill D. *Thomas Jefferson and the New Nation: A Biography.* New York, 1970.

Rutland, Robert, et al., eds. *The Papers of James Madison: Secretary of State Series.* 4 vols. to date. Charlottesville, Va., 1986–.

Sheridan, Eugene R. *Jefferson and Religion.* Charlottesville, Va., 1998.

Smith, James Morton, ed. *The Republic of Letters: The Correspondence of Thomas Jefferson and James Madison, 1776–1826.* 3 vols. New York, 1995.

Smith, Page. *John Adams.* 2 vols. Garden City, N.Y., 1962.

Sowerby, E. Millicent. *Catalogue of the Library of Thomas Jefferson.* 5 vols. Charlottesville, Va., 1952–9.

Stewart, Donald H. *The Opposition Press of the Federalist Period.* Albany, N.Y., 1969.

Syrett, Harold C., et al., eds. *The Papers of Alexander Hamilton.* 27 vols. New York, 1961–1987.

Warren, Charles. *Jacobin and Junto, or Early American Politics as Viewed in the Diary of Dr. Nathaniel Ames, 1758–1822.* New York, 1968.

Woodress, James. *A Yankee's Odyssey: The Life of Joel Barlow.* Philadelphia, 1958.

Acknowledgments

In the research for this book I have had the support and assistance of many persons and institutions. Among the scholars, archivists, and library specialists who have aided my research, I am greatly indebted to Nicolò Russo Perez and Malcolm Sylvers, University of Venice; Thomas C. Albro II, Carol Armbruster, Frederick Bauman, Gerard Gawalt, James Hutson, John McDonough, Lyle Minter, David Wigdor, and Mary Wolfskill, Library of Congress; Georgia Barnhill, American Antiquarian Society; Margaret Cook, Sweem Library, College of William and Mary; Roderick McGrew, London; Charles T. Cullen, president, Newberry Library; James Horn, director, and Douglas L. Wilson, former director, of the International Center for Jefferson Studies, Monticello; Bonner Mitchell and Charles Nauert, University of Missouri–Columbia; and Anne Edwards and Margaret Howell, Ellis Library, University of Missouri–Columbia.

My research has been supported by the University of Missouri through my appointment as the Curators' Professor of History. I am very appreciative of this important aid and the supportive working conditions of the Department of History and the Ellis Library.

I am grateful to my wife, Dana, for her interest in, and support of, my research and writing. To Daniel P. Jordan, president of the Thomas Jefferson Foundation, Monticello, Virginia, I am indebted for his leadership in advancing scholarship in the age of Jefferson and the support of this project by the Thomas Jefferson Memorial Foundation. To Beverly Jarrett, director and editor-in-chief, and Jane Lago, managing editor, of the University of Missouri Press, I am greatly appreciative of their outstanding editorial talents.

I am indebted to the following institutions and libraries for making available for study the sources on which this study is based and for permitting the reproduction of documents and other items illustrated.

Alderman Library, University of Virginia
American Antiquarian Society
Beinecke Library, Yale University
Biblioteca di Storia Moderna e Contemporanea, Rome
Biblioteca Universitaria, Bologna
Bibliotheque Nationale, Paris
Chicago Historical Society
City of Manchester Art Galleries, England
Duke University Library
Ellis Library, University of Missouri
Institut für Zweitungsforschung, Dortmund
Library of Congress
Library of Virginia
Massachusetts Historical Society
National Museum of American History, Smithsonian Institution

Newport Historical Society, Rhode Island
New-York Historical Society
New York Public Library
Princeton University Library
Staats Bibliothek zu Berlin
Staats- und Universitats Bibliothek Carl von
    Ossietzky, Hamburg

Staats- und Universitats Bibliothek, Bremen
Sweem Library, College of William and Mary
Thomas Jefferson Memorial Foundation,
    Charlottesville
White House, Washington, D.C.

Index

Unions and Economic Crisis:
Britain, West Germany and Sweden